Game of Love

Edited by
Harjinder Singh

First Published 2008
Sixth Edition Published 2020

British Library Cataloguing in Publication Data
A catalogue record for this book is available from the British
Library

ISBN 978-1-9996052-2-3

Akaal Publishers is a not for profit publisher which publishes
books with timeless messages, based upon Sikh history, ethics and
philosophy. For further information see our website:
www.akaalpublishers.com

Dedicated to all Sikhs,
who laid down their lives,
for the freedom of others.

Acknowledgements

The writing of this book started with the blessings of the Late Baba Thakhur Singh Jee, Acting Head of Damdami Taksal. Baba Jee had said such an endeavour should be undertaken to preserve the history of the great Sikhs who sacrificed their lives in the Sikh Freedom Struggle.

Baba Thakhur Singh was a great soul whose whole life was dedicated to Sikhi; he told many Singhs to go on missions of assassinations and fully supported the Sikh Freedom Movement. Baba Jee's traits and character were such that he kept a lot of this information secretive, but those Singhs who have spent time with Baba Jee, who still live to tell their tales, know the real value of Baba Thakhur Singh after Operation Blue Star[1].

I have not authored this book; rather I have compiled what has been written by a variety of authors and collated this information in a way that I would like to portray it. I would like to thank the UK based weekly Punjabi newspapers of Awaze Quam, Des Pardes, Punjab Times, and Wangar Magazine. A lot of material has been translated from these print media. I would also like to acknowledge the foresight of Bhai Anokh Singh Babbar who was one of the first Sikh Insurgents to start writing about the Sikh Insurgency and its warriors. His writings inspired others to also raise the pen and record the History of the Sikhs over the last 20 years or so. More recently the monthly magazine of Damdami Taksal 'Khalsa Khandeydhar' started the resurgence of writings about the bravery of Sikhs.

Authors and magazines of recent times that need to be acknowledged are: Narain Singh (Akaal Federation), Baljit Singh Khalsa, Amardeep Singh Amar, Maninder Singh Baja, Inderjeet

---

[1] Please see Annex 1 at the end of the book to view a short biography of Baba Jee

Singh Jaijee, Khalsa Khandedhar (magazine), Fatehnama (magazine), Sikh Shahadat (magazine) and www.tapoban.org, from which Balpreet Singh, Zorawar Singh, and the numerous anonymous posters on this websites message board. Much of the translations have been drawn from www.tapoban.org. Where translations were not available I translated articles/tracts myself.

For the photos used throughout the book, a special thanks to www.shaheedkhalsa.com and www.sikhtoons.com. A special thanks to the sevadars who provided assistance throughout the compilation of this book and those who tirelessly read the numerous drafts and gave constructive feedback. I apologise for any omissions of people who have contributed, as a lot of the material was taken from back issues of newspapers and translated. Subsequently some of the authors of the original articles may have been omitted and this is partly due to full articles not being available.

Harjinder Singh
May 2015

Sixth Edition

We have deleted the photos from this edition of the book and we suggest readers buy 'The Sikh Martyrs Volume 1' from www.nsyf.org.uk/shop for high quality pictures of the Sikhs mentioned in this book.

This edition is a reprint to keep the paperback in circulation – we will hopefully bring a new updated edition out in the coming months.

Harjinder Singh
June 2020

Preface

Those that have become imbued with the Love of God,
Have realised him, attained self-realisation
(Sri Guru Gobind Singh Jee, Tva Prasad Svaye)

Love is the greatest human emotion and love can be seen in a number of different lights. Sikhi teaches us that there is only one type of true love or true romance and that is with God. There is a saying that, 'Lightning only strikes once'. I would argue that this can be seen in the uttering of Sri Guru Gobind Singh Jee,

Those that meditate upon God even for one second,
They become liberated from the transmigration of the soul

When we have complete and pure love for God then we can realise him in a second, and it is this level of concentration that Sikhs endeavour to achieve. One can only learn what this true concentration and consciousness of purity of mind and thought are by developing a thorough grasp of the teachings and spiritual undertones of Sri Guru Granth Sahib Jee.

The following chapters will outline what defines this true love and I will give examples of great souls who played this game of love. Their love for the Guru and the belief that Sikhs fight against injustice and for the freedoms of all, is what shines through in their lives.

The story of the last 20 years or so, is not simply of personal political gain for the Sikhs (to gain Khalistan) but, on the contrary, it is part of a continuum in Sikh History where Sikhs have had to wield the sword to uphold righteousness as all other peaceful means had been exhausted. The History of the Sikhs which will be described shows that the Sikhs as a nation have always wielded the sword as a defence and have never gone on the offence to follow political aims.

Readers are reminded that from 1984 – 1993 many Sikhs entered a battle against the Indian government for the freedom of Sikhs. Thus, certain instances of Sikhs taking up arms that will be later mentioned need to be taken in the context of a whole scale insurgency in India's Punjab. The majority of Sikhs who lived through this period felt that all peaceful means had been exhausted and it was only just to draw the sword or gun to protect the honour, freedoms and history of the Sikh nation. I would suggest that readers read further books and articles of the recent Sikh Freedom Struggle to gain a full grasp of the cases and history that will be touched upon in this book.

CONTENTS

1. The Gurus

Foundations of Faith

Sri Guru Nanak Dev Jee (1469 – 1539AD) came to this world to dispel the mist and make a new dawn in which the light would enthral and enlighten all. Bhai Sahib, Bhai Gurdas Jee[2] describes the coming of the first Sikh Guru, Sri Guru Nanak Dev Jee thus:

"With the emergence of the True Guru Nanak, the mist cleared and the light scattered all around. As if at the sun rise the stars disappeared and the darkness dispelled. With the roar of the lion in the forest, the flocks of escaping deer now cannot have endurance." **(Bhai Sahib, Bhai Gurdas Jee, Var 1, Pauri 27)**

Sri Guru Nanak Dev Jee was respected and is still respected by both Muslims and Hindus. Sri Guru Nanak Dev Jee's teachings were based on simplicity, faith in truth, truthful living, and meditation, sharing with others, righteousness, humility and above all being obedient to One God in all that one does.

Sri Guru Nanak Dev Jee rejected the traditional ritual initiation into the Hindu fold by rejecting to wear the Janeoo – a thread which is put on as part of an initiation ceremony. The Guru rejected the thread and said,

"Make compassion the cotton, contentment the thread, modesty the knot and truth the twist. This is the sacred thread of the soul; if you have it, then go ahead and put it on me. It does not break, it cannot be soiled by

---

[2] One of the most famous Sikh Scholars, there were two Bhai Gurdas's who were contemporaries of the Gurus, they have writings of ballads and prose which are to be seen as the key to Sikhi., the first in this instance is quoted.

filth, and it cannot be burnt, or lost. Blessed are those mortal beings, O Nanak, who wear such a thread around their necks. You buy the thread for a few shells, and seated in your enclosure, you put it on. Whispering instructions into others' ears, the Brahmin becomes a guru. But he dies, and the sacred thread falls away, and the soul departs without it." **(Sri Guru Nanak Dev Jee, Ang 471)**

Sri Guru Nanak Dev Jee had come with the divine mission of enlightening the world of the eternal truth, which had become mystified in complexities of religious rituals and falsehoods. I refute the proposition of many contemporary authors that Sikhi became a fusion of the Hindu and Islamic faiths. I argue that Sikhi is a simplification of the Eternal Truth and all the Gurus did, was show mankind the path to this Eternal Truth, the realism of God and ways in which to obtain self-realisation.

For all the great fetes of Sri Guru Nanak Dev Jee – one can go and write much prose, but here I will concentrate on the nature of the social reformer and the courageous, which is usually brushed over by many historians. Here I refer to the eternal historical proofs given to us in Sri Guru Nanak Dev Jee's own writings, which are included in Sri Guru Granth Sahib Jee.[3]   Sri Guru Nanak Dev Jee was well aware of the atrocities and sinful actions being committed by rulers in modern times:

"The Dark Age of Kali Yuga is the knife, and the kings are butchers; righteousness has sprouted wings and flown away. In this dark night of falsehood, the moon of Truth is not visible anywhere. I have searched in vain,

---

[3] The eternal spiritual guide of the Sikhs, an anthology of the word of God/prayers

and I am so confused; in this darkness, I cannot find the path. In egotism, they cry out in pain. Says Nanak, how will they be saved? **(Sri Guru Nanak Dev Jee, Ang 145)**

These words rang true in the times of Sri Guru Nanak Dev Jee when he was referring to the Mughal Raj/Rule, and they are true for the modern Indian state which mercilessly murdered thousands of Sikhs between the years of 1978 – 1995, and still persecutes minorities. These teachings of the great Guru also ring true in reference to oppressors such as Hitler, Milosevic and Indira Gandhi. These leaders had common features in being rulers with an iron fist, having only morals of self-preservation and dictatorial rule. The great Guru talked of his contemporary Ruler as follows (which applies also to those aforementioned):

"As the Word of the Forgiving Lord comes to me, so do I express it, O Lalo. Bringing the marriage party of sin, Babar has invaded from Kabul, demanding our land as his wedding gift, O Lalo. Modesty and righteousness both have vanished, and falsehood struts around like a leader, O Lalo ... The wedding songs of murder are sung, O Nanak and blood is sprinkled instead of saffron, O Lalo." **(Sri Guru Nanak Dev Jee, Ang 722)**

"Having attacked Khuraasaan, Baabar terrified Hindustan. The Creator Himself does not take the blame, but has sent the Mughal as the messenger of death. There was so much slaughter that the people screamed. Didn't you feel compassion, Lord? O Creator Lord, You are the Master of all. If some powerful man strikes out against another man, then no one feels any grief in their mind. Pause. But if a powerful tiger attacks a flock of sheep and kills them, then its master must answer for it. This priceless country has been laid to waste and defiled by dogs, and no one pays any attention to the dead. You

THE GURUS

yourself unite, and you yourself separate; I gaze upon Your Glorious Greatness. One may give himself a great name, and revel in the pleasures of the mind, but in the Eyes of the Lord and Master, he is just a worm, for all the corn that he eats. Only one, who dies to his ego while yet alive, obtains the blessings, O Nanak, by chanting the Lord's Name." *(Sri Guru Nanak Dev Jee Ang 360)*

Above, the great Guru is talking of the genocide that Baabar was committing to extend and maintain his rule. Similarly today modern rulers propagate draconian laws that restrict human rights, and in extreme cases genocide and ethnic cleansing are pre-planned and implemented. A Sikh living in India between the years of 1983-1993 was viewed as a terrorist. The outward appearance of Sikhs made them easy targets of abuse and murder by the authorities. The Great Guru has emphasised that such rulers are truly worth nothing in the afterlife:

"*... The kings are tigers, and their officials are dogs; they go out and awaken the sleeping people to harass them. The public servants inflict wounds with their nails. The dogs lick up the blood that is spilled. But there, in the Court of the Lord, all beings will be judged. Those who have violated the people's trust will be disgraced; their noses will be cut off.*" **(Sri Guru Nanak Dev Jee, Ang 1288)**

Only that person that effaces his/her ego whilst alive attains true union with God (a concept I will explain further in succeeding chapters). The social scene of the coming of Sri Guru Nanak Dev Jee has been set and we shall now go onto discuss the aspects of the pre-requisites of being a Sikh and what level of commitment the Guru instructs his Sikhs to have.

THE GURUS

The Sikhs of Sri Guru Nanak Dev Jee

Anyone who wants to enter the path of Sikhi as laid by Sri Guru Nanak Dev Jee must adhere to the following, which is accepted as the first step to initiation:

"If you desire to play this game of love, then step onto My Path with your head in your hand. When you place your feet on this Path, give me your head and do not pay any attention to public opinion." **(Sri Guru Nanak Dev Jee, Ang 1412)**

A Sikh must be willing to sacrifice everything in their life that they may call their own, in pursuit of self-realisation. Saying this in mere words can be easy, but it is only when this faith is put to the test that one realises the true value of such oaths to the Guru. The Guru does not ask for half-cocked commitment, the Guru demands 100% and nothing else will do if we are to become true Sikhs, like the many martyrs and saints of Sikh history. Thus Sikhs must strive to undertake and live each and every teaching of the Gurus, and then Sikhs can become the living embodiment of the Guru themselves (as the Khalsa, as taught by the tenth Guru). Sikhs have no fear of worldly powers, but have much fear of violating the rules of God, and it is their love for God that makes them persevere in the quest of self-realisation:

"He Himself creates the world, and He himself takes care of it. Without the Fear of God, doubt is not dispelled, and love for the Name (of God) is not embraced. Through the True Guru, the Fear of God wells up, and the Door of Salvation is found. Through the Fear of God, intuitive ease is obtained, and one's light merges into the Light of the Infinite. Through the Fear of God, the terrifying world-ocean is crossed over, by

reflecting on the Guru's Teachings. Through the Fear of God, the Fearless Lord is found; He has no end or limitation. The self-willed manmukhs[4] do not appreciate the value of the Fear of God. Burning in desire, they weep and wail. O Nanak, through the Name, peace is obtained, by enshrining the Guru's Teachings within the heart." (Sri Guru Nanak Dev Jee, Ang 1288)

This is the birth of a Sikh in the house of Sri Guru Nanak Dev Jee. A birth in which, one relinquishes everything to the Guru. But then how should the death of a Sikh come?

"Death would not be called bad, O people, if one knew how to truly die. The death of brave heroes is blessed, if it is approved by God. They alone are acclaimed as brave warriors in the world hereafter, who receive true honour in the Court of the Lord. They are honoured in the Court of the Lord; they depart with honour, and they do not suffer pain in the world hereafter. They meditate on the One Lord, and obtain the fruits of their rewards. Serving the Lord, their fear is dispelled. Do not indulge in egotism, and dwell within your own mind; the Knower Himself knows everything. The death of brave heroes is blessed, if it is approved by God." (Sri Guru Nanak Dev Jee, Ang 579)

The death or martyrdom of Sikhs fighting for a righteous cause is praised and highlighted as being truly blessed. Although these Sikhs are not mere warriors, they are also imbued in meditation, making them Saint Soldiers. Liberation is not restricted to those who take up this honourable path, it is also rewarded (liberation) to those who undergo deep meditations and become one with God, or those who undergo a self-sacrificing process by doing

---

[4] Those led by their minds rather than their Guru

voluntary work in the name of God. I will not elaborate on the latter two paths to liberation, as much literature concentrates on these aspects, but will remain focussed upon Sikhs who take up arms in defence of their faith.

These great Sikhs, who take up the honourable path of joining God's army to uphold righteousness, have an undying spirit which Sri Guru Nanak Dev Jee describes:

"If my body were afflicted with pain, under the evil influence of unlucky stars; and if the blood-sucking kings were to hold power over me - even if this were my condition, I would still worship and adore You, and my longing to chant Your Praises would not decrease." **(Sri Guru Nanak Dev Jee, Ang 142)**

This is the spiritual strength that is manifested in these Great Warriors. Even if they were boiled alive, as was Bhai Gurdev Singh Jee Debu, their children murdered on ice-blocks, yet they still did not flinch in their repose and stood firm in their loyalty to God and Panth/Nation. It is these Great Sikhs that we will learn of and how they lived up to the ideals that the Gurus had laid down for us to follow as Sikhs.

Sri Guru Nanak Dev Jee started the social reform that was later to become formalised into Sikhi, but from its very inception Sikhi principles were based upon speaking up for one's beliefs and having no fear of mankind, but having much fear of God (in that one always tries to reflect the tenets of Gurbani in one's life).

Sikh Language

Sri Guru Nanak Dev Jee blessed Sri Guru Angad Dev Jee (1504 – 1552AD) with the Guruship prior to ascending to Sachkand (abode of truth). This second Guru of the Sikhs started the clear step towards creating a defining mark of separatism of Sikhs. He created the Gurmukhi script. Gurmukhi is the language of the Sikh scriptures, and in East Punjab today this script is the standard for writing Punjabi.

But again the social reform and vocal nature of the Gurus did not die down; on the contrary, Sri Guru Angad Dev Jee reflected Sri Guru Nanak Dev Jee's thoughts:

> *"The beggar is known as an emperor, and the fool is known as a religious scholar. The blind man is known as a seer; this is how people talk. The trouble-maker is called a leader, and the liar is seated with honour. O Nanak, the Gurmukhs know that this is justice in the Dark Age of Kali Yuga."* **(Sri Guru Angad Dev Jee, Ang 1288)**

He was also as unflinching as Sri Guru Nanak Dev Jee about the level of commitment a Sikh needs in order to get union with God. He famously says in Asa Di Var:

> *"One, who offers both respectful greetings and rude refusal to his master, has gone wrong from the very beginning. O Nanak, both of his actions are false; he obtains no place in the Court of the Lord."* **(Sri Guru Angad Dev Jee, Ang 474)**

He also encouraged the Sikhs to keep fit and ardently promoted wrestling to Sikhs. He gathered the writings of Sri Guru Nanak Dev Jee and began teaching Sikhs the newly formed Gurmukhi script. Thus education became integral to each Sikh household. The Sikhs would become an educated people who did not have to rely on any form of religious clergy; rather, each Sikh was to be a clergy man/woman themselves.

Equal Rights for Women

Sri Guru Amar Das Jee (1469 – 1574AD) continued the revolutionary evolution of the Sikh way of life by challenging discrimination against women and implementing practises that went against this discrimination. He made it a sin for any Sikh women to be veiled and taught the Sikhs that Sati (the self-mortification of a woman on the funeral pyre of her husband) is inhumane and was outlawed for Sikhs by the Guru. He took the equal rights of women one step further than Sri Guru Nanak Dev Jee – who had argued women were equal to men, here his predecessor actually appointed Sikh Missionaries who were women.

The other great teaching of Sri Guru Amar Das that stands out is that of selfless Seva (voluntary service). The Guru himself did Seva of Sri Guru Angad Dev Jee for 13 years, before being bestowed the Guruship. Sri Guru Amar Das was the living embodiment of selfless Seva and was forever engaged in Seva even when he became the Guru of the Sikhs.

These two teachings were later to be enshrined in the armed struggles of Sikhs, in that Sikh women would urge their men to go to battle and would also take up arms if needed, as they were not deemed inferior. Also the living memory of the old Guru tirelessly fetching the water and carrying the pitcher on a daily basis, would make Sikhs persevere in the hardships they faced when doing Seva themselves.

The Pool of Nectar – Amritsar

The fourth Guru, Sri Guru Ramdas Jee (1534 – 1581AD) built the sarovar of Sri Amritsar Sahib, which is the heart of the Sikhs. This sarovar (water tank, pool of nectar in this instance) has healing powers, and each and every Sikh in the world daily supplicates to visit Sri Amritsar Sahib and do Ishnaan/bathe there. This added to the nation building of the Sikhs, with the formation of this shrine Sikhs would have a place they would always see as the capital of their religious affairs.

Sikh Warriors would and do always long to bathe and visit Sri Amritsar Sahib, and it has become central to both attacking the Sikhs and liberating them. Sikh warriors have and do secretly enter the shrine to bathe in its sacred pool, even in times when it has not been in the control of Sikhs.

The First Sikh Martyr

Sri Guru Arjan Dev Jee (1563 – 1605AD), the fifth Guru of the Sikhs, would have a lasting effect on the polity and spiritual practices of the Sikhs. This was due to two achievements in his worldly life, first the collation of Sikh scriptures into Sri Aad Granth Sahib Jee and secondly, peacefully achieving martyrdom whilst undergoing torture. He continued the work of His Father Sri Guru Ram Das as he built the shrine of Sri Harmander Sahib in the centre of the Sarovar that had been built. This Gurdwara would become the holiest shrine for Sikhs, due to its divine sarovar, its nature of open access to the world, and the continuous recitation of prayers.

Sri Harmander Sahib was built under the supervision of Sri Guru Arjan Dev Jee; it was purposely built with four doors - each door in a geographical direction, indicating that this Gurdwara was open to all people of the world regardless of any social status, race, caste, sex or physical differences. The Gurdwara was also built on a lower level than the rest of the city, symbolising that one must efface ego and come in humility to meet God. Amritsar as a city derives its name from the shrine, which literally translates to 'Amrit' Nectar of Immortality and 'Sar' which means pool, thus Amritsar = pool of nectar. Sikhs believe that this nectar is revived daily by the recitation of prayers, which are continuous in the shrine. It is commonly referred to as Golden Temple as it has gold plating on it which was not part of the original design but added by a Sikh ruler Maharajah Ranjit Singh in the 19th century.

Sri Guru Arjan Dev Jee made another clear step towards consolidating the evolving way of life of Sikhs by collating the prayers of the Gurus who had gone before him, and those of Saints of the Sufi and Bhagti traditions and of other Sikhs. By doing this, Guru Jee made a clearly defined anthology of prayers that Sikhs would revere for eternity. It was this compilation that was revered to as Sri Aad Granth Sahib Jee and installed at Sri Harmander Sahib in August of 1604AD. This anthology would have minor editions of Sri Guru Hargobind Sahib adding 'Dhunis' (mentions of musical tunes) and the Gurbani of the Ninth Guru, Sri Guru Teg Bahadur Sahib Jee to it, which would then be given the Guruship for eternity by Sri Guru Gobind Singh Jee (the tenth Guru, who concluded the process of Physical Guru's).

The Guru made a clear distinction that Sikhs were not Hindus or Muslims:

"I do not keep fasts, nor do I observe the month of Ramadan. I serve only the One, who will protect me in the end. The One Lord, the Lord of the World, is my God Allah; He administers justice to both Hindus and Muslims. (Pause.) I do not make pilgrimages to Mecca, nor do I worship at Hindu sacred shrines. I serve the One Lord, and not any other. I do not perform Hindu

worship services, nor do I offer the Muslim prayers. I have taken the One Formless Lord into my heart; I humbly worship Him there. I am not a Hindu, nor am I a Muslim. My body and breath of life belong to Allah - to Ram - the God of both. Says Kabeer, this is what I say: meeting with the Guru, my Spiritual Teacher, I realize God, my Lord and Master. **(Sri Guru Arjan Dev Jee, Ang 1136)**

The shrine of Sri Harmander Sahib and the many shrines within its complex, have multiple historical significances to the Sikhs and we have yet to mention the Sri Akaal Takhat Sahib, which is the highest temporal seat of the Sikhs. All these factors (of historical importance) would add to the backlash against the Indian Government when they committed suicide by sending in their troops to attack Sri Harmander Sahib/The Golden Temple in June 1984. The most shocking aspect was that the Martyrdom day of Sri Guru Arjan Dev Jee fell on the days of the attack. The government knew of the festivities being planned, yet took advantage of this to ensure that as many innocent Sikhs who came to pilgrimage on this auspicious occasion, could be caught and murdered in the cross-fire.

With the Martyrdom of Sri Guru Arjan Dev Jee we need to look at the undying and unflinching spirit of a Sikh that Guru Jee mentioned in his own divine utterances:

"First, accept death, and give up any hope of life. Become the dust of the feet of all, and then, you may come to me."
(Sri Guru Arjan Dev Jee, Ang 1102)

Again the same spirit of sacrificing all to the Guru is demanded in order to follow the path of the Guru and to have extreme humility at the same time. Sri Guru Arjan

Dev Jee was the living epitome of the utterance mentioned above. He peacefully attained martyrdom from the Emperor Jahangir, his only crime being that he would not appease the Emperor in his requests to convert to Islam. The Emperor was jealous of the rise in popularity of the Guru. The Emperor's son Khusrau also made a rebellion against his father and he stayed the night at Goindval where Guru Jee was. This shelter was not given in support of the rebellion but rather in the spirit of the Sikh beliefs of giving anyone food and shelter who came to a Gurdwara (Sikh place of worship). It is also mentioned historically that the main culprit for the cause of such harsh torture against the Guru (seating him on a hot plate, pouring heated sand over his head and throwing him in cold water afterwards) was Chandu, an advisor to Jahangir, who had been outraged at the refusal of his daughter's hand in marriage to the son of the Guru, Sahibzada Sri Hargobind Sahib Jee (who would become the 6th Guru).

Guru Jee peacefully sat on the hot plate (of iron) and withstood all the torture they could cruelly administer and peacefully attained Martyrdom. He did not compromise his principles. This would turn a new chapter in Sikh history and start the tradition of martyrdom in Sikhs, the Guru being the first Martyr. Bhai Sahib, Bhai Gurdas Jee writes of the Guru's martyrdom:

"As fishes are at one with the waves of the river, so was the Guru, immersed in the River that is the Lord: As the moth merges itself at sight into the flame, so was the Guru's light merged with the Divine Light. In the extreme hours of suffering, He was aware of nothing but the Divine Word, like the deer who hears no sound but the ringing of the hunter's bell. Like the humming-bee who is wrapped inside the lotus, He passed the night of his life as a casket of bliss; never did He forget to utter

the Lord's word, as the chatrik[5] fails never to utter its cry; to the man of God joy is the fruit of devotion and meditation with equanimity in holy company. May I be a sacrifice unto Guru Arjan." (Var 24, Pauri 23)

Political & Righteous

The martyrdom of the Fifth Guru led to a stark change in the practices of Sikhs – the Gurus had previously praised the warrior spirit but had not actually indulged in warfare themselves. Now Sikhi was under direct attack and new tactics befitting the situation had to be undertaken. Thus Sri Guru Har Gobind Sahib Jee (1596 – 1638AD), when being anointed the Sixth Guru told the Master of the Ceremony – Baba Buddha Jee, that he should bring him two swords. These two swords were worn by the Guru throughout His life. The swords depicted the belief in a harmony of the temporal/political powers and the righteous ones (religious), giving birth to a concept of political activism and saintliness (Miri/Piri). This decision was taken in reaction to the oppression of the Mughal Rule and any act of drawing arms in the future of Sikhs would always be defensive and not offensive. The Guru now asked the Sikhs to bring arms and horses to His Court, things that would add to the attire of a ruler. The Emperor had made many laws of oppression that the Guru would go and flaunt such as:

- Nobody could keep an army
- Nobody could sit on a raised platform (as a sovereign would)
- Nobody could wear a Kalgi (worn on the turban showing sovereignty)

---

[5] A bird found in the tropics that continuously cries for rain to satiate its thirst.

The Guru went ahead and broke these directives in direct challenge to the leadership to show that he would not bend to their rules, on the contrary, he engaged in battle with the Emperors forces on four different occasions. The outlawing of sitting on a raised platform led to the building of the highest temporal point of faith for Sikhs the Akaal Takhat (Immortal Throne)[6]. This was purposely built opposite the highest religious point – Sri Harmander Sahib – showing one must first become saintly then get direction from the Akaal Takhat to become worldly. All decisions of polity would become to be taken at the Akaal Takhat in years to come by Sikhs.

It was from the Akaal Takhat that the Guru sent out directives to Sikhs. Thus another aspect of nation building was concreted adeptly by the Sixth Guru, the Sikhs now had both religious and political centres of gravity – in which their nation would evolve.

The Guru was imprisoned at the fort of Gwalior by the Emperor, early in His reign as the Guru. There are differing accounts given for the imprisonment, the most plausible being that the Emperor paid much credence to his astrologers – some of whom had a bitter dislike of the Guru. The astrologers advised the Emperor that he should imprison the Guru and make him meditate to alleviate bad luck that he was about to encounter. There are again differing accounts of the length of imprisonment the Guru underwent, but He did ensure the freeing of another 52 princes[7] along with himself – thus He is fondly referred to as *'Bandi Shorr'* – *'The Liberator.'* After being released from Gwalior Fort the Guru made His way to Amritsar and reached there on the night of Divali, and thus Sikhs

---

[6] It's original height as in the times of the Guru was between 9 – 13 feet high.

[7] Who were also being held for whimsical reasons.

celebrate Divali as a celebration of freedom and upholding the rights of others. This memory of Divali would give fortitude and inspiration for generations to come, especially to those who would also undergo imprisonment at the hands of unjust rulers.

The Guru was called many a name by the rulers of the day, due to his challenging nature – terrorist would have probably been one of the names used, even though the Mughal Rule was terrorising the masses. The taking to arms of Sikhs was in defence of faith and never have arms been drawn by Sikhs in offence. When the time came the Sikhs would recall this tradition started by the Guru and draw arms if necessary to uphold justice. If the Guru had not taken this decision – Sikhs probably would not exist today – as peaceful means had been exhausted – the peaceful Martyrdom of Sri Guru Arjan Dev Jee had proved this.

Conservation & herbal remedies

Each Guru brought a new facet to Sikhi and each was revolutionary in thought and practise. The seventh Guru, Sri Guru Har Rai Sahib Jee (1630 – 1661AD), introduced the concepts of conservation, animal welfare and herbal remedies. He promoted the conservation of nature, set up reserves for wildlife, and treated sick or injured animals. He also promoted the use of herbal remedies, created many remedies, and opened a dispensary.

He maintained an army of 2000 soldiers, but this army was never called into action. He brought a unique essence of preservation to Sikhi, which included that of our environments. The Sikhs had been taught by successive Gurus to preserve their history and look after their environments. However both these aspects were attacked to the root, when the Indian Government took the reckless move of pressing self-destruct, when they attacked the Harmander Sahib complex in June 1984 and looted and burnt the Sikh Reference Library. Thousands of Sikh manuscripts haven't been returned to date.

The Child Guru

The Eighth Guru, Sri Guru Har Krishan Sahib Jee (1656 – 1664AD) was appointed the Guru at the young age of 5, which shocked many. It was groundbreaking for a person of such a young age to become a spiritual and political head of a community in South Asia. But the Guru was very wise and he showed this when in court, and many a wise man went away over-awed by His knowledge and spirituality.

When there was an outbreak of smallpox in Delhi and other parts of what we now refer to as the Indian subcontinent, the Guru spent a lot of time tending to the sick, and he healed many sufferers of the disease. He built a well and blessed it with healing powers – many took water from the well and were healed of their ailments – and to this day this practise continues at Gurdwara Bangla Sahib in Delhi. To alleviate sickness he took the disease upon himself, thus taking away the ailment from many others, and left his worldly body. Thus he sacrificed himself for the welfare of others. The ethos of helping others in terms of being altruistic would be reflected by Sikhs time and again, even if it would be detrimental to them. For example, when Sikh soldiers would save the daughters of fellow countrymen (usually Hindus who were largely pacifists) from the Afghan invaders who would come and loot wealth and kidnap women to make them slaves (this was during the 18th century). Sacrifices of children would also become common place in Sikh history.

Human Rights

Sri Guru Teg Bahadur Jee (1621 – 1675AD) is famous for his bold stance of protecting the rights of others, and for his utterances of the Holy Word, which are embodied in detachment from the world and attachment to God. In His younger years the Guru was a great warrior, thus the name of *'Teg Bahadur'* - 'Warrior of the Sword' was attributed to him (even though He was originally named Tyag Mal). His Father was the 6th Guru and he had seen the reigns of three Gurus in total. In the time after the departure of His Father to His Heavenly Abode (Sachkand), Sri Guru Teg Bahadur spent most of His time immersed in deep meditations at Bakala (later known as Baba Bakala, Amritsar).

The Guru reminded Sikhs that the world was a mere illusion:

"The mortal is entangled in Maya; he has forgotten the Name of the Lord of the Universe. Says Nanak, without meditating on the Lord, what is the use of this human life? **(Sri Guru Teg Bahadur Jee, Ang 1428, Stanza 30)**

We are given this human life as a gift to merge with God. Through dedicated meditation and practise of the teachings of the Gurus we can achieve this objective. The Guru talks of the reality of death:

"O dear friend, know this in your mind. The world is entangled in its own pleasures; no one is true to you[8]. Pause. In good times, many come and sit together, surrounding you on all four sides. But when hardships

---

[8] God & Guru is the only reality we can rely on at all times – all others are false.

come, they all leave, and no one comes near you. Your wife, whom you love so much, and who has remained ever attached to you, runs away crying, ""Ghost! Ghost!"", as soon as the swan-soul leaves this body[9]. This is the way they act - those whom we love so much. At the very last moment, O Nanak, no one is any use at all, except the Dear Lord." **(Sri Guru Teg Bahadur Jee – Ang 634, Sorath)**

"In good times, there are many companions around, but in bad times, there is no one at all. Says Nanak, vibrate and meditate on the Lord; He shall be your only Help and Support in the end." **(Sri Guru Teg Bahadur Jee, Ang 1428, Stanza 32)**

Most of our so-called family and friends do leave our side at times of hardship and this is especially rings true for people who stand up for the truth and are revolutionary in the fact that they speak the truth and only heed the rules of the Lord and not those of any worldly rulers. These eternal truths have and do give inspiration and reasoning to Sikhs to continue in their endeavours regardless of the hardships they may undergo, including torture, rape, being displaced from their homes and family. The true Sikh will sacrifice all, including ones mortal body if the need arises.

Sri Guru Teg Bahadur lived in the turbulent times of the Mughal Rulers who were forcing conversion to Islam and persecuting those of differing faiths and practises. The Guru had spent much time away from Punjab enlightening the masses in the East of India in Assam, Bihar and surrounding areas. The Guru returned to set up camp in Sri Anandpur Sahib and the Mughal rulers had started persecuting the masses, to the extent that even places of

---

[9] As soon as death takes the soul out of the body.

worship of faiths other than Islam were also forcibly being demolished.

It was in this social setting that the Hindus were afraid of being made extinct in India (as most Hindus believed in Ahishma – non violence, thus would not stand up to the challenge by taking up arms). They came in their hour of need to Sri Guru Teg Bahadur Jee and begged him to listen to their supplication and protect them; this Hindu delegation of Pandits came from Kashmir. The Guru said that he would give them strength and protect their rights – not because the Guru believed in their beliefs but rather for the upholding of the freedom to practise whatever faith one wishes and the protection of basic human rights. The Guru sent a message to the Mughal Emperor Aurangzeb that if they could convert Him, all the Hindus and Sikhs of the country would follow in conversion.

The Emperor thus called the Guru to Delhi – to try and persuade the Guru to convert to Islam. He offered many riches and threatened the Guru with torture, but Guru Jee did not flinch. The Emperor then said that the Guru thought he was a Holy man – to prove this he should perform a miracle – but the Guru declined to perform any miracle as this was not in the will of God to perform miracles for mere entertainment. The Emperor then proceeded to torture to death three close associates of the Guru. The three Sikhs were Bhai Mati Das, Bhai Dayal Das and Bhai Sati Das Jee. Bhai Mati Das Jee was bound between two pillars and cut in two. When the saw was applied to his head, he calmly started uttering: "Ik Oankar" and started to recite "Sri Japji Sahib." The recitation of Sri Japji Sahib continued throughout the sawing and even continued until the completion of the prayer, even though two distinct halves of the body had been made.

Next, Bhai Dyal Das and Bhai Sati Das were executed. Bhai Dyal Das's hands and feet were tied firmly and he was thrown into a cauldron of boiling water. Not a sign of grief was uttered by this beloved disciple of the Guru. Bhai Sati Das was wrapped up in cotton and set alight. Thus these three great Sikhs attained martyrdom peacefully whilst undergoing the most inhumane tortures, but these efforts could not stir the Guru into surrendering his principles for worldly pleasures.

Thus the Emperor continued with his murderous intention and ordered the beheading of Sri Guru Teg Bahadur Jee – Guru Jee peacefully attained martyrdom in Chandni Chowk, Delhi, for the upholding of freedom of basic human rights, such as the right to practice one's faith without persecution.

King of Kings

Sri Guru Teg Bahadur knew of the treacherous times ahead and had made arrangements for His son, Gobind Rai, to be enthroned as the next Guru. Thus the tenth Guru of the Sikhs was Sri Guru Gobind Rai Jee (1666 – 1704AD), later known as Sri Guru Gobind Singh Jee. He was to be the last Human Guru of the Sikhs and was to lay the foundations for the future manifestations of the Sikhs and Sikhi.

It was the young (Guru) Gobind Rai who had made the first response to the Kashmiri Pandits who were supplicating to His Father (Sri Guru Teg Bahadur Jee) to protect their religious freedom. Gobind Rai had said there was no person of higher esteem than Sri Guru Teg Bahadur Jee, thus He should offer His head in weight of getting a compromise with the Mughal Empire to allow the Pandits to have religious freedoms. Thus it was the future 10th Guru at a tender age of 9 years, who had made the suggestion that only the sacrifice of Sri Guru Teg Bahadur would bring the issues of human rights abuses to the fore. Sri Guru Teg Bahadur seeing this inspirational response had decided at this point that Gobind Rai was ready to take on the throne of Sri Guru Nanak Dev Jee. This was the first sacrifice of Sri Guru Gobind Singh Jee. His greatness is incomparable. Is there any other son in the History of the World that would send His Father to a sure death and do this with pride?

Sri Guru Gobind Singh Jee decided to make a Nation that would fight to the death rather than compromise an inch of their faith and beliefs. This decision was taken when the Sikhs who were living in Delhi had been silent and anonymous at the public execution of His Father (as the Sikhs had no distinguishing features from the general public).The Sikhs had quietly watched the execution and had not protested against this injustice. This first hand report was given to the Guru by Bhai Jetha who had daringly taken the decapitated head of Sri Guru Teg Bahadur Jee and brought it to be cremated at Sri Anandpur Sahib (where Sri Guru Gobind Rai was residing). The body of Sri Guru Teg Bahadur Jee had been cremated by Bhai Lakhi Shah Lubana; He had burnt his whole house down to allow the cremation to take place (as they could not have an open cremation by order of the Mughal authorities and had secretly taken the body of Guru Jee). These grave circumstances had thrust upon the Guru the decision that such a nation would be created that would stand out and stand up for it's rights and not passively stand by whilst oppression of the masses occurred – this gave birth to the Khalsa Panth (Nation/Order of the Pure).

In 1699, Sri Guru Gobind Singh Jee created the Khalsa at Sri Anandpur Sahib. Again, the tradition of asking for nothing less than complete commitment was asked for from the Sikhs. Sikh belief is that the Guru asked for the offering of a head and he then decapitated the Sikh that offered his head. In turn, this was done five times. After slaying these five Sikhs the Guru recited prayers over an iron vessel that had water & sugar cakes (patase) in it, whilst stirring the mixture with a double-edged sword (Khanda). This Immortal Nectar (Amrit) was then administered to the Five Sikhs (Panj Pyare) who had been slain and they were brought back to life by drinking the Amrit. This account is historically accounted for by Abu-ul-Turani who was a spy of the Mughal Emperor Aurangzeb posted in the court of Sri Guru Gobind Singh Jee. Abu-ul-Turani would routinely send reports back to Aurangzeb of developments. Abu-ul-Turani states that Sri Guru Gobind Singh Jee decapitated the Panj Pyare in full view of the congregation. He then cleaned all the blood from the stage and surgically joined the heads back to differing bodies and placed white sheets over their bodies. He then went on and prepared the Amrit and after giving it to each Pyara and asking them to recite Vaaheguroo Jee Ka Khalsa Vaaheguroo Jee Kee Fateh, each Pyara was brought back to life roaring the Fateh. This was the last spy's report that Abu-ul-Turani sent back and he was overawed by what he saw, he warned Aurangzeb that Sri Guru Gobind Singh Jee is one with God and he should end his useless enmity towards the Guru. Abu-ul-Turani begged for the boon of Amrit and Sri Guru Gobind Singh Jee blessed him and he was known as Ajmer Singh from that day on. Dr Ganda Singh, a great Sikh Scholar and historian supports this historical account and argues that it is the most authentic account of the Amrit Sanchar of Vaisakhi 1699 AD. From this point on, initiation into the Sikh faith would be done by Panj Pyare in the presence of

Sri Guru Granth Sahib Jee, and the form of the Guru for Sikhs after the passing of Sri Guru Gobind Singh Jee to the abode of truth in 1708AD became Sri Guru Granth Sahib (Spiritual form of the Guru) and Panj Pyare (Physical form of the Guru). Thus guidance from five Sikhs would be seen as guidance directly from the Guru – this would be the basis of Sikh polity in generations to come. Nation building was enacted by giving Sikhs a distinct and common identity, in that anyone who became an initiated Sikh would have the following common features:

- o Father   Sri Guru Gobind Singh Jee

- o Mother   Mata Sahib Kaur Jee

- o Place of Birth   Sri Kesgarh Sahib,

                          Sri Anandpur Sahib

- o Surnames   Kaur (princess – for women),
                          Singh (tiger – for men)

- o Colours to wear   Blue, black, white, yellow/saffron

- o National Flag   Nishan Sahib

During torture, many Sikhs would only reveal the above information when interrogated. Thus they would frustrate the authorities as they would not give out any other personal information which may lead to them being identified or helping in their enquiries.

Articles of Faith

Kesh (unshorn hair), Kanga (wooden comb), Kirpan (iron sword), Kacchera (Sikh underwear), Kara (iron bangle worn on the wrist). All initiated Sikhs would keep these articles of faith upon them at all times and never part with them. Each of these articles of faith has deeper moral and spiritual messages;

Kesh – tied as a top-knot commonly on the top of one's head, with which a turban is complemented. The turban should be worn by both males and females. This tradition did die down in Sikh women but is being revived once again. The uncut hair and turban reminds a Sikh that he/she should remain humble at all times and live in the will/command of the Guru. The turban outwardly reminds the Sikh that he/she is distinct and a constant representative of the Guru. Keeping the hair is humbling in that one submits to the will of God in allowing nature to take its cause by not cutting one's hair.

Kanga – A Sikh will comb his/her hair twice daily. This is not a ritualistic practice. Rather, the Sikh is reminded that he/she should break bondage/attachment with the world in the same way that broken hairs are taken out with the act of combing one's hair in the morning and evening.

Kacchera – The underwear is a constant reminder of one's moral obligations.

Kara – The bracelet is like a handcuff to the Guru, showing one's serfdom to the Guru and is a constant visual reminder that a Sikh should not indulge in greed.

Kirpan – Sword of mercy is a constant reminder that one should remember that the Guru is with one at all times as, in Sikhi, weapons are also seen as a form of the Guru. Additionally the Kirpan reminds a Sikh that he should stand up to tyranny and injustice and only draw the Kirpan in defence of these principles. The Kirpan is also used to bless food and signifies the acceptance of the offering by the Guru, when the Kirpan blesses the food.

Cardinal Sins

There are four cardinal sins that cannot be committed by initiated Sikhs. If one of these sins is committed, a Sikh must go and ask for forgiveness at an initiation ceremony and receive punishment from the Panj Pyare. The cardinal sins one must refrain from are:

1. **Cutting one's hair, dying it, surgically removing it or plucking it. Also a Sikh must not deface the body in anyway, for example a Sikh cannot get body piercing or tattoos.**

2. **Consuming intoxicants – including drugs, alcohol, and tobacco.**

3. **Eating meat, fish or eggs (in survival circumstances they may be consumed but Halal meat is still outlawed)**

4. **Committing adultery or having sexual relationships outside of marriage.**

National Anthem – the Sikh national anthem authored by Sri Guru Gobind Singh teaches and inspires a Sikh to be an optimist and take on life's challenges with courage and never refrain from righteous acts or be scared to do so:

> *Grant me this boon O God*
> *May I never refrain from the righteous acts;*
> *May I fight without fear all foes in life's battles*
> *With confident courage claiming the victory!*
> *May thy teaching be grained in my mind,*
> *That I remain forever greedy to sing thy praises;*
> *When the time comes for me to die*
> *May I die fighting with limitless courage.*

Sri Guru Gobind Singh Jee's whole family were sacrificed for the upholding of Sikhi. His four sons (Sahibzade) were martyred and the Guru entered battle four times with the Mughal Emperors. He left a lasting impact on the future of the South Asian sub-continent and the world at large. The Guru had clearly stated that Sikhs should pursue their freedoms and fight for them and that without rule/complete freedom they will not be prosperous:

> *Without sovereignty Dharam (righteous principles)*
> *cannot prosper*
> *Without Dharam chaos rules*
> *No-one gives anyone sovereignty*
> *Those that become sovereign do so, by their strength.*
> (Sri Guru Gobind Singh Jee)

Sikhs are, though, ardent believers that arms are only drawn as a last resort:

> *When all other means have been exhausted*

It is then just to take out arms
(Sri Guru Gobind Singh Jee)

Battle Victories of Sri Guru Gobind Singh Jee

Sri Guru Gobind Singh Jee led a peaceful life until 1689 AD when he defended Anandpur Sahib in his first battle, the battle of Bhangani. This battle was against the Hindu Hill Rajas (Kings) who despised the Guru for raising all castes on a common platform and they wanted to dislodge the Sikhs from Anandpur. They were successfully routed and rebuffed by Sri Guru Gobind Singh and his brave warriors. The Hill Rajas called on the Mughals to support them to defeat Sri Guru Gobind Singh Jee who was branded as a common foe to the Muslims and Hindus by the respective rulers.

In 1704 the combined forces attacked the Sikhs but knew that they could not defeat the Sikhs in open battle, as they had been rebuffed once again. Thus they laid siege to Anandpur in the summer of 1704. The Sikhs and Sri Guru Gobind Singh Jee were in a fort called Anandgarh for months during this siege. There was a deadlock - the opposing forces could not draw the Sikhs out of Anandgarh and could not see any breaking of the impasse. Thus, after solemn oaths, taken upon the Cow and Quran by the respective enemies, that no attack would be launched, Sri Guru Gobind Singh Jee agreed to leave the fort. This was on the 20 December 1704, but the treacherous enemy forces broke their 'solemn oaths' and attacked the Sikhs. However, the Sikhs manfully rebuffed their attacks once again and Sri Guru Gobind Singh Jee reached Chamkaur on the 21 December 1704 after crossing the Sirsa stream.

Sri Guru Gobind Singh Jee and forty surviving Sikhs raised a defensive position in a raised mud house (Garhi). The Sikhs showed exemplary bravery in battle from the

Chamkaur Garhi, but many of the Sikhs were martyred. Nonetheless Sri Guru Gobind Singh Jee still managed to escape unscathed. In His own words Sri Guru Gobind Singh Jee narrates victory in letters to Aurangzeb the Mughal Emperor. These are called Fatehnama and Zafarnama, namely meaning prose of victory. Firstly I will quote the whole of the Fatehnama and provide commentary where necessary:

In the name of the Lord who manifests Himself as weapons of war viz (through) the sword, the axe, the arrow, the spear, and the shield. The Lord is with the brave warriors who, mounted on their horses, fly through the air. The Lord who has bestowed upon you the kingdom[10], has granted me the honour of protecting the faith. Where as you are engaged in plunder by deceit and lies, I am on the path of truth and purity. The name "Aurangzeb" does not befit you, since a king who is supposed to bring honour to the throne, will not indulge in deceit Aurangzeb! Your rosary is nothing more than a bundle of beads and thread. With every move of a bead, you entrap others in your snare Aurangzeb! By your grisly act, you have put your father's name in the dust; by murdering your own brothers, you have added (to the list of your evil deeds) and from that (by imprisoning your father and murdering your brothers) you have laid a weak foundation of your kingdom. Now by the grace of the Lord, I have made the water of steel (Amrit for my warriors) which will fall upon you like a torrent and with this (torrent of Amrit), your sinister kingdom will vanish from this holy land without a trace. You came thirsty (defeated) from the mountains of South; the Rajputs have also made you drink the bitter cup (of defeat). Now you are casting your sight towards this side (Punjab). Here

---

[10] Referring to Aurangzeb

also your thirst will remain unquenched I will put fire under your feet when you come to Punjab and I will not let you even drink water here. What is so great if a jackal kills two cubs of a tiger by deceit and cunning?[11] Since that formidable tiger still lives, he will definitely take revenge (from the jackal). I no longer trust you or your God since I have seen your God as well as his word. I do not trust your oaths anymore and now there is no other way for me except to take up the sword[12]. If you are an old fox, I will too keep my tigers out of your snare. If you come to me for detailed and frank talks, I shall show you the path of purity and truthfulness. Let the forces from both sides array in the battlefield at such a distance that they are visible to each other. The battle field should be arranged in such a manner that both the forces should be separated by a reasonable distance (of two furlongs). Then I will advance in the battle field for combat with your forces along with two of my riders. So far you have been enjoying the fruits of a cosy and comfortable life but never faced the fierce warriors (in the battle field). Now come into the battle field with your weapons and stop tormenting the people who are the creation of the Lord. **(Fatehnama, Sri Guru Gobind Singh Jee, translation from www.zafarnama.com)**

This challenge from Sri Gobind Singh Jee of an open and face to face battle was never taken up by Aurangzeb. From the wording of the Fatehnama, one can see complete

---

[11] It is unclear if Sri Guru Gobind Singh Jee is referring to the older or younger Sahibzadas (His sons) here, but regardless of this the Sahibzade were all martyred due to treacherous false oaths taken by the Mughals & Hill Rajas in battle.

[12] All the battles that Sri Guru Gobind Singh Jee was victorious in were all defensive, in that the Sikhs were attacked and the Sikhs (in the times of Sri Gobind Singh Jee) never made any territorial land claims even when they were victorious in battle – this is unparralled in history.

defiance and the spirit of victory of Sri Guru Gobind Singh Jee, even though he had at this time sacrificed his beloved close associates in Chamkaur and his four sons and mother. This is the greatness of the Father of the Sikhs, an undying rising spirit. I will now quote directly from Zafarnama of how Sri Guru Gobind Singh narrates the events of the battle of Chamkaur:

"What can forty hungry men do, when suddenly ten-lac[13] strong army pounces upon them? That the promise breakers launched a surprise attack with their swords and arrows and guns. It was out of sheer helplessness that I came in the battle field. (Having thus decided) I came with all the battle plans and munitions.

When the entire stratagem employed for (solving) a problem are exhausted, (only) then taking your hand to the sword is legitimate.[14]

What trust can I have on your oath on Koran? Otherwise you tell why I should have taken this path (of taking up the sword). I do not know that this person (Aurangzeb) is cunning like a fox. Otherwise I would never have come to this place i.e. Chamkaur (by vacating Anandgarh on the false oaths of Aurangzeb and his men). If any person believes an oath on Koran, he should neither be tied (arrested) nor killed.

They (the enemy) dressed in black and like flies came suddenly with great uproar. Any person who came out from behind the wall, took one arrow (on his body) and

---

[13] 1,000,000

[14] This is the most quoted verse of Zafarnama. 300 years ago, Guru Gobind Singh Ji had laid down the circumstances when a person or a nation can pick up the sword against the other. (Comment taken from original translation)

was submerged in blood. Any person who did not come out from (behind) that wall, did not take an arrow and (hence) did not become miserable (die). When I saw that Nahar had come out from behind the wall for battle, he immediately took one of my arrows on himself (and died).

Many Afghans who used to tell tall stories (about their bravery) also ran away from the battlefield. That large number of other Afghans came for the battle like a flood of arrows and bullets. They launched many a brave attacks. (However) some of these (attacks) were intelligently launched but some were sheer madness. They launched many attacks and they took many wounds upon themselves. They killed two (of my) men and also gave their own lives as well.

That coward Khawaja (who was hiding behind the wall) did not come out in the battlefield like a brave man. Alas! If I had seen his (Khawaja's) face, I would have sent him to the other world just with one arrow.

In the end many fighters from both sides died quickly after being wounded by arrows and bullets. The battlefield was full of (severed) heads and legs, which gave the impression as if these were balls and sticks.[15]

The whizzing of arrows and vibrations of the strings of bows produced huge commotions. And cries of "hai-hu" were coming from the whole battle field. And the dreadful noises of weapons had their affect on the bravest of brave men who gave the impression as if they had lost their mental balance.

---

[15] If the battle field was full of severed heads and legs (which could not be counted), it again reflects on the heavy price the Mughal forces had to pay at the hands of the defenders of Chamkaur. (Comment taken from original translation)

And finally what could the bravery of my forty warriors do in battle when countless of these (Afghans) fell upon them." (**Zafarnama** – verses 19 - 41, **Sri Guru Gobind Singh Jee, translation from** <ins>www.zafarnama.com</ins>)

Sri Guru Gobind Singh Jee shows no relenting even though his sons have been sacrificed,

What happened that you have killed four children (my sons); the coiled snake (in the form of my Khalsa) still remains. What manliness you have shown by extinguishing a few sparks (Sahibzadas). You have made the conflagration brighter and more furious. How nicely the sweet-tongued poet Firdosi has said that "to act in haste is the work of a devil."[16] When I meet you in the court of your Lord, you will appear as a witness there (and answer all the crimes committed by you)." (**Zafarnama** – verses 78-81, **Sri Guru Gobind Singh Jee, translation from** <ins>www.zafarnama.com</ins>)

One final comment on the Chamkaur battle that needs to be noted is that Sri Guru Gobind Singh Jee is a truly a unique Father who could have saved his older sons from being sacrificed in the battle. Yet, He happily let them enter battle and attain martyrdom. He truly treated all Sikhs as his children and when leaving the Chamkaur Garhi he took his shoes off so he would not step on any of the martyred Sikhs with his shoes on. This was the love He had for His Sikhs.

Another misconception about the Sikhs and especially the battles of Sri Guru Gobind Singh Jee that needs to be clarified is that the Hindu Hill Rajas were as much against

---

[16] Guru Jee is referring to the summary execution of the young Sahibzadas at Sirhind which he has termed as an act of a devil. (Comment taken from original translation)

the Muslim Mughals, sometimes the Islamic element is over-emphasised and the Hindu Hill Rajas are given a convenient oversight. In the Guru's words,

> *"I am also the annihilator of the hill rajas, the idol worshippers. They are idol worshipers and I am engaged in defeating "the very concept" of idol worship."* **(Zafarnama – verse 95, Sri Guru Gobind Singh Jee, translation from www.zafarnama.com)**

I would like to also clarify that Sri Guru Gobind Singh Jee fought against tyranny and did not undertake battle to attack any faith or faithful. Sikhs in their zealous nature sometimes refer to the battles of the Guru as being against Muslims, but this is mistaken. The battles were to uproot tyranny regardless of the faith allegiance of those being fought.

I think it would also be fitting to quote how Sri Guru Gobind Singh Jee narrates that the faithful are protected by the Almighty in battle and dire circumstances:

> *"In time of need, He blinds the enemy and takes out the helpless without an injury to him; even from a thorn (a thorn cannot prick him if God does not ordain it).*[17] *The Compassionate Lord always showers mercy upon any person who follows the path of truthfulness. Anyone who serves the Almighty with total devotion is blessed with peace and tranquillity. What deception can an enemy inflict on a person who is under the protection of Lord Himself."* **(Zafarnama – verses 100-103, Sri Guru Gobind Singh Jee, translation from www.zafarnama.com)**

---

[17] Guru Ji is referring to his escape from Chamkaur. (Comment taken from original translation)

The above lines are universal and apply to the faithful, regardless of their religious allegiance.

I thought it would also be fitting to finish this chapter with the narration of the story of the final martyr of Chamkaur battle – Bibi Harsharan Kaur,

"… in village Khroond, a daughter of Guru Gobind Singh, Bibi Harsharan Kaur, asked for her mother's permission to perform the final rites for the Shaheeds. Her old mother replied, "it is total darkness outside and soldiers are everywhere around the fort, how will you even go near?"

Hearing this, Kalgeedhar's[18] lioness daughter replied with resolve "I will avoid the soldiers and perform the cremation, and if need be, I'll fight and die." The mother gave her courage and hugged her daughter and then explained the maryada[19] to follow for the cremation. After performing Ardas, Bibi Harsharan Kaur left for the Chamkaur Fort.

The battlefield, which saw iron smashing against iron, heard the bellows of elephants, the trotting of hooves and calls of "Kill! Capture!" was now totally silent, and enveloped in complete darkness. In such a situation, the 16 year old girl Bibi Harsharan Kaur avoided the guards and arrived at the Fort. She saw that bodies were lying everywhere and distinguishing between Sikh and Mughal was very difficult. She still had faith and began to find arms with Karas and torsos with kachheras and heads with long Kesh. As she found a body, she would wipe the face of every Shaheed. Both Sahibzadas and about 30 Shaheeds

---

[18] The plume wearing Sovereign – reference to Sri Gobind Singh Jee
[19] Rites

were found and then she began to collect wood. Fearing the approaching light of dawn, Bibi Harsharan Kaur worked very quickly and soon prepared a pyre. She then lit the fire.

Seeing the rising flames, the guards were shocked and advanced towards the pyre. Bibi Harsharan Kaur was seen in the light of the flames sitting beside the pyre. She was quietly reciting Kirtan Sohila. The guards were shocked and confused as to how a lone woman could come into the fort on such a dark night.

The guards asked in a loud voice,
"Who are you?"

Bibi Jee:	*I am the daughter of Guru Gobind Singh*
Officer:	*What are you doing here?*
Bibi Jee:	*I am cremating my martyred brothers.*
Officer:	*Don't you know about the order that coming here is a crime?*
Bibi Jee:	*I know it.*
Officer:	*Then why have you disobeyed that order?*
Bibi Jee:	*The orders of a false king do not stand before the orders of the Sachay Patshah (True King)*
Officer:	*Meaning?*

36

Bibi Jee:	*Meaning that I have respect for the Singhs in my heart and with the Guru's grace I have done my duty. I don't care about your King's orders.*

Hearing such stern answers from Bibi Harsharan Kaur, the infuriated Mughal Soldiers attempted to capture her and attack. Bibi Jee grabbed her Kirpan and fought back with determination. After killing and maiming many soldiers, Bibi Harsharan Kaur was injured and fell to the ground. The soldiers picked Bibi Harsharan Kaur up and threw her into the pyre, burning her alive.

The next day the cordon around the Fort was lifted because it was clear that the Sahibzade and most of the Shaheed Singhs had been cremated. The ancestors of the Phulkiaan family, Rama and Triloka, then cremated the remaining Singhs. The story of Bibi Harsharan Kaur reached Guru Gobind Singh Jee Maharaj in Talvandee Sabo (Damdama Sahib).

Upon hearing of her daughter's martyrdom, the old mother thanked Akaal Purakh (Immortal Lord). She said, "My daughter has proven herself Worthy." The story of the cremation of the Chamkaur Shaheeds will forever serve as a glowing star of inspiration for all Singhs and Singhnees." (Adapted from Mahinder Singh ChachraaRee in Soora December 1997, Translated by Admin www.tapoban.org)

Eternal Guru

Sri Guru Granth Sahib Jee is the eternal Guru of the Sikhs. In 1708 at Nanded Sri Guru Gobind Singh Jee gave the spiritual Guruship to Sri Guru Granth Sahib Jee and ordained that the physical Guru would be Panj Pyare. Thus the Guru being present in full glory, where there would be Panj Pyare and Sri Guru Granth Sahib Jee, as in Amrit

Sanchars (initiation ceremonies). The Sri Guru Granth Sahib Jee is truly universal and includes the writing of Sufi Saints and Bhagats of the Bhagti tradition. The Sri Guru Granth Sahib Jee was completed in its present form by Sri Guru Gobind Singh Jee and it includes the writings of the first five Gurus' and Sri Guru Teg Bahadur Jee (the ninth Guru).

The Sri Guru Granth Sahib is the guide of Sikhs in all their affairs and a Sikh will take a Hukamnama - a command from random - when he/she wishes to gain guidance from the Guru. I will not delve too much into the teachings of Sri Guru Granth Sahib Jee at this point as various quotes will be used consistently throughout this book. However I will quote a verse which has consistently been received as a Hukamnama by Sikhs when they have been preparing to punish a tyrant:

All demons and enemies are eradicated by You, Lord;
Your glory is manifest and radiant.
Whoever harms your devotees, you destroy in an instant.
I look to you continually, Lord.
O Lord, Destroyer of ego,
Please, be the helper and companion of your slaves;
Take my hand, and save me, O my Friend! ||Pause||
My Lord and Master has heard my prayer,
And given me His protection.
Nanak is in ecstasy, and his pains are gone;
He meditates on the Lord, forever and ever.
(Sri Guru Arjan Dev Jee, 681 Ang, Dhanasree)

2. 1708 – 1947

Baba Banda Singh Bahadur's Rule

Baba Banda Singh Bahadur (1670 – 1716AD, see page 134 for picture) led the Khalsa armies after Sri Guru Gobind Singh Jee. He successfully routed Sirhind – the place of the execution of the younger Sahibzade who were aged 5 and 7 years old respectfully, and he managed to create a Sikh state that covered Amritsar, Kalanaur, Batala and Pathankot, overrunning the Sutlej and Ravi rivers.[20] . This period is looked upon favourably, as immediate retribution was meted out to the Mughal tyrants and the Sikhs successfully enjoyed the glow of freedom, even if it was short-lived. This Sikh state reigned from 1710 – 1716AD until Bhai Banda Singh Bahadur was executed by the Mughal emperors. The genocide of the Sikhs proceeded this reign and a price was put on Sikh heads; anyone who came forward with information about the whereabouts of Sikhs or brought the heads of dead Sikhs forward to the Mughal authorities, were awarded bounties. Due to these treacherous circumstances many Sikhs were reduced to living in jungles, and Sikhs who kept their faith had to undergo serious hardships, such as exposure, starvation, having no income or fixed abode.

Shaheed Bhai Bota Singh Jee & Shaheed Bhai Garja Singh Jee

Two great Sikhs who did not compromise their faith in this period of persecution were Bhai Bota Singh and Bhai Garja Singh. They underwent hardships and had set up camp in a jungle. One day they were hiding out in the jungle and some soldiers of the Mughal Empire passed them. The soldiers were saying that the Sikhs have become extinct and there are no Sikhs left in the Indian sub-

---

[20] 'History of Sikh Struggles,' Gurmit Singh, 1989

continent. These two Sikhs were infuriated by the remarks and decided that their lives were useless if they could hear such insults and do nothing about it. Thus they decided to stand up and be counted. They set up a mini-state in the small enclave that they were living in and they started levying tax on any passers-by; to go past the enclave a Khalsa tax had to be paid in order to maintain this mini-Sikh state (of their enclave). Obviously news reached the Mughal authorities who were infuriated at the audacity of these two Sikhs and they deputed forces to undertake battle with them. The two Sikhs maintained their mini-Sikh state for 7 days without hindrance and it was only on the 7th day that they were martyred defending their faith and state (in 1739AD).

The above is a small example of the sheer audacity and bravery of true Sikhs, where two Sikhs set up and ran a Sikh state, even if it were only for 7 days. In real terms setting up a Sikh state should not be that hard if we have the strength and determination of these two great role-models.

Sikh Raj

In the 1760s different Sikh leaders started to re-assemble themselves and to reclaim land, which led to the development of "Misls", which were basically districts that were governed by Sikhs such as Sardar Jassa Singh Ramgharia & Sardar Jassa Singh Aluhwalia (it was now that the term Sardar became prevalent for Sikhs, basically meaning leader/ruler).

Maharajah Ranjit Singh tenaciously created a kingdom by getting other Sikh leaders to join him in a confederation of regions. His reign lasted from 1801 to 1837 and it was finally annexed in 1847 after two Anglo-Sikh wars. This reign was short lived and the Maharajah died of disease.

The British only attacked on the death of the king as they feared attacking whilst he was alive because of his excellent military skills.

"The principalities the Sikhs had carved out were integrated into the sovereign state of the Khalsa by Ranjit Singh. Born heir to one of these confederacies, he had the foresight to visualise a united Sikh kingdom. By his superior military genius and political acumen, he succeeded in integrating the existing Misls and joining the people of Punjab into a strong nation." (Harbans Singh, 1994:130)

Some argue that this Raj was not a Sikh Raj, but I argue that it was as it was based upon the principles of equality and the King himself took direction from the Akaal Takhat Jathedar who was Akali Phula Singh Jee. The Sikhs were a minority in this Raj and treated Hindus and Muslims with equality and no preference was given to Sikhs. The Raj's decision making was based upon democratic decision making, in that a court would be held in which the leaders of the different principalities would meet, discuss and decide matters of polity.

The British ruled over Punjab for the next century between 1847 and 1947.

Uprisings against British Raj

The Sikhs looked favourably upon their recent history as being "Sardars", and thus could only take so much British rule before starting uprisings against them. Their strong history of bravery and being revolutionaries led them to spearhead such uprisings ,both in guerrilla warfare and in organised political uprisings.

Namdhari Movement - The Namdhari movement was initially a strict reform movement of Sikhi and was led by Baba Ram Singh (1816 – 1885AD). He led this movement from 1857 onwards. The distinct features of the Namdharis and their political programme were that they differed from orthodox Sikhs in dress because they had a distinct style of turban, wore only hand woven dress, had simpler weddings and all their clothing was white in colour. Namdharis were forbidden to join government service or to go to courts of law or learn the English language. The Namdharis developed an alternative political system, having their own law courts that were based on religion and their own postal system. All that was British was shunned by the Namdharis, which proved an immense commitment by them to their own cause, no matter what the difficulties or obstacles faced in opposition to their beliefs and practices:

"Its chief inspiration was, in fact, derived from opposition to foreign rule and everything tending to remind one of it was shunned. English education, mill-made cloth and other imported goods were boycotted. In its advocacy of the use of the Swadehsi[21], the Kuka movement forestalled, in the sixties of the last century, an important feature of the nationalist struggle under the leadership of Mahatma Gandhi." (Harbans Singh, 1993: 193)

This peaceful political movement laid the foundations for what Mahatma Gandhi would re-enact some 70 years later as part of the Indian National Movement. The Namdharis were also organised geographically, having 12 missions with distinct geographical jurisdiction. Their movement was initially peaceful, but they started to take up arms in

---

[21] The use of indigenous goods only

defence of their faith and beliefs when the British started to persecute them.

Towards the end of 1871 the Punjab government placed a ban on Namdharis assembling for any fair or festival outside of Bhaini town, where the Namdhari headquarters were situated. On the morning of January 15, 1872 Namdharis numbering more than a hundred attacked a store of state armoury in Malerkotla. In this attack eight police officials and seven Namdharis lost their lives. From this incident 68 further Namdharis were arrested and blown up by cannons (they were tied to the mouths of the cannons) by the British, to show what would happen to those rebelling against the British. Ram Singh along with ten Subas (commanders of different districts) was exiled from Punjab. (Harbans Singh, 1993)

The Namdhari movement was the first truly international movement for emancipation from British imperialism. Contact was made with Russia and ambassadors were appointed in Afghanistan and Nepal. The British quashed the movement with barbaric tactics and it became a docile/peace-loving movement. This form of it lives on today and it has become cult-like with a living Guru. It has lost all its revolutionary fervour and has become a cult that is viewed as heretical by mainstream Sikhs.

Ghadar Party & Babbar Akalis - The Ghadar Party was essentially a secular party that was joined by many Sikhs, in the hope of freeing "India" from the British. The publication of a newspaper, the Ghadar, meaning 'revolution,' led to the founding of the Ghadar party. In August 1914 in Sacramento, USA, the party had a meeting in which it was declared that Indians would go back to India in large numbers in order to cause revolution and armed disturbances. It was declared in the following manner in the Ghadar:

"Now is the time to rise and put Europeans to death and free your country of them ... I am telling you of a war declared ... It has spread all over India ... Can you sit idle while a war is going on? You will join in this war ... You should unite together, uproot the present Raj and establish a Republic." (Rai, 1984:61)

It is estimated that by the beginning of December 1914 nearly one thousand Ghadarites had entered India. Most activists were from Punjab and the majority Sikhs as they made up the largest immigrant group. The party aimed at stirring up the emotions of the people to rebel against the British. They actively encouraged armed rebellion. In their writings they attempted to stir up rebellious thought in the following way:

"Why do you disgrace the name of Singhs? How come!
You have forgotten the majesty of 'lions'
Had the like of Dip Singh been alive today
How could have the Singhs been taunted?"
(Puri, 1983:84)

This is an extract of one of the poems published in the 'Ghadar' newspaper. By 1915 the uprising had virtually been smashed. But it was the first secular movement which had aimed at liberating India by the use of arms. The movement was largely significant for the Sikh community and they did have a large participation in the activities of the party. It marked the end of unquestionable loyalty to the British by the Sikhs on a political level, as the Ghadar party were more popular with the masses than the Namdhari movement ever was. It arrived at a time when the people were tiring at the hands of British imperialism. Even though the rebellion was quashed it re-emerged in the form of the Akalis in the reform of the Gurdwaras and the Babbar Akalis who used violent means to achieve their ends.

The Babbar Akalis used guerrilla tactics to free the Gurdwaras from the control of the British. They made sporadic attacks against the British and against those abusing their power as caretakers of the shrines. The Babbar Akalis were the first organised armed resistance against the British. Their ranks were mostly drawn from those present in Punjab, unlike the Ghadar party whom were drawn mostly from Sikh Diaspora. The Babbar Akalis were quashed but they did give a shock to the British, that the Sikhs could be organised and start such resistance. The end of this movement led to the development of a peaceful movement for freeing the Gurdwaras which did reap more fruits.

Birth of Shiromani Gurdwara Parbandhak Committee (SGPC) & Shiromani Akali Dal (SAD)

The British established new land settlement records when they came to power in Punjab. Thus land and property that were attached to Gurdwaras[22] were entered as the property of the priests. These priests then began to misuse the Gurdwaras, turning them into brothels, dens of gamblers and criminals. To counter these anti-Sikh practices by the priests who were in most cases not practising Sikhs themselves, the Shiromani Gurdwara Parbandhak Committee[23] was founded on 15 November 1920 in which a committee was set up to manage all Sikh shrines. Some priests stepped down and handed control over to the SGPC whereas others entered into confrontation

---

[22] Place of worship for Sikhs
[23] Abbreviated to SGPC henceforth

with the SGPC. On 14 December 1920 the Shiromani Akali Dal[24] was founded. This was to be the political wing of the SGPC, thus two bodies were made - one solely religious and the other political - both to further the interests of the Sikh nation. (Kushwant Singh, 1977)

In 1921 a violent confrontation between the Sikhs and the priest's mercenaries took place at Nanakana Sahib, the place of birth of Guru Nanak, where 130 Akalis who were peacefully protesting were murdered by the priest's mercenaries. The keys to the shrine were immediately handed over to the SGPC. This incident triggered off the Gurdwara reform movement that lasted over four years. The British opposed this movement, thousands of Sikhs being arrested and beaten in their peaceful protests.

The Guru Ka Bagh incident is one of much terror and courage on the part of the Sikhs. They were trying to get control of this shrine by peaceful means. Many Sikhs were peacefully walking to the shrine and then getting beaten to a pulp by the British police. This continued for nineteen days. When the police brutality stopped, 5,605 Akalis had been arrested and 1,650 hospitalised. (Kapur, 1986)

Incidents like this led to the Sikh Gurdwaras and Shrines Act of 1925, which handed over the control of Sikh shrines to the SGPC. (Tatla, 1999) During the Gurdwara reform movement the Sikhs developed a passion for politics. Though the movement was supposed to be religious, the anti-government stance gave it a complexion of a political movement. Wallace (1989) argues that the temple reform after World War One became the major political activity of the Sikhs and this is viewed by many as the basis for Sikh separatism.

---

[24] Abbreviated to SAD henceforth

3. Independence?

Indian & Pakistani Independence

Although Sikhs spearheaded the initial freedom movement of India with mass protest (in the Gurdwara freedom movement) and guerrilla uprisings, after freeing Gurdwaras from British control the majority of Sikhs became a silent majority who took a step back from political involvement. This led to Sikh leaders having a less radical support base and led them to compromising Sikh concerns. Sikhs were a minority and setting up a minority-rule to appease Sikhs was unlikely. The Sikhs had no option but to make a critical choice of either joining the Indian or Pakistan National Movement(s) leaders. The Sikh leaders in the end had very little bargaining power.

There were many complexities to the claim of a Sikh state, and it was the Sikhs who suffered the most in the independence of India. They lost half of their historical shrines to Punjab of Pakistan, they lost fertile lands and many had to move from their homes. Many were killed in the partition violence and they lost any political privileges they had gained under the British rule. Half a million people were killed when the partition of India & Pakistan took place, in communal violence that ensued between communities who had to migrate from their homes (see page 134 for pictures relating to the partition).

It did not matter if the Sikhs could not have their own state, but what did matter was that their interests as a minority were insured and that their shrines were given proper respect in independence, but this was not achieved. The Sikhs ended up salvaging whatever they possibly could.

What was the role of the other communities and the British? The Congress party made many promises to the

Sikhs that Sikhs would enjoy the glow of freedom but when independence dawned they did not achieve any special concessions to Punjab, which they thought would be semi-autonomous. Their language was denied the status it should have had in constitutional terms and the Sikhs were termed Hindus in the new constitution. In reality the Sikhs were the ones who made most sacrifices to free India/Pakistan from British Imperialism:

"During the freedom struggle, 73 of 121 persons executed were the Sikhs and 2147 of 2664 sentenced to life imprisonment in the Andamans were the Sikhs. In the Jalianwala Bagh massacre which brought to a head the demand for freedom, out of 1302 men, women and children gunned down by General Dyer, 799 were the Sikhs." (Sangat Singh, 1995: 502)

The Sikhs made sacrifices for freedom in an excessive manner yet they were not rewarded for their heroics and their political leaders did not have either the political acumen or courage to demand justifiable returns. What the Sikhs got in return were broken promises and inequalities in the form of India. Please see the Sikhtoon on page 134.

Free India – Discrimination of Sikhs

What did Sikhs specifically get when "India" got freedom in 1947, in terms of policy formulations?

- **Article 25** – Indian Constitution states that Sikhs are Hindus (as are Christians, Jains and Buddhists). The constitution drawn up in 1950 has never been accepted or signed by the Sikhs, as it broke promises made prior to independence.

- **Hindu Marriage Act** – there is no Sikh Marriage Act (even the British recognised this basic need of the Sikhs)

- **Shiromani Gurdwara Parbandhak Committee (SGPC)** – is governed by Indian Law and is not an independent body and the Deputy Commissioner of Amritsar can intervene at any time when he/she pleases. Thus the Sikhs have not even got religious freedom and state interference with matters of Sikh faith is common place.

- **Linguistically** – in 1956 the states of India were reorganised on a linguistic basis. The mother tongue of the state was made the language of each respective state, but this wasn't done with Punjab. Sikhs protested and after much deliberation, they agreed Punjabi Suba in 1966 (which was a much smaller sized Punjab to ensure Sikhs made up about 60% of the population, as the Hindus voted for Hindi as their mother tongue over Punjabi when consultation took place). Punjab was divided into 3 states of Haryana, UP and present day Punjab to get this linguistic right promised in Independence. Please see page 95 for a picture showing Sikhs protesting for the creation of Punjabi Suba.

- **River waters** - Punjab's only natural resource is the river water that flows through it, yet this water is diverted to other states and used to generate energy for other parts of India and Punjab gets nothing in return for this water sharing. In return farmers suffer and Punjab has energy deficiencies that it shouldn't have.

Sikhs on the whole did just put up with their lot and put hard work into establishing themselves economically. Punjab became the bread basket for India, becoming the supplier of about 60% of all wheat . Even this hard work has not been looked upon favourably and farmers do not get fair prices, nor has inward investment from central government been forthcoming to invest in technology to bring Punjab into the global economy. What has been forthcoming are alcohol production (and sales) and excessive expenditure to control any uprisings/agitations asking for just rights.

State of Emergency
On the 26th June 1975, Indira Gandhi called a state of emergency, which was done to stop the corruption enquiry that could have invalidated the election and subjected Indira to criminal charges. She suspended the constitution to stay in office and avoid imprisonment. The state of emergency lasted 19 months. Sikhs spearheaded the non violent protest against the self-imposed state of emergency. 50,000 Sikhs courted arrest during this period.

Sant Kartar Singh Jee Bhindranvale was a leading figure in the protests against the state of emergency and he organised 37 protest marches in which the Sikh masses were mobilised. Alongside this, Sant Kartar Singh travelled extensively to preach the teachings of Sikhi and stop the rise of apostasy in Sikhs. This was the first time that the Damdami Taksal came to the forefront in terms of a joint political and spiritual movement in the 1970's and it started its steady rise to be recognised as a serious political and religious force.

In Delhi on 7 December 1975 AD – to commemorate the 300th anniversary of the Shaheedi of Sri Guru Teg Bahadur

Jee, in the Ram Lila ground, a procession of 2.2 million people arrived and P.M. Indira Gandhi came onto the stage. In the presence of Sri Guru Granth Sahib Jee all those on the stage arose to welcome and respect her, but it was only Sant Kartar Singh Jee who remained seated. On the stage Sant Jee spoke passionately about this anti-Sikh act of the Sikh leaders rising to greet Indira Gandhi in the presence of Sri Guru Granth Sahib Jee, as for a devout Sikh no-one deserves higher reverence than Sri Guru Granth Sahib Jee. By rising to greet the prime minister they had belittled Sri Guru Granth Sahib Jee – this is portrayed in history by the Emperor Akbar being told to partake in the free kitchen prior to meeting Sri Guru Amar Das, the Emperor did so and ate alongside common people and he was only then granted a meeting with the Guru. Many leaders who spoke on the stage said that P.M. Indira Gandhi had built an excellent relationship with Punjab, after which she said the Delhi government[25] got Sri Guru Teg Bahadur martyred and today the Delhi government[26] prostrates to Sri Guru Teg Bahadur Jee. The same Delhi government[27], who were given reports against the Sikhs, today respects and reveres Sri Guru Teg Bahadur Jee.

Sant Jee's time to speak was after P.M. Indira Gandhi, he began with,

"May my head be sacrificed, but not my Sikhi"[28]

First Rajput Kings used to give their daughters to get rewards. Today Sikhs are disgracing themselves if they do the same. For this reason no Sikh is to marry their daughter to an apostate and the rehatnama says:

---

[25] The Mughal Empire of the time ruled from Delhi
[26] Reference to the Modern Indian Government led by Indira Gandhi
[27] Again reference to Mughal Empire
[28] A famous Sikh Slogan that would have been sung in a high melody

INDEPENDENCE?

Sri Guru Gobind Singh Jee says that the Sikh that marries his daughter to a Sikh and does not take any money/dowry; he is a true Sikh of mine and will reach my abode in Sachkand[29]. (Bhai Sahib Singh Rehatnama, p.160)

He further questioned, *"We want to ask Indira Gandhi, who achieved the rule of the Delhi government?" If you have come here to prostrate to Sri Guru Teg Bahadur you have done no great act. If Guru Jee had not become martyred the master of this throne would have been a Muslim and everywhere all would be greeted with Salema Lekham (Islamic greeting). You yourself would have been under a Burka/Hijab."*

The number of hairs that are on the body of the P.M., even if she was to cut her head off that many times and placed at the feet of Guru Jee, she still would not be able to remove the debt owed to Sri Guru Teg Bahadur Jee. Regardless of how powerful the P.M. is, no-one is more powerful than our Guru. She should prostrate to our loved one, the light of the 10 Kings - Sri Guru Granth Sahib Jee, not that we get up and pay respect to her." Upon this Jakaras[30] were heard from all areas of the arena.

The truth being spoken by Sant Kartar Singh Jee led to disputes between P.M. Indira Gandhi and the Damdami Taksal. Please see page 96 for a picture of Sant Kartar Singh Jee). If anyone disrespected Sri Guru Granth Sahib Jee, Sant Jee never tolerated it, regardless of who they were. Thus they spoke up against the Nakali/Fake

---

[29] Abode of truth
[30] Slogans of victory

52

Nirankaris and did programmes to tackle their onslaught on Sikhi. (Source: www.damdamitaksal.com)

Indira never forgot this defiance against her dictatorial rule (protests during the emergency) and she saw the Sikhs as an enemy from this day onwards, even though Sikhs were simply being good citizens in trying to uphold the freedoms of India which were being exploited by Indira Gandhi.

The Landmark - Anandpur Sahib Resolution
Sikhs had agitated for equitable rights and treatment for their nation, in terms of practice of their faith and equity in the way that Punjab is served by the Centre (Punjab having the majority of the Indian Sikh population). Since the inception of Indian independence, agitations were started, and to date they continue in some shape or form. What was to become a pivotal point for the modern claim to a Sikh state or Khalistan was to be a lengthy document asking for more autonomy and equal rights for Sikhs, namely the Anandpur Sahib[31] Resolution.

The Anandpur Sahib resolution was initially adopted at Anandpur Sahib on October 16th/17th 1973 and was endorsed at the 18th All India Akali Conference of Shiromani Akali Dal in Ludhiana on 28th/29th October 1978. The following excerpt from the resolution summarises the basic principle of the resolution:

"... The Sikhs therefore demand, firstly, that an autonomous region in the north of India should be set up forthwith wherein the Sikh interests are constitutionally

[31] Anandpur Sahib is the historical Gurdwara where Sri Guru Gobind Singh created the Khalsa. Creating the Khalsa in 1699 was revolutionary and now the Sikhs made a resolution that would lead to a revolutionary movement of great fervour

recognised as the fundamental State policy. Secondly, that this autonomous region includes the present Punjab, Karnal and Ambala districts of Haryana, inclusive of Kangra district of Himachal Pradesh, Chandigarh, Pinjore, Kalka, Dalhousie, Nalagarh Desh, Sirsa, Gulha and Ratia areas of Ganganagar district of Rajasthan, thus bringing continuous Sikh population and Sikh habitats within this autonomous region as an integral part of the Union of India, and, thirdly, this Sikh autonomous region may be declared as entitled to frame its own constitutions on the basis of having all powers to and for itself except Foreign Relations, Defence, Currency and General Communications which will remain subjects within the jurisdiction of the Federal Indian Government."

Thus the main crux was to get Sikhs to formulate a state where they would form a majority and would encapsulate Sikh populations currently outside of Punjab who could enjoy the glow of freedoms within a united state of Sikh interests. This demand for more autonomy came due to the continual discrimination Sikhs had been undergoing since Indian independence. Other resolutions were:

- Redefining the Central and State relations so India can become a truly federal and geographical entity, which safeguards the fundamental rights of religious and linguistic minorities.

- Chandigarh[32] which was originally the capital of Punjab should be handed back to Punjab.

- Economic reforms should be made, namely opening an International Airport in Amritsar[33] and a Stock Exchange in Ludhiana.

---

[32] It is the shared capital of Punjab & Haryana

- Punjabi language to be given second language status in Haryana, Himachal, Jammu, Kashmir and Delhi, where major parts of the population speak Punjabi.

- Proper representation given to Sikhs in other states in government service, local bodies and state legislatures, protecting minority interests.

- Equity in distribution of river waters of Ravi and Beas.

- Relay of Kirtan from Sri Harmander Sahib for Sikhs worldwide, which would be paid for by Sikhs, the government merely approving this resolution.[34]

Thus the resolution was in no means separatist, as it was arguing for more autonomy within the Union of India and was calling for a truly Federal system. The resolution remained the flagship resolution of the Shiromani Akali Dal and did not receive much support from other political parties, as the other parties were not the ones who were being discriminated against en masse. Thus they were happy to proceed as they were.

---

[33] An International Airport was subsequently built, but expansion has been limited and one gets a stark example of how wide the gap between two comparable cities prior to Independence can be, in that the Lahore International Airport (Pakistan), is a truly International Airport and has been invested in heavily, whereas the Airport in Amritsar doesn't resemble much more than one that can only be described as definitively third world.

[34] This has now happened due to a private TV company airing the Kirtan and All India radio does also relay the Kirtan at set times.

INDEPENDENCE?

Akhand Kirtani Jatha

The Akhand Kirtan Jatha is a Sikh organisation/movement that promotes Sikhi through the singing of Gurbani/Kirtan. It promotes Sikhi through Kirtan programmes, initiation ceremonies and prayer recitals (Akhand & Sehaj Paths). It has a world-wide coverage and is popularly seen as an organisation with highly disciplined and principled Sikhs.

Bhai Randhir Singh was a member of the Ghadar Party and a freedom fighter of Indian independence. He is seen as a founding father of the Akhand Kirtan Jatha Thus the Jatha draws inspiration also to be a politically motivated organisation demanding more rights for Sikhs. Bhai Randhir Singh spent many years in jail and never faltered in any of his principles, continually fighting for the freedoms of Indians to break their shackles from British Imperialism.

The Akhand Kirtani Jatha's political involvement came to the fore in the mid-1970s with the rise of a spirited and charismatic Sikh, called Bhai Fauja Singh. Bhai Fauja Singh stood up for the rights of Sikhs and thus colleagues of his, who were also members of the Akhand Kirtani Jatha and/or those attending programmes of the Akhand Kirtani Jatha, started to become jointly involved in political and armed resistance against anti-Sikh practices and enemies of the Sikhs. Some of these Sikhs would become the founding Fathers of what would later become known as Babbar Khalsa.

Bloody Vaisakhi

Vaisakhi is celebrated by Sikhs to celebrate the revelation of the Khalsa by Sri Guru Gobind Singh Jee in 1699 AD and it falls usually on the 13th April annually.

The Vaisakhi of 1978 is remembered for different reasons. This Vaisakhi was the catalyst for Sikhs becoming more vocal and aware of the discrimination they were facing in a so-called "free and democratic" India.

A heretical sect called the Nirankaris or Narakhdharees (those going to hell as they are commonly referred to) and their leader Gurbachan, were making attacks on the Sikh faith at the behest of Indira Gandhi's Congress party and were receiving full government patronage to carry out their heretical mission to malign Sikh Gurus and history. Some of the attacks being made on Sikhi were:

- Gurbachan was referring to Sri Guru Granth Sahib as a mere bundle of papers.
- He said Sri Guru Gobind Singh had Panj Pyare (5 Beloved ones) but he will make "Sat Sitare" 7 stars.
- He also disrespected Sri Guru Granth Sahib by putting his foot upon Guru Jee.

The above are just a few examples of Gurbachana's open disregard for the Sikh faith and his open challenge to Sikhs. I think it would be pertinent to quote Bhagat Kabir Jee who talks of fakes like Gurbachan,

> *Kabeer, shave the mother's hair of that guru,*
> *Who does not take away one's doubt.*
> *He himself is drowning in the four Vedas;*
> *He drowns his disciples as well. ||104||*
> **(Sri Guru Granth, Ang 1369)**

In the Indian sub-continent, to shave a woman's hair off is to take away her honour (and this would have especially been so in Bhagat Kabir Jee's time), so Bhagat Jee is telling us to dishonour the mother of such a Fake Guru who has given birth to such a "Guru." Gurbachan was leading his followers into sinful actions and was committing profanities. Sant Jarnail Singh in one of his speeches talks of when the Narakhdharees recruit into their sect, they put the recruits in a room with the lights off and get them to hug each other. Both sexes are recruited together (taking part in the hugging initiation), nobody under the age of 25 years is allowed to enter this ceremony, but I presume Gurbachan as the "Guru" would be allowed in to "bless" this ceremony!

This Fake had the audacity to hold a march through the city that holds the citadel of the Sikhs in Amritsar. He had a procession through the city and then had a conference at a stadium, and to rub salt in, this was all done on Vaisakhi, 13th April 1978. Sikhs learnt of this event and assembled at Darbar Sahib, Amritsar. After having a short meeting, they made resolve to go and peacefully protest. The Sikhs were led by Bhai Fauja Singh and in total there were about 200-300 Sikhs. They made their way to where the procession was to pass, but were late and the procession had already got to the stadium.

The Sikhs made their way to the stadium, to be stopped by the Police, who returned with the lynch men of Gurbachan and they opened indiscriminate fire upon the Sikhs with guns, spears, swords, acid bottles, homemade bombs and arrows. The brave Sikhs made their way forward as much as they could and resisted as long as they could. 13 Singhs were martyred and over 70 were injured in the onslaught. Bhai Fauja Singh was still alive when his body was put with the other martyred Sikhs, but the police would not allow the Singhs to remove his body and he succumbed to his injuries without any treatment. See pages 135-136 for photos of the 13 Singhs and their funeral. Another Sikh who was wounded in the attack on the Nirankaris was Bhai Harnam Singh (the brother of Sant Kartar Singh). He was injured and was placed with the Sikhs who had been martyred, but he was still alive. He was taken to the mortuary with the martyred Sikhs. Due to his serious injuries he could not do anything about the predicament he had been placed in by the oppressive authorities. Bhai Amrik Singh, his nephew, persisted in getting access to him and fortunately got there in time for him to get medical treatment.

This event led to the Sikhs becoming more conscious of the government oppression being meted out against them, and the blood of these 13 Sikhs would inspire the Sikh masses to stand up for their rights. These 13 Sikhs paid the ultimate price for their courage, but this would plant seeds of dissent for many. Their martyrdom was not futile. On the contrary, it was the catalyst for the Sikh insurgency that followed.

I think it would be poignant to take up the opportunity of elaborating a little on the inspirational lives that these Sikhs led. They were not merely 13 everyday Sikhs - they were a special elite deputed by the Guru. I will firstly give a few inspirational highlights from the lives of some of the 13 Singhs and will then go on to explain Bhai Fauja Singhs character and teachings.

Bhai Raghbir Singh (Bagupur) was so spiritually enlightened that he listened to a Sri Akhand Path Sahib (48 hour recital of Sri Guru Granth Sahib Jee) the whole way through, without eating, drinking, or sleeping and did this all whilst sitting in one stance throughout. He then listened to a further 6 hours of Kirtan (devotional hymn singing). These are not the feats of a normal Sikh, but an extraordinary Sikh. Someone referred to Bhai Raghbir Singh as being very generous, in that he used to give 9 tenths of his earnings to charitable causes and used to live a modest life by surviving on 1 tenth of his earnings (yet Sikhs are required to only give tithe to charitable causes).

Jathedar Ranbir Singh Fauji was another of the Sikhs who was also martyred. He knew of the forthcoming event and that his death would be caused by it (thus he was of such spiritual prowess that he knew that his time had come to leave this mortal world). He therefore, went to Sri Goindval Sahib on 11th April 1978 and completed the recital of Sri Japji Sahib on all 84 steps and did a supplication to the Guru that his body be sacrificed in the service of the Guru. His wish was granted and he attained martyrdom on 13th April 1978.

Bhai Avtar Singh (Kuda Kurala, Hoshiarpur) was one of these great Sikhs. He received a shot and simply got up and sat down in meditation and embraced martyrdom, peacefully meditating whilst the merciless Narakhdharees continued to attack this elderly Sikh gentleman who was putting up no defence.

Another example of sacrifice is that of ***Shaheed Giani Hari Singhs wife***, Giani Jee was Shaheed on Vaisakhi of 1978 and in turn all the families of the martyrs were called to Sri Akaal Takhat Sahib to be honoured on 23 April 1978. When Giani Jee's wife was honoured for Giani Jee's sacrifice she did not say she felt sad for his loss but instead offered her sons to the Panth should their heads be needed, she said,

"My husband has given his life for Guru Jee and my three sons are also ready to sacrifice their lives, whenever the Panth needs them."

Such is the undying spirit of these Sikhs who make futures and are honoured in history as extraordinary figures. They could always go that extra few miles than the thousands of us who just live the rat race of life and go unnoticed.

Bhai Fauja Singh was one of these Sikhs who is even today talked about with awe and a twinkle in one's eye, just mentioning his name gets one to sigh with exception such was the spirit of Chardi Kala (high spirits) in him.

I will start to talk of Bhai Fauja Singh by quoting his poem of Kurbani which was written shortly before his martyrdom,

O True Guru we will serve your everlasting Sikhi with our every word, thought and deed. We will devote our youth, wealth and all worldly possessions to the cause of the Panth. My body, preserved since childhood, will be sacrificed now the need has arisen. By continuously repeating and sincerely following Gurbani, we will get rid of all our evil-mindedness. If you keep your Grace my Graceful Lord, we will sacrifice ourselves limb by limb. We will endeavour to fly the wonderful flag, which marks the treasure of your Name, all over the world. The light of faith that seems to be dwindling will be rekindled with our blood, by forsaking our mind's wisdom O Lord, we will blend our soul with yours. With your divinely ordained faith we will overcome all evil. By sacrificing ourselves we will revive and renovate the fading symbol of our faith. The Khalsa speaks with your Grace; our inner-voice will be heard by all.

Sikhi is immortalising nectar and we will serve it with the five Kakkars to our last breath. When all else fails, in the hour of need, we will sacrifice our heads at your altar.

The above depicts the faith, devotion and sacrifice of Bhai Fauja Singh Jee. These are the words of a lover - a devotional lover who sacrifices everything at the altar of his beloved and keeps nothing to himself not even his mortal body; all is sacrificed and nothing less. Bhai Fauja Singh Jee was a strict adherent of Sikhi and partook in many missionary activities such as organising Kirtan programmes and Amrit Sanchars (initiation ceremonies) and he led a revival of Sikhi in villages that he visited. He also organised Sikh training camps on his farm which was fondly named Khalsa Farm and he practised Shastar Vidiya (the art of warfare) and believed firmly in the use of arms in protection of faith and this belief included using modern technology to combat modern tyrants.

The camps that he held led to the birth of Babbar Khalsa after his martyrdom. The founders of Babbar Khalsa and future leadership had all met Bhai Fauja Singh and participated in these camps and missionary activities. The infamous martyrs that took inspiration from Bhai Fauja Singh included Bhai Anokh Singh, Bhai Sukhdev Singh and Bhai Talvinder Singh (all Babbars) to name a few. But Bhai Fauja Singhs legacy was not just for Sikhs of Punjabi origin, he was also very close and like a father figure to many Americans (white Americans) who had discovered Sikhi. Bhai Fauja Singh was imprisoned prior to Vaisakhi of 1978 for attacking police officers who had cowardly raped a young Hindu lady. Whilst in prison he sent many letters to these American Sikhs who he was very fond of:

"Dear Sister Sat Kirpal Kaur Ji ... The Khalsa does not exist under the protection of the S.G.P.C. or the police. The Khalsa is able to face loneliness, separation, hunger, fatigue, the piercing sun and the biting cold. The Khalsa exclaims the Truth; remaining unperturbed if they insult him, ignoring opposition if they oppose him, gets dragged if they drag him and stoned if they stone him. The Khalsa can cross the mountains of the Himalayas on foot in order

to preach in Tibet, without any protection. The Khalsa can penetrate the dense forests of Brazil for the same purpose, even if he has to sacrifice his life. The Khalsa does not mind death for the True cause. In fact it is profitable, enjoyable and pleasurable for the Khalsa to give his very life in pursuit of this duty. This is positively healthy, happy and holy for him. (Bhai Fauja Singh is here alluding to 3HO, the Yogi Harbhajan Singh organisation)

I do not think I need to give a narrative to the above, as the words speak for themselves and Bhai Fauja Singhs spirit can be experienced by reading them. One has to remember this letter was written when he was in prison and had no knowledge of what could happen with the proceedings against him. Finally I quote a commentary by someone who went to visit Bhai Sahib whilst he was in prison:

"As we got off the bus in Gurdaspur, Bibi Amarjit Kaur told me to go onwards to the jail. The mid-afternoon sun was as blinding as the entry way was dark. I just stared at the man dressed in perfect white Bana. He opened the barn-like door of the prison, so I naturally assumed he was a warden or perhaps even the jailer. He was smiling at all the Akhand Kirtani Sikhs as they came in and as it turned out; he was the prisoner sentenced to life imprisonment for defending a woman who had been mercilessly gang-raped. This incident illustrates why Bhai Fauja Singh could never be contained within a prison cell. He was the host of the jail, generating Chardi-Kala and the Akhand Kirtani Sikhs were in soaring high spirits when they met him. His wife Bibi Amarjit Kaur led the American Sikhs on a tour of the prison. It was a tremendous relief to see that Bhai Fauja Singh was under such light security, that he could organize the prison's Gurdwara. He proudly showed us his private cell and the cell next to it for the devoted Sevadars. Such a leader of righteousness could never be imprisoned. He

fought and fasted to attain his cell for meditation. It was a dark square shaped room containing a huge mattress. There was a little hole in the roof but otherwise no windows. The door opened out into a private yard where he set up a stove (one rectangular oil tin) with a round steel water pot on top. This was where he prepared his own food. The walls were painted yellow. This cell contrasted greatly to the modern red brick walls holding back shorthaired men who ganged together at the opening of the wall to stare at us.

Bhai Fauja Singh was the light of the prison, an inspiration for the prisoners as well as us! The men who rediscovered Sikhi under his influence were elevated from prison life. Their faith in Dharam took them beyond their situation. They were eternally grateful to their leader for their new beards. His concern for his fellow inmates was so deep and intense that when he left jail,
they were still a major concern for him."
Bibi Harikrishan Kaur Espanola, New Mexico

"Memories of Bhai Fauja Singh: Interview with Bibi Amarjit Kaur" – Taken from "So Kaheeat Hai Soora" August 2004. Translated by www.taponban.org

Bibi Amarjit Kaur, the wife of Bhai Fauja Singh in a recent interview in 2004 reminisces that in the Khalsa Farm residential retreats all the Singhs would wake up at about 2am and did Amrit Vela, after which they performed Kirtan, Gatka and discussions that lasted all day. When the camp would end, the Singhs would be sad to be separating and would even begin to cry. They did not feel like leaving.

Fauja Singh used to say this was the place of Shaheed Singhs (Khalsa Farm) from the small Holocaust. Many others felt the patrol and presence of Shaheed Singhs. The Khalsa Farm was a very peaceful place because it was isolated and was thus very good for doing Simran and Kirtan.

He knew of his Shaheedi approaching he would say, *'Don't cry when you see my body ... this is going to happen. Accept Bhaanaa (the will of God).'*

He would describe the roots of injustice as, *"There's Gandhi, there is Nehru and there is Nehru's daughter (Indira Gandhi). They are all just Gangoo what else is there here?"*

He said they would try to bring Sikhi down anyway possible and that to stop them, every Singh would have to be Shastardhari (carrying weapons at all times).

He used to also say that: *'If the Sikh Nation becomes solid in Banee, Bana, Seva & Simran, Satguru Jee is willing to give them rule/Raj even today.'* He said that as soon as the Sikh Nation becomes pure, Khalsa Raj will follow.

4. 1984 – Operation Blue Star

Meteorical Rise of the General of the Sikhs

The 20th century's great General, the heart of the Sikh youth, charismatic personality, Sant Jarnail Singh Jee Bhindranvale was born in 1947 at village Rode, Dist Faridkoth to Baba Joginder Singh and Mata Nihal Kaur Jee. Baba Joginder Singh Jee was a dedicated sevadar of the Sikh Nation.

Sant Jarnail Singh Jee took Amrit when he was about 5 years old and remaining committed to prayer was made his life-long aim. Daily he would recite 110 Japji Sahibs and the Panj Granthi whilst doing his farming duties. He remained at his village and was engrossed in meditations for 11 years. He had little formal education but his memory was astonishing. Sant Jee memorised the following Banee's, Dakhani Oankar in 1 day, Sukhmani Sahib in 13 days, and Sidh Gosht in 1 day and Asa Di Var in 8 hours.

When Sant Gurbachan Singh Jee Khalsa arrived at village Rode on his annual tour, he took in one of the 7 sons of Baba Joginder Singh to live in Jatha Bhindra on a permanent basis, who was Sant Jarnail Singh Jee. Sant Jarnail Singh Jee was educated in the knowledge of God, by Sant Gurbachan Singh Jee Khalsa. In 1 year he learnt the correct pronunciations of Gurbani and Gurus history. His Anand Karaj was performed in 1966 at Village Bilaspur with Sardar Sucha Singh's daughter, Bibi Pritam Kaur. He has two sons who are Ishar Singh born in 1971and Inderjeet Singh born in 1975. After Sant Giani Kartar Singh Jee Khalsa ascended to Sachkand, Sant Jarnail Singh Jee was appointed the Jathedar of Damdami Taksal. Baba Thakhur Singh tied the turban of leadership on Sant Jarnail Singh Jee, after which Takhat Sri Patna

Sahib's Jathedar Bhai Mohan Singh Jee presented Sant Jee a Siropa (robe of honour) on behalf of the Takhat Sahib.

Under his leadership of Damdami Taksal, Sikhi Parchar (preaching) with much fervour and passion began. For eight months they did Parchar touring Punjabi villages/cities, Madh Pradesh U.P, Bombay and Calcutta and other areas. They were about to embark on their second tour of Parchar when on Vaisakhi in 1978, the Nirankaris had announced a large gathering. Sant Jee accepted the challenge of the Nirankaris. The Government and anti-Sikh sentiments started to say that Sant Jee was an extremist and terrorist, but still Sant Jee came out untarnished and the Damdami Taksal's fame and respect kept rising. To see a photo of the most popular Sikh of the 20th Century please see page 137.

The Damdami Taksal were the first to take note of the anti-Sikh practises of the Nakali Nirankaris. Damdami Taksal's Jathedar and Singh's in 1953 had discovered that the Nakali Nirankaris were distorting the message of the Sikh Gurus, Sikh history, Sikh religion and discipline. The discoveries of Damdami Taksal were never acknowledged or attempted to be understood by many. About 18-19 years ago, in Tamil Nadhu, some low-caste Hindus became Muslims, and the whole of the Hindu society was angered and worried by this act. Even in Indian Parliament the question was raised as why the low castes Hindus were converting to Islam. As a direct result of which, organisations such as Vishav Hindu Pareeshaad and Verat Hindu Samelan were born.

In Hindustan about 87% of the population (approximately 60 billion) are Hindus. If out of the Hindu nation, some convert to Islam then this is seen as a threat.

If the Sikhs, who are 2% of the population, are attacked ideologically, this is not seen as a threat.

To get to this conclusion does not need much assessment. This threat was first pointed out by the Damdami Taksal, whose aim, from its onset has been to tackle those opposed to Sikhi. To make opposition to those opposing Sikhi is not to oppose other faiths. It is similar to the Hindu faith opposing followers of low castes converting to Islam; it is not necessarily opposing Islam. Damdami Taksal's prime duty has been to tackle attacks on Sikhi - regardless if they are sects of Sikhi or exterior threats, but it is not to oppose other faiths.

Sant Jee found out that the Nakali Nirankaris were going to hold a procession in Amritsar, in which their leader and his wife will be seated in a canopy and that much anti-Sikh propaganda will be carried out. Singhs sent by Sant Jee and the Akhand Kirtani Jatha went peacefully to protest against the Nirankaris, but the Nirankaris met their peaceful nature with gun fire. 13 Singhs were martyred and many were injured. After this bloody encounter their event still carried on for more than 3 hours. The government openly supported the Nakali Nirankaris. On 24th April 1980 the Nakali Nirankaris leader was assassinated and for this assassination both the government and the Nakali Nirankaris made Sant Jarnail Singh Jee a prime suspect. On 9th September 1981, Lala Jagat Narain was assassinated and a warrant for arrest was issued for Sant Jarnail Singh Jee. Sant Jee voluntarily courted arrest on 20th September 1981. He was taken to many places and questioned on many issues whilst in custody. But no evidence was produced against Sant Jee and he was released without charge.

On 26th April 1982, a Morcha (campaign) was started to get Amritsar holy city status. Some Singhs of the Jatha and Bhai Amrik Singh Jee (AISSF) were arrested. Sant Jee began the Dharam Yudh Morcha on 19 July 1982 to get the innocent Singhs freed (to see a photo of Bhai Amrik Singh & Baba Thara Singh, upon their release from imprisonment please see page 137). The Dharam Yudh Morcha was also adopted by the Shiromani Akali Dal on 4th August 1982 and they declared that the Morcha would continue until all demands of the Anandpur Sahib resolution were met. In the first three months of the Dharam Yudh Morcha 40,000 Singhs courted arrest. The Delhi government were not giving an inch and not even one of the demands was met. Due to the press coverage and mass participation in the Dharam Yudh Morcha, the government began to criminalise and persecute the Sikh community, through its propaganda and tools of state machinery. The government propagated the view that Sikhs wanted the whole of India to be divided into many nations and that Sikhs were enemies of Hindus. They propagated the view that the lives of Hindus in Punjab were under threat and that an exodus of Hindus from Punjab had begun.

The Asian Games of November 1982 were being held in New Delhi. The Sikh leaders had expressed their desire to inform the world media at the Games that Sikhs had been discriminated against since independence in 1947. Prior to independence Gandhi, Nehru and the like, who had given promises to the Sikhs, had not fulfilled these promises. Indira Gandhi hinted to Bhajan Lal that Sikhs should be discriminated against during the games. Due to Bhajan Lal's orders, every Sikh was interrogated prior to entering Delhi, to ascertain if they were terrorists or not. They were treated very badly, they were rigorously searched and questioned, to the extent that Ex-Cabinet Minister Swaran Singh, Retd. Air Chief Marshal Arjan Singh, Retd. and

General Arora was even interrogated. Sikhs were given a strong message that they are 3rd class citizens and that they are unwanted residents of India. This disrespectful, unwarranted treatment was not criticised by state or central government. The press or intellectuals did not question this disgraceful treatment. No Sikh Congress Minister resigned in protest. Only one conclusion could be drawn from these events: Sikhs are an oppressed minority in India.

Indira was convinced that the Congress Party Sikhs were so low that even if she ordered an army assault on Sri Harmander Sahib, they would remain silent and would tow the party line. She was confident that the Shiromani Akali Dal would be taught a lesson and they would not dare step out of line again. Leading Akali leaders gave assurances to Indira Gandhi that Sant Jee would run scared when faced against the might of the Indian Army and that they will not support him, in the event of the attack. Many leading personalities of India and abroad, discussed the Dharam Yudh Morcha with Sant Jee. Sant Jee would make all those who visited him content with his responses. Dr Subarmanim Swami who was a member of the Indian Parliament had to say after discussions with Sant Jee, *"If Sant Jarnail Singh is a terrorist then so am I."*

The government were failing in their propaganda attempts because they were losing to intellectual and well grounded arguments. They were becoming frustrated and thus they sent the army into Punjab and ordered a state of emergency.

For the nation, the 9th Guru, Sri Guru Teg Bahadur Jee was sacrificed (as a matter of human rights) and in the independence of India92% of those who were killed by the British were Sikhs. Instead of being grateful they attacked Sri Harmander Sahib and Sri Akaal Takhat Sahib on 1st

June 1984. Thousands of army personnel and tanks were used in the army assault and a fierce battle raged until 6th June 1984.

Some leading Akalis had informed the government that when they (the army) win the battle, upon gaining control of Sri Harmander Sahib, then Sant Jee and his associates will join their hands and surrender and the heroics of the Taksal will end. In 1983 one journalist even had the audacity to write that the heroic stories that the Sikhs narrate at Gurpurabs and never tire in re-telling, are myths like the Puranic myths. The Delhi government were convinced that Sant Jarnail Singh would surrender and that Sikhs would be totally disheartened after the attack and will become apathetic and controllable. The outcome of the attack they thought would be an end to the rebellious nature of Sikhs and an assimilation of Sikhs into the Hindu fold, Sikhs simply becoming long-haired Hindus.

In March 1983 Sant Jee learnt of all these evil plans and the prevalent threats to Sikhs, and he devised strategies to lead the Sikhs through this critical and historically definitive period. He attempted to ensure that the dreams of the enemies of the Panth were not prosperous, and that the cause of the Sikhs received global media attention. In the eyes of the world, the Sikhs made a unique victory with Operation Blue Star, as the government had to stoop so low in attempting to silence the Sikhs. This made history. In the battle that occurred, Baba Thara Singh (Damdami Taksal), Bhai Amrik Singh (President AISSF), General Subegh Singh and many others were martyred[35].

---

[35] Courtesy of www.damdamitaksal.com

Dharam Yudh Morcha

The Dharam Yudh Morcha (campaign to get just rights) was launched officially in August 1982 under the dictatorship of Sant Harchand Singh Longowal, to whom all Akali Dal members of the Punjab Legislative Assembly and Parliament had submitted their resignation. The Morcha was supported by all Sikhs regardless of their political and/or spiritual allegiances and was more a political than religious movement. It aimed at getting Sikhs and Punjabis just rights that they deserved and it was led by the moderate Shiromani Akali Dal Party.

To fully comprehend the demands of the Anandpur Sahib resolution and the Dharam Yudh Morcha one has to assess the underlying causes of these demands and protests. The Punjabi masses did support these campaigns on the whole and the reasons are varied and sometimes simplified as faith issues. However, when one delves a little deeper one learns of multi-faceted problems that all Punjabis faced. At a:

1) Household level the problem was primarily economic.
2) State wide level the problem was legal and constitutional
3) National level the problem was perceived to be religious/communal, '…and this construction is mainly the product of the actions of the central government, more specifically the government of the late Indira Gandhi and not the people or the politicians of Punjab.'[36]

---

[36] The Punjab Crisis, Murray J. Leaf (Asian Survey Vol.XXV, No.5, May 1985, page 475)

At the household level the rural masses and farmers had a long list of grievances which were unresolved. These included price supports for their produce, lack of technical investment into agriculture, water and power supplies, and lack of industrial development. At the state level the problem was legal and constitutional due to the misappropriation of the river waters of Punjab and the pricing structures that were forced upon farmers, which did not take into account the financial input needed to make agricultural gains. To add fuel to the fire, the Central government only seemed to pillage Punjab for its resources and not return any inward investment that would make Punjab a forward looking industrially developed state.

At the national level the Congress government led by Indira Gandhi played the dirty trick of communal politics, using faith as a dividing factor to gain popularity and complicate the "real" underlying issues. This policy was played out in the light of the upcoming elections of January 1985, in which Indira wanted to be seen as a national hero destroying the "separatist Sikhs" who were tarred with the image of being hell bent upon destroying harmony and unity in India. Some commentators argue that Sant Bhindranvale was used by the Congress as a tool to help add to this image but I would argue that the Congress manipulated the image of Sant Bhindranvale and painted a picture of him being some sort of gun-laden terrorist. To the contrary Sant Jee was revered by some MP's.

There was also the lack of national concern at the deaths of the Sikhs at the hands of the Nirankaris, yet Indira Gandhi went to the funeral of the leader of the Nirankaris and was pictured in Punjabi papers laying flowers on his grave. *'And compared to the lax handling of the murders of the Sikhs, prosecution of this case was vigorously undertaken by the Central Bureau of Investigation, and the papers were full of stories of torture of suspects and the like.'[37]*

Many Sikhs lost their lives during the period of the Morcha. In April 1983 in a road block protest (Rasta Rokho), 21 people died whilst peacefully protesting. Between the years 1981 – 1984, more than 250 Sikhs were killed in fake encounters. More than 250,000 were arrested, who were peacefully agitating as part of the Morcha for more state autonomy and a just share of Punjab's river waters as envisaged by International Riparian Laws.

In October 1983 the Central Government imposed President's Rule in Punjab. Thus the Punjab legislature was suspended and Punjab began to be administered directly by the Central Congress Government. This further fuelled the polarisation of the Sikhs and Punjabis and led to the unrest that was to follow for years to come. One could argue that all that happened in Punjab in the 1980's could have been avoided through diligent and honest dialogue, as the Sikhs were not looking for a stand-off with the state government but were merely pursuing their constitutional rights, but the Congress was not sincere in its negotiations and would always withdraw from talks when a settlement seemed to be approaching.

"The problem is a basic anti-farmer and ant-rural bias in the structure of the Indian Government. The solution is "federalism." It is absolutely crucial to realise that this is the view of by far the most important mainstream groups in Punjab, Sikh and non-Sikh, and of most political parties. It is equally important to note that this view is not based on

---

[37] Ibid P.490

"Sikh fundamentalism," "separatism," or any sort of terrorist ideology."[38]

The really sad fact is that even now the same issues that have been outlined so far as the cause of the unrest that arose still exist, and this has even been noted by commentators who are seen as pro-Congress such as the author Kushwant Singh. The underlying causes for the unrest have still to be resolved and all it will take is a few triggers to re-ignite the whole unrest again. The Indian government needs to take sincere steps to resolve the demands of the Anandpur Sahib resolution and the unjust treatment that Punjab and Punjabis receive, the majority of the issues being around economic development.

Sant Bhindranvale's last known recorded speech - 24th May 1984

On the 14th April 1984, one of Sant Bhindranvale's closest associates Surinder Singh Sodhi was assassinated. This killing was carried out by two people one referred to as Shinda and a female accomplice. Sant Bhindranvale described Surinder Singh Sodhi as his right arm and said he had been deprived of his right arm, i.e. one of his most useful assets, when Sodhi was assassinated. Sodhi was known for carrying out secret missions on behalf of Sant Bhindranvale and is fondly remembered as the handsome Singh who rode his motorbike on a railway line track (the single beam) to make an escape from a pursuit.

The female accomplice was supposed to then go on to assassinate Sant Bhindranvale but she hesitated and her plan was foiled. Both of these assassins were swiftly put to death within 3 hours of Sodhi being assassinated.

---

[38] Ibid P.491

It was later learnt by Sant Bhindranvale that Shinda had been sent by a Gurcharan Singh who was an Akali Dal member. Thus Sant Bhindranvale turned on the Akalis and knew clearly that the government wanted him dead, but now even the Akalis were scheming to get him assassinated. The Sant then decided to move to Sri Akaal Takhat Sahib and dig his heels in for what would become the most significant event in Sikh history in the twentieth century.

I will summarise some of the points that Sant Bhindranvale makes in his last speech which will clarify his mood just days before Operation Blue Star, but also clarify his inner feelings of what had been going on (the full speech can be accessed on www.sikhunderground.com);

Sant Jee & the Babbars

There is much debate on whether Sant Jee got along with the Singhs who later became known as Babbar Khalsa. Sant Jee mentions that Bhai Sukhdev Singh Babbar (referred to as Sukha in the speech) spent 10 days with him and that he would help any Singhs who had done honourable acts of upholding the Sikh Spirit and who had warrants out for their arrests.. Later on in the speech, Sant Jee mentions the great service that Bhai Talvinder Singh Babbar had been performing by preaching Sikhi, and that warrants were out for his arrest. He mentions that Bhai Talvinder Singh escaped to Germany but then was arrested due to an informant. He goes on to say that Talvinder Singh is a great warrior who has done a brilliant service for the Sikh Nation and that, if he is deported/extradited to India, he will be eliminated by the Indian Government and the government will drink his blood like it has done of other Singhs. Sant Jee then names the following Singhs who are all seen as Babbar Khalsa members who had already laid down their lives – Amarjit Singh Daheru, Kulwant Singh Nagoke, Gurmit Singh, Bhola Singh, Kashmir Singh, Jasdev Singh, Sukhdev Singh and states that if Talvinder Singh is sent back to India he will face the same fate as his colleagues. Sant Jee then goes on to say that the government is trying its hardest to arrest Talvinder Singh, Tarsem Singh (Kala Sangha) and Vadhava Singh (current leader of Babbar Khalsa International), but even if it does capture and eliminate these Singhs, it will not fulfil its aim of destroying the Sikhs.

Sant Jee may have had minor differences with the Singhs of Babbar Khalsa but they were not of major concern and there were many forces at work trying to keep them apart. One of the key culprits in this was Sant Longowal as the Babbars had a close relationship with him and the SGPC.

Sant Longowal & Akalis

Sant Jee clearly states that the Akalis were going to Delhi to do deals with the government and compromise on their demands. Sant Jee asks the following questions of the Akali Dal:

1) Why did the Akali Dal order the assassination of Surinder Singh Sodhi?
2) Why is the Akali Dal labelling Sant as an agent of the Congress Party? Sant asks the Akali Dal to provide a shred of evidence to substantiate their shallow claim. In the 22 months of the Dharam Yudh Morcha Sant says he has never made a single press statement against the Akali Dal yet there are numerous statements against Sant Jee made by the Akali Dal – thus who is at fault?

Sant Bhindranvale goes onto argue that, out of 400 court cases of Sikhs in relation to the Dharam Yudh Morcha,

Sant Jee is fighting (providing monetary aid to) 375 of these. He asks if the Akali Dal can even substantiate that they are assisting 25 court case proceedings in defence of the Sikhs.

Sant Jee questions the sacrifices of the Akali Dal as a party – he asks why in the last 37 years there has not been a single Shaheed who was from the Akali Dal.

Sants mission

The Dharam Yudh Morcha was about fighting injustice and getting equitable rights for Sikhs in Punjab as part of India. But Sant does clearly state that the day the government attacks the Golden Temple, the Sikhs should then raise arms and start a full frontal attack.

He criticises the Akalis for visiting the Nirankari head Gurbachna. They were seeking his blessings in order to get votes in the elections. He clearly states that Sikhs should not associate with such leaders.

He questions why he is being labelled a Congress agent, with the following questions:

- o 12,000 people got initiated on Vaisakhi, is this the work of the Congress Party?
- o Keeping hair, giving up intoxicants is what I promote.
- o It has been 8 months since I've been allowed on the stage at Manji Sahib to address the congregation.

Making residence in Akaal Takhat Sahib

Many people criticised Sant Jee for taking up residence in Akaal Takhat Sahib and said, and still do argue, that he violated the Maryada/Code of conduct by doing so. Sant replies by arguing that Jathedar Mohan

Singh, Sant Fateh Singh and Granthi Jasbir Singh (along with his family) have all lived in Akaal Takhat Sahib. Sant Jee was angered at the attempt of slur and tarnishing his image by unscrupulous elements.

Sant Jee also learnt from Sevadars of 20 years of Akaal Takhat Sahib that, apart from at Divali and Vaisakhi, there were never more than 400 people present at the Initiation Ceremonies (Amrit Sanchars) held at Akaal Takhat Sahib. Yet now (whilst Sant was residing there) every Sunday there were a minimum of 400 initiates. This displays the influence and support Sant had and the effect he was having on the masses.

Bearing Arms

Sant Jee had been promoting the bearing of arms by Sikhs as a right of being a Sikh (as bearing arms is a Sikh tradition). He argued that as part of the demands of the Anandpur Sahib Resolution it was argued that a Sikh would not need a license to bear arms. He goes on to say that if Sikhs follow this advice and then are stopped by the police they should keep a copy of the Anandpur Sahib resolution on their person and display this as proof of their right to bear them. He replies to Sikhs who have made requests of where to get arms from? He says that there are arms factories everywhere - the CRPF (Central Reserve Police Force) can be seen everywhere, they are walking factories of arms. Singhs should approach them and take by force the arms they feel are befitting from the CRPF.

Operation Blue Star

Operation Blue Star was the army name given to the suicidal attack that the Indian government launched on the holiest shrine for Sikhs, which has fondly come to be known as the Golden Temple (please see the Sikhtoon on page 137). To put the army operation into context, we need to first examine the circumstances under which the government launched this attack and, secondly, we need to examine who the Sikhs were who gallantly defended the Golden Temple.

Context of the attack

Indira Gandhi had raised the stakes of her suicidal mission of maligning the Sikh community to get her electoral victory and again be seen as the Goddess Durga (as she had been idolised when defeating Pakistan in the war to create an independent Bangladesh) by crushing the Sikh demands for more rights. President's rule had already been declared in Punjab and tensions were high, with the police increasing its illegal killings of young Sikhs who could be suspected of being involved in the Dharam Yudh Morcha or sympathizers of Sant Jarnail Singh's mission.

Sant Jarnail Singh had taken up residence in the Golden Temple complex and was delivering speeches (in the complex at Manji Sahib Gurdwara) to awaken the Sikh masses to the facts of the persecution that they were undergoing (the majority of these speeches were delivered to Sikhs who were about to court arrest as part of the Dharam Yudh Morcha). These speeches and extracts can be accessed from various books and internet sites, but the general tone was to inspire Sikhs to demand for justice that they deserved as citizens of India.

Sant Bhindranvale moved his residence within the complex and eventually took up residence in Sri Akaal Takhat Sahib. The government had had numerous failed assassination attempts on the Sant. Sant Bhindranvale had become very popular and could mobilize thousands of Sikh Youth and sympathizers with ease. This was helped by his closeness to Bhai Amrik Singh who was the President of the All India Sikh Students Federation. The Akalis, including Sant Longowal, were not happy with Sant Bhindranvale's popularity and knew they could not control or manipulate him for their own political aims.

All in all, everything that was happening in and around Punjab and in the Golden Temple had led to this false whole-scale threat posed by Sikhs, which had in actual fact been presented by the Congress government to seem like a credible threat to national security. They were merely creating an atmosphere in which they could build up support to launch an attack against the Sikhs as a people, a faith, and a geographical community as Punjabi's. This was to ensure that discrimination against Sikhs could be used as a political vote winning move and ensure that tyrannical tactics could be implemented without outcry from other Indians. It was also to ensure the economical suffrage for Punjab in order to feed the prosperity of other parts of India.

The official reason given by the government for attacking the Golden Temple was that armed terrorists had violated its sanctity by taking refuge there and were refusing to leave. Sant Bhindranvale was seen as the leader of these so-called "terrorists." In response to the accusations made, I would like to point out that there are arms/weapons of historical significance displayed at the Akaal Takhat and it is a duty for a Sikh to be armed, to wear a Kirpan, and the Guru's instructed to Sikhs to treat weapons as they do their Guru. To revere the weapons is a key practice of the faithful.

Sant Bhindranvale had courted arrest once before and if legal charges were brought against him once again, then one could assess if he were at large or refusing to co-operate, but no such step was taken by the government to consolidate the issues that lay ahead. The Akalis, such as

Gurcharan Singh Tohra (President Shiromani Gurdwara Parbandhak Committee) and Sant Longowal, invited the Indian forces to attack, as they could no longer control the situation and were hungry to retain their political posts. Sant Bhindranvale had become a real threat to their stronghold on the Sikh Community's leadership.

The attack was unnecessary. If they had wanted to simply draw out the so-called "terrorists" all they had to do was to cut off all the food, water, and energy supplies to the Golden Temple and they could have slowly drawn them out. However, this was not part of their agenda as they planned to humiliate and crush the Sikh Spirit. The whole of Punjab was sealed off from the rest of India and an additional 70,000 troops were called in. A simultaneous attack on about 40 other shrines was launched. Complete press censorship was established and martial law was declared[39].

The army was given orders to shoot anyone breaking the curfew and the whole of Punjab was placed under military siege, starting from the 1st June 1984 for the next few days through to the 10th June 1984. One has to ask were there "terrorists" in the other 40 or so Gurdwaras that were attacked simultaneously and why had the government launched the attack so close to the Martyrdom of Sri Guru Arjan Dev Jee, which was to be celebrated on the 5th June 1984: the simple fact is that the attack was premeditated and calculated. Please see the Sikhtoon on page 138.

The Akali leadership, Jagdev Singh Talwandi, Sant Harchand Singh Longowal, Gurcharan Singh Tohra and Parkash Singh Badal were all colluding with the

[39] The Punjab Crisis. Murray J. Leaf, Asian Survey Vol.XXV, No.5, May 1985, p.495

government and asking the government to actually attack the Golden Temple. The Dharam Yudh Morcha was becoming more and more vociferous and there was rising civil tension as there was deadlock and no progress in talks with the government.

The government carefully created the siege like situation, and Sant Longowal declared that he would launch a campaign of civil disobedience from the 3rd June 1984, curtailing the non-payment of taxes. Food grains and trains would not be allowed to move out of Punjab. In simple terms, mass civil disobedience. This was just a drama played out to allow Indira Gandhi to attack. This statement of launching this campaign was done as part of the wider campaign to precipitate the attack. Indira Gandhi went on to national television appealing for calm and telecommunications were cut for the whole of Punjab. All foreign journalists were shipped out of Punjab so they could not witness and/or report what went on. She went on to national television saying, 'Let us not shed blood, shed hatred.' General Brar, one of the army generals in charge of the offensive on the Golden Temple says that troops were already moving in. How hypocritical and convenient for Mrs Gandhi. For a full description of the attack and accounts of what happened please refer to "Politics of Genocide" (1999, Inderjeet Singh Jaijee, pages 32-71).

In October 1983, the Indian Army selected 600 men from different units and sent them to rehearse the assault on a replica of the Golden temple at a secret training camp in the Chakrata Hills about 150 miles north of Delhi. Two officers of the RAW, the Indian secret service, were sent to London to seek expertise from the SAS (Mary Anne Weaver, Sunday Times, June 1984). The army trained well in advance and thought their planning would mean an easy attack that would annihilate the Sikhs within a few hours. How very wrong they were.

Gallant Defenders

I will give a brief outline of the key Sikh personalities who fought against the Indian armed forces in the attack on the Golden Temple and of their involvement in the Sikh freedom struggle prior to the attack. The two personalities that I will give brief biographies of will be Bhai Amrik Singh and General Subegh Singh. Others who fought and died valiantly will be covered in later chapters.

Bhai Amrik Singh Jee
President of All India Sikh Students Federation (AISSF)

Bhai Amrik Singh was the son of Sant Kartar Singh Jee Bhindranvale and Mata Niranjan Kaur. At the age of 5 years Bhai Amrik Singh started to attend Jaddi Village Poora Kohan School. He studied here until Middle School. When he had passed his Year 5/5th Grade exams, he was taken out of school and inducted into Damdami Taksal by Sant Gurbachan Singh Jee. He studied Sikhi for 2 years under the guidance of Sant Gurbachan Singh Bhindranvale. He was taught the correct pronunciations of Gurbani and he learnt about Sikh history and the meanings of Gurbani. He was religious from a young age and he memorized the 5 morning prayers as a child. He went on to study at Khemkaran Government School where he passed his 10th Grade.

He then went on to study at the Khalsa College, Amritsar - he passed his MA here. During his studies he had to undergo considerable financial hardship. This was due to the fact that the family had little land to farm and any money that was generated from the farming was mostly donated in Seva by Sant Kartar Singh Jee. Sant Kartar

Singh Jee told Bhai Amrik Singh to do a PHD in Gurbani. He was studying this PHD when Sant Kartar Singh had a fatal accident and ascended to Sachkand. He never submitted the thesis for his PHD as he got heavily involved in the promotion of Sikhi.

During his time at Khalsa College, Bhai Amrik Singh became a member of the All India Sikh Students Federation (AISSF) and held honorary positions. In 1977 at the Tagore Theatre, Chandigarh at the AGM of the AISSF, Bhai Amrik Singh was appointed the President of the AISSF. Under his leadership the AISSF became a force to be reckoned with and a very powerful voice for Sikh Youth.

There was a rise in apostasy of Sikh Youth in Punjab and an increasing tide of Sikh Youth becoming communists. Bhai Amrik Singh started Gurmat Camps to reinstate faith in Sikhi, in the Sikh Youth. This campaign to re-introduce Sikh Youth to their roots bore fruit and practicing Sikhs (Amritdharees) became to be a visible presence once again in schools, colleges and universities. A new rule for all members of the AISSF was introduced by Bhai Amrik Singh, whereby all members had to be Amritdharees and reciting their daily prayers (7 prayers). When Amrit Sanchars (Sikh initiation ceremonies) were organised, 50% of the new initiates used to be youth. This was due to the influence of AISSF and Sant Jarnail Singh's preaching.

The AISSF also protested against the poisonous Fake Nirankaris and raised numerous memorials in memory of the 13 Sikhs who were martyred peacefully protesting against the Nirankaris on Vaisakhi in 1978. The actual site where the 13 Sikhs were martyred is in B-block Amritsar, where a Gurdwara (Shaheed Ganj) is present in commemoration to the martyrs. This memorial Gurdwara only became possible due to the efforts of the AISSF, under Bhai Amrik Singh's leadership. The AISSF vowed to raise a memorial on the actual site where the Singhs were martyred. The problem was that the land was owned by the government and the government would not sell the land to the Sikhs for this purpose under any circumstances. The AISSF Singhs started visiting the site at night and building a wall around the site so that they could claim the land by force, Sikh youth used to come in tractors and spend all night constructing the wall. The authorities got wind of what was occurring and the police began to intervene. The Sikhs used to build the wall at night and the local government agencies would come in during the day and knock the wall down. A stand-off was developing and the police began to give threats that they would shoot anyone who participated in raising the wall. Bhai Amrik Singh said that the AISSF will not compromise and will do whatever it has to in order to raise a memorial in the name of the 13 Sikhs who had spilt their blood. In the end the authorities had to accede to the demands of the Sikhs and the memorial Gurdwara stands tall today in honour of the 13 Sikhs.

In 1979, a Gurdwara in Uttar Pradesh (UP) was forcefully sealed off by the government due to protests against the Fake Nirankaris. Bhai Amrik Singh led the protest to get the Gurdwara freed from government control. The UP government had to concede to the protests and were forced to re-open the Gurdwara and the Sikhs were victorious.

To get Amritsar Sahib it's holy city status, AISSF in partnership with Sant Jarnail Singh Jee Bhindranvale and other Sikhs participated in an anti-tobacco protest. Thousands of Sikhs participated in the protest and the government was pressured to ban the sale and use of alcohol and tobacco around the Golden Temple/Darbar

Sahib[40]. Bhai Amrik Singh worked closely with Sant Jarnail Singh; they had much love for each other. They would always consult each other on matters of importance and work out solutions together. This love for one another was portrayed when Bhai Amrik Singh and Baba Thara Singh were arrested and imprisoned in Amritsar. Sant Bhindranvale was in bad health, but not heeding to his ill-health Sant Jee left Mehta and went straight to Amritsar. After discussions with the Singhs of what forward strategy should be implemented, Bhai Harminder Singh Sandhu and other AISSF leaders performed an Ardas at Sri Akaal Takhat Sahib to begin an agitation to get the Singhs freed. Immediately a Jatha of 51 Singhs was deputed to protest on 9th July 1982. It was this protest that snowballed and came later to be known as the Dharam Yudh Morcha.

During the Dharam Yudh Morcha, the fame and popularity of AISSF and Damdami Taksal became widespread and they became known worldwide. Operation Blue Star followed, in which Bhai Amrik Singh fought valiantly and attained martyrdom. The AISSF learnt of General Subegh Singh and the way that he had been treated by the Indian government and they introduced him to Sant Jarnail Singh. Bhai Amrik Singh had a dream that Gurmat Camps would be held the world over, to teach children, youth and all Sikhs about their great history and the practices of Sikhi. We all need to work to fulfil this dream. To see a photo of Bhai Amrik Singh please see page 138.

Major General Subegh Singh

General Subegh Singh was an exemplary soldier who became a close aide of Sant Jarnail Singh and fought valiantly in Operation Blue Star. He co-ordinated the

---

[40] This is no longer the case and people can be seen smoking very close to the proximity of the complex

defences and set up the fortifications in the Golden Temple to protect against the Indian Forces.

He had been a national hero who had been instrumental in the Bangladesh war, in which Bangladesh got independence from Pakistan. He fell out of favour, in his own words; with the Prime Minister due to him making a statement that no-one was indispensable during the emergency. He felt this statement was used against him to ensure that he did not get the recognition and promotion he deserved after the end of the Bangladesh war.

He was discriminated against and unceremoniously removed from his post and his pension cancelled. He appealed even to Indira Gandhi that he be court-marshalled or tried if he had made an indiscretion that credited such treatment, but his appeals fell on deaf ears. Bhai Subegh spoke of Sant Bhindranvale in the following way:

'But the fact is that there is hardly a Sikh in this world who does not accept him as a leader. I also accept him as a leader. I firmly believe that he is the only Sikh born after Guru Gobind Singh who can get justice for the Sikhs as a community, in this country, in this country where we have been persecuted ever since independence. We are suspected individually and as a community.''[41]

General Subegh Singh masterminded the entire defence of Darbar Sahib and was an expert in Guerrilla warfare. He knew the Singhs would fight a retreating battle, thus he designed the defences in such a manner that the Singhs could retreat and leave traps and problems for the advancing soldiers.

---

[41] Summarised responses of an interview with Miss Tavleen Singh, The Telegraph, 1984

He taught guerrillas in Bangladesh to assist them to get independence from Pakistan. He did this as part of his work as an army officer. He even went to the extent of cutting his hair to complete this task - this was his level of commitment to the Indian army. He had frontline experience of leading and training guerrilla insurgents. He knew how to make best use of limited resources and how to inflict the most damage so, for example, he taught the Singhs to shoot the parachutes of the incoming commandos who were being dropped from aircrafts, which meant that the commandos were most likely critically injured when landing, The parachute was an easier target to hit rather than the commandos themselves and less bullets were used.

He organized the fortification and co-ordinated attacks over a walkie-talkie. He would give commands to forge forward or retreat to the battling Singhs. He would look at the oncoming soldiers and from their uniforms and weapons he would differentiate between the different ranks, and would command the Singhs accordingly. The commandos that first entered Darbar Sahib were covered in body armour but the great General knew that their legs were unprotected, so he ordered the Singhs to shoot them below the waist, thus disabling them. To see photos of General Subegh Singh please see page 138 .

The Army Assault

Both the government and the Sikh leadership knew that the inevitable attack would take place. Sant Bhindranvale had been mentioning in speeches from 1983 that the day the Indian Government attacks the Golden Temple complex, on that day the foundation for Khalistan would be laid.

The Sant had been an asset for the Akalis early on in the Dharam Yudh Morcha, but he had become a thorn in their side as he was uncompromising on demands, unlike them who would compromise at every opportunity. Thus the scene was set. The Akalis were inviting in the army to attack, Indira had misrepresented the Punjab issues as threats to national security by Sikh fundamentalists who were determined to break up the union of India and, last but not least, the government allowed the Sikhs to fortify the complex by relaxing checks on goods in and out of the Golden Temple.

The attack started on 1st June 1984 when the Golden Temple complex was surrounded by the army and light gunfire was instigated by the army to try to tease out the positions of the Sikhs defending the shrine and to see what sort of ammunition they had. The army gave no warnings of the opening of fire and pilgrims were stuck in the complex and had to undergo inhumane treatment or death by cross-fire. Bhai Kulwant Singh AKA Mehnga Singh Babbar was the first Sikh defending the shrine to fall to the bullets of the army; he was valiantly martyred on the 1st June 1984.

The attack would continue for the next five days, with the majority of intense fighting being between 3rd June – 5th June 1984. There were only about 100 Sikhs defending the shrine against the might of the Indian army who experienced massive fatalities in relation to the operation at hand. Tanks and aircraft had to be used by the army to make progress in their despicable operation.

Many Sikhs who were defending the shrine left on the 5th June 1984, as they could not see any point in fighting on, as they were fighting a losing battle and thought it better to continue the freedom struggle by leaving the complex, rather than being martyred. There were only pockets of Sikh fighters remaining in the complex on the 6th June

1984. The majority of them were in the Akaal Takhat along with Sant Bhindranvale. The army used tanks to destroy the Akaal Takhat and the attack came to an end on the 6th June, 1984, with the Sikh fighters either being martyred, captured, or on the run. To see photos of some of those martyred defending the complex please see page 100.

The Akali leaders peacefully courted arrested during the attack, Sant Longowal and Gurcharan Singh Tohra, but they did not assure the safety of pilgrims/Sikhs that they represented, who were stuck in the army assault. They once again showed their true colours of looking after themselves over the Sikhs, although they were jailed after the attack. Some days after the attack, at a Sikh convention, one of the Granthis of the Golden Temple, Giani Puran Singh narrated his own experience of the attack:

"... The Singhs carried on fighting until they were Shaheed even when their ammunition finished they carried on. Bhai Avtar Singh of the Akhand Kirtani Jatha (AKJ) was shot and Shaheed whilst doing Kirtan in Darbar Sahib, some AKJ Singhs kept the Kirtan going as is the Maryada ... On the 6th June at 4pm the army were throwing gas grenades at the Akaal Takhat. Even after the bombings of tanks Singhs were still firing back, as a result gas grenades were being used to flush out the remaining Defenders of Faith. On 7th June – we came back. The Ramgharia Bunga had a trench dug up, 4 Singhs had created it under there. 3 troops entered the trench and did not re-surface. The soldiers told the Singhs to get out, they refused and said they would be willing to co-operate with me, if I were bought to talk to them. I asked the officers that if I negotiated with the Singhs to leave the trench, what would come of the Singhs. They replied that they would not be killed here; I thus refused to negotiate their coming out of

the trench as I knew it would mean their deaths as a result of my assistance. The officers then said to me that if I could just ask them what had happened to the 3 soldiers who had entered the trench, one of which was a doctor who the army needed to be alive. I agreed to ask the Singhs, the Singhs said that they had killed anyone from the army who entered the trench, I then left and the Singhs, who carried on fighting until the 10th June. The army first tried shooting them, they then bombed the trench, but none of this had any effect. In the end the army used poisonous gas to draw the Singhs out and they were all martyred."

Other Sikh Fighters in the attack and innocent pilgrims

Many Sikhs had come to Sant Bhindranvale to join the ranks of the Sikhs who would be enlisted to defend the Golden Temple. Some of these Sikhs came from Hazur Sahib, Nanded. Others were from Nihang Dals, such as that of Baba Deya Singh (Bidhi Chand) and many were drawn from AISSF and Damdami Taksal. In all about 60 Sikhs who were defending the Golden Temple were martyred. Some Sikhs were told they could not participate in the attack and were sent out of Amritsar and told by Sant Bhindranvale that they must continue the fight after the attack.

Babbar Khalsa Sikhs, who made up about 20 in total, took up specific posts at the complex which were near the Sarais (accommodation quarters) and Gurdwara Baba Atal. Bhai Mehal Singh Babbar had set up a communications system so that the Singhs could communicate and know what was going on. This system was used by all the fighters and it was co-ordinated by General Subegh Singh. Bhai Anokh Singh Babbar was given the Seva of ferrying innocent sangat out of the complex during the 3 days of fighting.

He and his unit saved hundreds from the inevitable slaughter.

Many innocent pilgrims died in the cross-fire and, after the fighting ended, many Sikhs were mercilessly killed by the army, as they needed to boost up the numbers of fatalities of Sikh fighters because the fatalities of the army ran into the hundreds (a modest estimate). They also wanted to teach Sikhs a lesson; many women were raped and abused. Many innocent Sikhs died due to lack of food and drink, as there was extreme heat due to the Punjabi summer and they were stranded in the attack.

A full list of the Sikhs martyred in the attack can be found in the Ajaib Ghar (Museum) of the Golden Temple, where the names of all the Sikhs known to be martyred is engraved in marble at exit of the museum.

For a more in depth account of the attack and atrocities, readers are advised to read 'Politics of Genocide' pages 32-71 (Inderjit Singh Jaijee, 1999).

Innocent Pilgrims

Thousands of innocent pilgrims were entrapped in Operation Blue Star. I will now include a recent fictitious account of the attack that I wrote, which portrays the complexities of what innocent people underwent. All of the characters are fictitious, but all the places referred to in the narrative are real, including Ladha Kothi detention centre.

31st May 1984

Satwant could feel her clothes sticking to her, the heat was unbearable, she had spent the night tossing and turning trying to get goodnights sleep. She glanced at her watch, it was 4am, she thought, *I need to get up, help milking the cows so Bibi (mother) doesn't change her mind about letting me go to Amritsar.* She quickly rose to her feet and looked into her parents' bedroom and saw that Bibi was still sound asleep.

She quickly made her way over to the water pump and poured some water onto the top of it, to ignite the waters trajectory from below. She gave the hand-pump some quick bursts of arm-action and splashed the water over her face. This wasn't a nice sensation as she could taste salt from her perspiration of the night and the water was warm. Satwant placed a bucket under the pump she again energised the flow of water, with some hard and fast movements of her hands and arms. The water now collected was cool and refreshing, she again washed her face, and the sensation soothed her in the humid and windless surrounds of her village of Maheroo, Jalandhar. She filled 4 buckets of the cool water so her family could utilise it. Her Bibi had woken up and she walked over to her, Satwant quipped "Bibi, I'll start milking the cows," her Bibi replied, "fine, you go ahead and I'll join you shortly."

Satwant picked up some rope and took a bucket of water over to the feisty kicking cow. Satwant quickly grabbed the cows back legs to tie them with the rope, but in her haste she forgot about the cow's tail and she received a whipping blow of the cow's tail in the eye. She shuddered and immediately felt perspiration on her neck, she swooned backwards. She resolutely gathered herself and squinting through one eye, still managed to tie the cow's legs with the rope. After tying the cow's legs she got up grabbed a stick and gave the cow some vicious blows to let her know who the boss was. The cow resigned to her fate and allowed Satwant to milk her, she first washed the udders which were covered in dung and mud.

Bibi walked over, "You are blessed my daughter, you took on the battle-axe cow," Bibi could work at double the pace of Satwant, so in the time that Satwant had milked the battle-axe cow, Bibi had finished milking the other two cows. Upon completion they emptied their buckets of milk into the milk-man's container and kept one-eighth of the milk for themselves.

5am   Bibi said to Satwant "Don't worry daughter you will go to Amritsar with your uncle today." Satwant's stomach churned with butterflies, she quickly hugged her mother and kissed her forehead, her mother jokingly said "Stop clinging to me, it is already too hot, do you want me to come down with heat stroke."

7am   Mama Jagjit and Mami Jasbir (maternal uncle & aunt) turn up with their 2 year old boy Suraj and 4 year old daughter Parveen. They had planned the trip to Amritsar and were to take Satwant and her brother Balwant. Satwant's duty for the trip is to look after Suraj and Balwant's got to help look after Parveen, that's why Mama and Mami had wanted to take them to go with them as the pair of children are quite a handful.

9am

Satwant, Balwant, Mama and Mami board the 'Shane Punjab' train at Phagwara Junction train station to Amritsar. After about 90mins of hustle and bustle in the train and the excruciating heat of travelling in cattle-class in the train, they all took a sigh of relief at the arrival at Amritsar. Thankfully the kids had perfectly slept the whole time.

10.30am

After alighting from the train, we all gasped for air and thankfully drank at the public water points at the Amritsar train station. The water was warm but we drank it nonetheless, as we were too poor to afford cold drinks. We had planned to return to Maheroo on the next day after a whirlwind visit.

Satwant:

We make our way out of the station on foot, I and Balwant have to carry the bags as Mama and Mami carry the children. It's about half a mile walk to Durgiana Mandir and we start the walk with a slow pace, in order to stay as cool as we can. It takes us about 30 minutes to get there. We enter the Mandir after depositing our shoes in the shoes-stand. I walk into the shrine and see the Mandir shining in the middle of the water tank, with it's gold plated dome.

Immediately, I realise the marble floor is burning hot and I run to whatever matting I can find on the walkway. We're not a particularly religious family, we are Sikhs but we also pay our respects at shrines of Devtas (Demi-Gods) and those of the Hindu Faith. My Mami had wanted to come to Amritsar for the well-being of the kids.

We pay our respects at the Mandir, offer parshad (holy offering, purchased at the entrance of the temple), and joyfully bathe in the water tank to cool ourselves, in the afternoon sun. I'm not too sure of the historical significance of the shrine and hear it could possibly be the original home of Mata Sita and her sons Luv and Kush, some aeons ago (the family of Lord Rama of the Hindu Faith). I wasn't particularly bothered any reason to get out of Maheroo was a God-send and Amritsar is one of the largest cities of Punjab, so I was just in awe of the city.

After leaving the shrine we find some shade under a banyan tree and eat our lunch which was handed to us by Bibi in the morning. She carefully packed misse parshade (lightly flavoured chapattis), we drank water from the public tap and Mama purchased milk from the street-traders tea stall for Suraj.

2pm The afternoon heat was at its worst now, but Mama and Mami decided we should travel on to the Golden Temple and then rest when we get there. We made our journey through the alley ways of Amritsar, the rich aroma's, rickshaws and glaring shopkeepers calling out for business, all defined the Amritsar experience for me, as we dodged people and street traffic in the alley ways to the Golden Temple.

We passed Lohgarh Gurdwara (Sikh place of worship), which was a commanding fort on our way and went past Gurdwara Guru Ke Mehal, arriving at the Golden Temple near the clock tower entrance, whilst seeing the roof-top of Akaal Takhat to our right. We deposited our shoes, washed our feet in the soothing water wash basin and when I saw the Golden Temple, butterflies stirred in my stomach and a cool soothing sensation ran through my spine. When seeing the Golden Temple I was so humbled and over-whelmed that I dropped to my feet and bowed. When my forehead hit the ground, I could feel static energy reverberate through my forehead and my whole body. I was quickly brought back to earth by Suraj violently slapping me in the head, he had done this to get my attention, I looked up in anger and then I heard Mami hollering at me, "Hurry up! What are you doing? We need to keep together as a group," I quickly got to my feet and we alighted the stairs to enter the Gurdwara.

We promptly entered the shaded areas of the walkway (parkarma), took water at the Punjabi Sevak Jatha Shabeel (water point) and decided to get some sleep in the shade there. We all peacefully slept here, on the hard marble surface, using our bags as pillows for the next 2 hours.

5pm

We awoke and then offered parshad at the Golden Temple, I was amazed at the intricacies of the frescos and embedded jewels of the whole Gurdwara. The gold artwork and cladding was fascinating as were the expensive throws and flowers around Sri Guru Granth Sahib Jee. I was used to going to the village Gurdwara and mechanically bowing, running to get parshad and leaving immediately. So this experience of being over-whelmed by the art and beauty of a Gurdwara was fresh and inspiring.

The Akaal Takhat intrigued me, with it's weapons and arms of Sikhs and Gurus. We saw the end part of the daily display of the weapons as we paid our respects. As night fell we had Langar (blessed free food) at Guru Ramdas Langar Hall and went to sleep again in the shaded area of the parkarma.

1st June 1984

We were woken by an elderly woman, frantic but cautious. She whispered to all of us to wake up and leave the Gurdwara. She said the Gurdwara has been surrounded by the army and a curfew is in place. She chillingly said, *"Leave and save your children in any way that you can to my Mama and Mami."* My Mama cursed my Mami, "Stupid woman, I told you to wait a little longer before making this trip, the power-mad Bhindranvale and Indira Gandhi are both going to get us killed," she lightly slapped him on his upper arm and said quietly "Keep your voice down, somebody could hear you."

The reality of what was going on around me, suddenly dawned on me. I looked around and now realised that, what I thought was normal for the Golden Temple and Amritsar was possibly more sinister. I thought of armed Sikh men I had seen around the complex and the large presence of security forces across Amritsar.

We spent the rest of the day in the sweltering heat, flittering from pillar to post and thinking of what to do next. We didn't leave, as there was indiscriminate fire from the army outside, into the complex. Luckily at this point the armed Sikhs in the complex were not firing back. This bamboozled me, as I had an image of gung-ho fire squads of Bhindranvale. To the contrary armed Sikhs across the complex were sheltering, guarding and guiding innocent pilgrims into safe havens across the complex. We ended up taking shelter in Guru Nanak Niwas and in rooms built to usually house about 3 people, about 20 of us were crammed in. There were literally thousands of pilgrims locked into the complex, a few brave pilgrims did leave through the exits near Baba Atal, the Sikh reference library and the Akaal Takhat as there were pockets of entry points through which they could risk leaving and not being detected or shot by the security forces.

I fell into a torrent of thoughts as night approached and we sweated profusely in the night hue and heat. I thought, *I am only 14 years old, I have not got married, finished schooling, had children, I do not deserve to die!* Even though I had never prayed before in my life, I mentally started reciting "Satnaam Vaaheguroo," (True is the Name, He is the wondrous enlightener).

9.30pm   We heard a loud knock at the door and someone shouting, "Open." Everyone in the room was scared and someone near the door opened it. To our shock an armed Sikh was standing at the door, he looked like one of Bhindranvale's henchmen. He mechanically looked around the room and ordered me and another girl, who was about 14years old also, to get up and leave with him. My Mama shouted "No way" he quietly replied "brother, we need her to do some Seva with us," my Mama's voice got louder and he still said "NO" but then quickly said "Take me instead!" The Singh firmly said "No, we need her, we can do this the easy way or hard," he pointed at his assault rifle. My Mama backed down, I and the other girl - Surjit, were ushered out of the room with the Singhs pointing their guns showing us the way.

The Singhs proceeded towards Manji Sahib Divan Hall, one in front of us and one behind us. As we approached we could see a fire, as we got closer we realised it was a funeral pyre, I shuddered in fear. Horrified I thought, *am I going to be burnt alive?* There were about 20-25 Sikhs gathered around the fire, we were stopped about 20 feet way. The Singhs then said to us *"He was a great Sikh, he was shot today on Baba Atal Gurdwara. He died a warriors death, his name is Bhai Mehnga Singh. We have brought you here, as we thought we can't help everyone, but if we can help some younger sisters then we should try to do that."* They then sternly spoke, *"More than likely you will die in the violence that is to follow. The government is hell-bent on killing innocent pilgrims and Sikhs, they have purposely decide to attack the complex now, as thousands are gathered here in preparation for the memorial programmes for the martyrdom of Sri Guru Arjan Dev Jee which is on the 5th June."*

I was now confused thinking what are they talking about, will they still kill us? The Singh continued, "You are young women and you may be abused by the army, we have two cyanide capsules," the Singh reached into his pocket and handed me a capsule, as he did Surjit, "You should take this capsule if the situation gets too bad and death is a better option." They then marched us back to the room, before re-entering our room at Guru Nanak Niwas, I requested that

I be allowed to talk to Surjit, the Singhs gave us some space. I whispered to Surjit "We can't tell our families about these capsules, we must conceal them and not tell anyone," Surjit nodded agreeing with the suggestion, she said "but what shall we say has just happened?" I said "Don't worry, leave the talking to me, just follow my lead," she again nodded in agreement. We signalled to the Singhs that we were happy to re-enter the room, they opened the door and we entered.

Both our families rushed to greet us, the Singhs just left without saying anything. I quickly said "The Singhs asked us to make chapattis in the Langar Hall and to tend to the wounds of their fighters, me and Surjit said we have never made chapattis and have no medical knowledge, so they brought us straight back." Surjit half-winked at me, showing approval of my cover-up story. My Mami started blabbering, "How dare they, they knew this room has been designated for families with young children, they should have gone elsewhere." I calmly put my hand on my Mami's shoulder and said, "We are back safely," and she hugged me and I could feel Suraj and Parveen clenching at my legs.

My brother Balwant, was very subdued and quiet. Once all my family had fallen asleep, I whispered to Balwant, "Are you okay?" he said "No! Did those militants do anything to you?" I replied, "No – they were very polite to us." He then gently stroked my head and said, "I love you, I know I haven't been a good brother ..." I could see the tears welling up in his eyes. I put my finger on his lips and said, "You don't need to say anything, I know. Don't worry we will get out alive." Balwant – "I sure hope so."

2nd June, 1984

We spent the whole of the next day in the room, only venturing out to the corridor to use the toilets. The men in the room went out of the room at 12pm to get food from the Langar Hall. They brought back enough food for one meal, for everyone in the room. A lot of us were now suffering from dehydration due to the heat.

3rd June, 1984

10am - We get a visitor to the room, he says he is an employee of SGPC (Shiromani Gurdwara Parbandhak Committee – the management committee of the Gurdwara complex). He says that there will be an announcement to allow innocent pilgrims to leave the complex, he says we can all leave then. We all rush after him, thinking we have a slim hope of survival. In all about 200 people join this sort of walk to freedom. We are all assembled collectively at Manji Sahib Gurdwara and eagerly await the announcement from the army.

At 11am the announcement is made by the army that innocent pilgrims can leave and no harm will come to them. The army announced that pilgrims leaving, must leave through the Brahm Buta Market exit gate. When signalled by the SGPC workers the whole procession started walking towards the gate, I had realised that the SGPC workers conspicuously ensured they were at the back of the procession. I halted Surjit's family and mine and said "Let's go to the end of the lines, like the SGPC workers," my Mami looked at me, as if to say, *are you crazy?* Fortunately, at this point I saw the same Singh who had taken me and Surjit standing on an upper floor of the Langar Hall with his gun in toe. I pointed him out to my Mami signalling he has told us to go to the back, my Mami quickly obliged, for fear of getting shot by the Singh, even though, he wasn't even looking at us.

All of a sudden, gun fire stared and about 40 of the people at the front of the procession were immediately gunned down. Everyone ran helter skelter, for cover. I grabbed Parveen and ran towards the Langar Hall, I dived to the floor, smashing Parveen's chin on the floor and cracking her front teeth. She whimpered, but bravely didn't cry. We then crawled our way to the Langar Hall. I lost my brother, mama, mami and Suraj in the chaos. I never saw them again. Surjit had followed my lead and made it to the Langar Hall with me. I later learnt from family members that Balwant had told them the following;

....

Balwant:	"Mama, Mami, Suraj and I made it back to Manji Sahib. Some of the leaders of the SGPC and Akali Dal (Sikh political party) were trying to reassure the congregation that they would assure a safe escape, but there was much incessant bickering due to the earlier calamity of the 40 innocent pilgrims being gunned down by the army. Then a few hours later, these leaders left the complex with their arms in the air and about 70 others they had not taken to arms and were not involved any firing against security forces. But this time the leaders were forced to the front of the procession. We were shocked by the earlier incident and decided not to try leaving again.

Suraj died on the 4th June from dehydration and Mami died from banging her head so hard in the wall, in anguish of his death. She was already weak from dehydration and trying incessantly to breast-feed Suraj. She was like a crazed woman when he died and banged her head with much fervour, into a wall 2 or 3 times and the bleeding killed her. Mama tried unsuccessfully to get her treated and took off his own turban in an attempt to bandage the wound.

I and Mama survived to 6th June, as we both took the drastic step of drinking bloodied water from the Sarovar (sacred water tank of the Golden Temple that pilgrims bathe in). It made my stomach churn and I was nearly sick, when I first drank it. When Mama realised this, he slapped me so hard on the face, that I got an instant scar, he hollered, *"You stupid boy, you will die! If you don't drink."*

On 7th June, the army took control of the whole complex. I and Mama had survived by playing dead. We used to lie down between dead bodies and went undetected like this. At times we were even trampled upon by army personnel and I and Mama both developed bleeding in our mouths due to biting in agony, whilst trying not to make a sound in the excruciating pain. At about 12pm we watched the army killing Sikh men by tying their turbans around their backs, these were non-combatant pilgrims. They were all shot at point blank range. After witnessing this, Mama grabbed me by the shoulder and said, "We are only going to survive this, if we pretend we are militants. We are going to have to find some guns and surrender to the army, they will not kill us then as they will try to extract information from us." I thought he was insane and looked musingly up at him. He then lashed a back-handed slap across my face. "Trust me, it is our only chance of survival!" he shouted and his voice broke as he said it. I could see he was desperate. He was at the end of his tether, I agreed with him as I thought we're dead anyway.

Mama's plan worked, we conducted a fake surrender throwing empty guns (we had recovered) on the floor in front of the army personnel and throwing our arms in the air. At this point of surrender, I stared straight at the guns of the soldiers, waiting for a gun to launch a bullet that would pierce my body. But Mama was right, the soldiers cautiously approached us and sent us to Ladha Kothi Jail. This was full of people from the Golden Temple, all the prisoners were from there.

Mama died on 17th July 1984. He died from the relentless torture he endured at Ladha Kothi. He would get hung upside down, then, they would start interrogating him, trying to force him to make confessions or give information that he simply did not have. To force him to speak they would beat him with metal rods, electrocute him, run wooden logs over his legs and sexually abuse him. The sleepless nights between 7th June - 17th July were unbearable for him. He persistently cursed his luck saying, "What possessed me to surrender as a militant, this place is worse than hell itself. God please bring my death!" He also used to caressingly beg for my forgiveness, *"Son, I am sorry, I shouldn't have slapped you, my stubbornness has led us here, please forgive me, please forgive me..."* This was our daily ritual and he used to fall asleep everyday begging my forgiveness.

I was labelled a hardcore militant due to my age. Eventually I was released from prison when I was 13years old. I returned to my village - a disturbed 13year old, due to all that I had witnessed and experienced. Due to continuous police harassment after returning to Maheroo, I took the step of trying to protect myself rather than be a victim of physical violence from the state machinery. I joined the Khalistan Commando Force as Bhai Manbir Singh was its leader and he was from the village Chaheroo, which is neighbours my village.

I was involved in militant actions until the age of 18 and eventually came to the UK, to escape from India. My parents were both killed by the police when I was 17 years old, as they kept harassing them about my whereabouts. They were both killed being tortured by the police. I had no real inclination to faith initially and became a practising Sikh, due to the unjust and inhumane way that the state treated me, faith was the only thing that gave me solace and some hope of a better future."

....

Balwant became mentally unstable and could not settle in to life when he arrived in the UK. He no longer had a recollection of what 'normality' was, he could not adjust to finding a job, working, buying a house and getting married – things we may take as a normal course of life. All that he had endured took its toll in the most unforgiving manner, he committed suicide at the age of 22.

....

3rd June, 1984

Satwant: When we entered the Langar Hall, the door
            was slammed shut by an armed Sikh. I
            looked around frantically and quickly
            realised that the Langar Hall was a mini
            fortress. There were sandbags piled next to
            openings and armed Sikhs were guarding
            the rations. I also saw wiring which had
            been erected and realised a mini wired
            network for communications had been set
            up.

            The Singh who had given us the cyanide
            capsules came over and greeted us saying,
            "Sisters are you okay?" I pointed at Parveen
            and she started crying and blood started to
            pour out of her mouth. The Singh quickly
            picked her up and ran with her behind some
            sandbags. Behind the sandbags there was a
            Sikh woman with a turban on. I was
            shocked at the sight of her turban as I had
            never seen a woman wear a turban before,
            she calmed Parveen down, cleaned her
            wounds and applied some cream to stop the
            bleeding from her mouth. The Singh came
            back after about 10 minutes and said "I am
            Seva Singh, if you want to survive, I suggest
            you stay here and I promise to ensure your
            safety." Me and Surjit were re-assured by
            Seva Singh and asked how we could be of
            help. He said we could assist the injured

pilgrims and we started helping the woman who had treated Parveen.

4th June, 1984

We stayed in the Langar Hall until 4th June. At about 12pm Seva Singh came over to us, he said "I have arranged for your escape you must come with me immediately and do exactly as I say." I and Surjit nodded in agreement. Seva Singh told us that there was an opening at the back wall of Baba Atal Gurdwara, he and another Singh would ferry us to the safe house. We followed his orders, our path from the Langar Hall to Baba Atal was treacherous as we had to dodge sniper fire and come under attack from commandos, who were parachuted down from aircraft. We witnessed about 20 commandos were making their descent down, the Sikh militants opened fire, firing at their parachutes so when they landed they were seriously injured. We had witnessed the army continuously kill Sikhs indiscriminately between the 1st June to 4th June and were coping the best we could, with the war-like situation and killing all around us. We couldn't believe that the Indian Army had turned the Golden Temple complex into a killing field. It beggared belief that a whole scale army operation against its own people was underway.

As for the journey to Baba Atal we also had to walk over dead bodies of Sikhs and Indian army soldiers. The stench of death was sickening and unforgettable. We successfully dodged sniper fire until Baba Atal Gurdwara, where Surjit was grazed on the arm by a bullet, thankfully she only sustained a minor injury. As for our escape, Surjit and I had to make separate ways out from the complex, both ferried by a Singh each. Surjit had made it safely in to a Sikh household and I never saw her again. Me, Parveen and Seva Singh waited for the other Singh (who had taken Surjit to the safe house) to return safely, before leaving ourselves. One Singh had to remain near to the wall opening, to guard it from the army entering the complex from it.

Now it was our turn, I and Parveen made it safely to a flat of a Hindu family who were sympathetic to innocent pilgrims. Seva Singh bid us farewell and I bowed and touched the dust of his feet raising it to Parveens brow and my own. I thanked Seva Singh, "May you live on, and have a good life, my brother," he was a little embarrassed and smirked, saying "Whatever God will's will happen," he turned and left, I peered out of a window of the flat to see Seva Singh leaving, about 40 yards from the house, he fell to sniper fire, a bullet had pierced his chest. I ran to him, the Hindu family tried to stop me for their own safety and mine, but I wasn't thinking of the consequences and my safety and ran to his aide. I raised his head in my lap and stroked his forehead, he looked up and said "Vaaheguroo." He then passed away in my arms. I cried and screamed in agony.

I was crying for somebody I didn't know, had known for only a few days, but he was the only adult who provided safety and a sense of family for me. At that point in time he was all I had. I sat there crying for about a minute, I glared back at the flat and saw Parveen staring at me. I signalled for her to stay there and made my way back to the flat. She innocently asked *"Where are mummy and daddy now?"* I replied, *"I am your mummy and daddy now"* and she said, *"But you are my deedi (sister)."* I said, *"I am now your sister, mummy and daddy. We have to live with these people until we save enough money to go and see mommy and daddy."* She was pacified temporarily.

For the next 6 years, I and Parveen lived with this Hindu family in Amritsar, we changed our names to Hindu ones and lived with them as their servants. They became our surrogate family and we were treated lovingly, but had to put up a pretence of being servants, in front of other people to not raise suspicion. The head of the household was a gentle kind-hearted man, who was sympathetic to the Sikh cause and he kept in touch with influential Sikhs in the militancy. These Sikhs in turn paid for our upkeep. This family had been helped earlier by Bhindranvale in a dispute about dowry demands in the marriage of their daughter. Living with this family changed my whole outlook on Bhindranvale and what I termed, *Sikh Terrorists.* Living in Amritsar, I had easy access to recordings of Bhindranvale's speeches and learnt that he was not the monster the media and government had projected him to be.

When I was 20 years old, I left Amritsar to go to Germany and had to leave Parveen in an orphanage. She was than 10 years old. I was married in Berlin to a Sikh through the contacts of my new family of Amritsar. I never tried to contact my real family or Parveen's, as we would have risked the lives of our new Hindu family and were grateful to just be alive.

I am now 40 years old and live in Birmingham, England. Parveen is now 30 years old and is married with one child. We did eventually make contact with our relatives in 1995 when Punjab turned to what some refer to *'normality'* at the end of the guerrilla warfare.

I am now divorced and can never forget June 1984. The famous verse of *"I have seen all other places, none compare to you,"* in reference to the Golden Temple, has very different connotations for me and Parveen.

I attend the annual remembrance march in London in June and rally in Trafalgar square. I mourn for what I witnessed, lived through and live through. I feel a numbness that is indescribable when I think of these events. My only solace in life is meditation, as that is the only escape I have found that works.

I pray for the safety and well-being of all humanity, "Nanak Naam Chardi Kala, Tere Bhane Sarbat Da Bhalla" (May the name of God gifted to me by Guru Nanak, keep me in high spirits and I pray for the betterment of all humanity, oh Lord). I have no hatred, enmity or anger towards those that killed my family and so many other Sikhs. My closure is not sought in viewing myself as a victim. Rather I spend my days with resilience as thousands of Sikhs before me have done. Sikhs have been persecuted throughout History.

I hope that Sikhs realise that what happened to us should lead them to take positive action to try and get some redress, or at the very least to not forget. They should open their minds and hearts to the human side of what happened to us as a people. Thousands suffered and live on with horrifying memories. As a community and a people, we don't like being victims and this is portrayed with the rightful glorification of martyrs. The point I'd like to make is, the martyrs make up a minority and the majority who survived have also suffered immensely but little has been done or is being done to unearth their stories and support them.

I still have the cyanide capsule that my brother Seva Singh gave to me. The small time I had with him, inspired me so much that he became my reference point or alter ego and I would think of how he would handle a situation and in this way I always found a solution to my problems. After years of searching I recently found photos of him. I take out the cyanide tablet every year at Rakhria (an Indian festival which marks the vow of protection that a brother gives to his sister and their love), the capsule is then placed in front of his photo and I place my fingers lovingly over his photo and wave my hand over my brow – in the hope that his dust still magically inspires me to live on and be an ounce of the Sikh that he was.

To see some Sikhtoons about Operation Blue Star please see pages 140 – 141.

Destroying the History of Sikhs

The government wanted to destroy any pride the Sikhs had in their faith and history. Thus the army needlessly proceeded after the 6th June 1984 to set fire to Sikh artefacts and destroy the history of the Sikhs. The government did admit to taking artefacts away from the complex after the attack, but to date nothing has been returned to the Sikhs.

I will now give a short account from Giani Kirpal Singh of what happened to different Sikh artefacts. This is taken from "Eye-witness account of Operation Blue Star," Translated and edited by Anurag Singh (1999). Giani Kirpal Singh was the Jathedar of the Akaal Takhat at the time of the attack:

- A historic Sri Guru Granth Sahib Jee that was hand-written in 1830 AD, during the reign of Maharajah Ranjit Singh received a bullet mark, which has made a hole up to Sukhmani Sahib, about 260 Angs in. To date the Shiromani Gurdwara Parbandhak Committee (SGPC) has not undertaken any restoration of this historic Sri Guru Granth Sahib.

- The historic canopy that was studded with many priceless jewels was damaged with gun fire. The canopy had been presented to Maharajah Ranjit Singh by the Nizam of Hyderabad. The Maharajah had in turn donated it to the Golden Temple as he felt it was only befitting that such a priceless canopy be used at such a venue. Giani Kirpal Singh states that he put the ashes and what was left of the canopy under lock and key. Again no statement of what has happened to the canopy has been made by the SGPC.

- The wooden wardrobe that used to be used to store historic weapons at Akaal Takhat was completely destroyed, being burnt and damaged.

- A gold plated palanquin (throne) that was used to display the historic weapons during the day at Akaal Takhat was completely destroyed with gun fire. To see a photo of the destroyed Akaal Takhat please see page 141.

o Some of the historic weapons were traced from the debris on 11th June 1984 and the army had 2 big swords and arrows in their possession which they returned.

o Bhai Teja Singh who was one of the longest serving employees of the SGPC serving at Akaal Takhat helped locate and identify historic weapons from the debris of Akaal Takhat. He found broad and straight swords, Khandas (double-edged swords) and Chakars (iron discs).

o 2 gold tipped arrows of Sri Guru Gobind Singh Jee were destroyed in the attack.

o Many historic paintings were destroyed in the attack. The army took away 103 such historical paintings and promised to return them after getting them restored. Again the paintings have not been returned nor have the SGPC made a concerted effort to get them back.

Many things happened after the attack but the SGPC has to take responsibility for not compiling a comprehensive list of artefacts damaged and/or lost in the attack. Nor have they made a strong campaign to have these artefacts returned. A concerted and continued effort is needed. The person who was in charge of the Sikh library in June 1984 where the majority of these artefacts were stored, is still employed by the SGPC, thus first-hand knowledge of the artefacts is still possible.

Co-ordinated Attacks on other Gurdwaras

The Indian government planned to destroy the morale of the Sikhs and the bogey of terrorism and religious fundamentalism were used as scapegoats to implement their plan. The government argued that attacking the Golden Temple was needed to flush out terrorists, but then the question has to be raised as to why Gurdwaras across Punjab were attacked? Were terrorists in all these places of worship?

"Coordinated with the attack on the Golden Temple were raids against 44 places of worship in the Punjab where terrorists were believed to be based." (P.132 **"Indira Gandhi in 1984, Confrontation, Assassination & Succession."** Robert L. Hardgrave, Jr. in Asian Survey, Vol.XXV, No.1, January 1985)

'Terrorists' were not in these shrines. There were Sikhs present. If the government wanted to equate being a Sikh with being a terrorist, then their plan of destroying the morale of Sikhs was counterproductive as a full-fledged guerrilla war was instigated as a result of these suicidal actions. Different commentators come up with different numbers of Gurdwaras attacked simultaneously with the Golden Temple, but these figures are between 38 – 75 Gurdwaras being attacked. Significantly Professor Uday Singh (August 1987) argues that Takhat Kesgarh Sahib and Takhat Damdama Sahib (two thrones of authority, out of the five thrones in Sikhi) were also destroyed by attacks by the government.

5. 1984 Halloween

Indira Gandhi had started a suicidal mission against the Sikhs that would ultimately lead to her death. She had tried to misrepresent the Sikhs and their demands, attempting to make them national social outcasts in India. This was all done in the selfish aim of trying to win votes and the upcoming elections.

Sikhs throughout the world were calling for the head of Indira Gandhi in revenge for the attack on the Golden Temple. She knew that her life was under threat and security was increased. But due to her ego and self-confidence, she refused to heed the advice of her advisors that all her Sikh bodyguards posed a threat and should be duly redeployed. She refused to heed this advice as she was confident that she had done nothing wrong and had faith in her bodyguards. To see a profile photo of Indira please see page 142.

Satwant Singh and Beant Singh, both bodyguards of hers, did in the end assassinate her. They were dismayed by her actions. They had visited the ruins of the Akaal Takhat and seen the damage to the whole Golden Temple complex. Firstly I would like to present an alternative view of why they assassinated her. It was due to their duty of protecting Indian national security, as they were employed by the government to perform.

This argument is made in "The Punjab Crisis" by Murray J. Leaf (Asian Survey Vol.XXV, No.5, May 1985). It is argued that they laid down their lives to defend their country, homeland and their religion. Therefore they acted out of the same convictions that led them to serve the Country in the first place. In their view Indira must have been representing a pressing threat to all three and so they gave their lives to stop her.

In the end, Indira Gandhi fell to the bullets of the Singhs on a befitting day, the woman that represented a witch to Sikhs was put to justice on Halloween. She had planned other acts of violence and oppression against the Sikhs and Operation Blue Star was just the tip of the iceberg of things to come.

In October 1984, Bhai Satwant Singh and Bhai Beant Singh visited the Golden Temple and witnessed the destruction that the army had caused upon the orders of Indira Gandhi. After seeing the destruction they had an awakening of faith. They both became practicing Sikhs and were initiated at an Amrit Sanchar in Delhi.

Satwant Singh and Beant Singh were both bodyguards of Indira Gandhi. After seeing the destruction at the Golden Temple Complex they started plotting to assassinate Indira Gandhi. They felt their mission in life was now to get revenge for the destruction of the heart of all Sikhs the Golden Temple Complex. They worked separate shifts where one used to finish his shift and the other used to start his shift so they were not together on bodyguard duty with the Prime Minister. To accomplish their aim they needed to be together on their shift, so Satwant Singh feigned illness saying that he had stomach ache. In this way he was able to swap guard duty with another soldier. Now Satwant Singh and Beant Singh were together on their duty and could proceed with the next stage of their plan.

On the 31st October at 9am, Indira Gandhi left her residence, without wearing a bullet proof vest. She refused to wear protective clothing and refused to dismiss her Sikh bodyguards. This was just an example of her arrogance and confidence in her actions. She felt she was invincible. She was going to her office on Safdarjang Road. Beant Singh saluted her, but today instead of his right hand opening the gate it went straight to his service revolver and in an instant he fired five bullets from his revolver. Indira tumbled upon impact of the bullets and fell to the ground. Satwant Singh then moved forward and fired 28 bullets from his Thomson Machine Gun into her.

The other guards cowardly ran haplessly in all directions when the bullets started being fired, and ran for cover even though they were all armed as well.

Beant Singh and Satwant Singh then threw their weapons on the ground and declared,

"We have done what we aimed to do; now you can do what you like with us"

They threw their arms in the air to show they were surrendering. The Indo-Tibetan Guards seeing the coast was clear then approached the Singhs and took them into custody. When in custody the arresting officers were repeatedly swearing at the Singhs and Satwant Singh got angered at their use of vulgar language and he lunged at one of the officers to disarm him. The arresting officers then opened indiscriminate fire on the Singhs. Beant Singh was shot first and he fell on top of Satwant Singh. Beant Singh was martyred on the spot. Satwant Singh was seriously injured but was saved, as Beant Singh falling on top of him, had saved him from the brunt of the bullets fired.

Satwant Singh was taken to hospital and treated for his injuries, but he was tortured and treated very badly by the authorities. He remained in custody for the rest of his life and was continually harassed at every opportunity. He could not even walk when his parents went to see him for the first time. Satwant Singh and Kehar Singh were sentenced to death by hanging for the assassination of Indira Gandhi.

Satwant Singh's final wish was,

"May I be born over and over to annihilate tyrants."

Satwant Singh and Kehar Singh asked for their faces to be kept uncovered for the hanging. They wanted to show that they were not afraid of being hung or of facing up to their actions. They walked onto the platform of where they were to be hung at 7.55am, 5 minutes early, as they were eager to receive their punishment. They even placed the rope around their necks so the executioner would not have to waste his efforts. They roared Jakaras before being hanged. Please see page 142 for photos of Satwant Singh, Beant Singh & Kehar Singh.

Their families were not allowed to witness their execution; their families had planned to conduct the funerals themselves. The authorities in haste immediately cremated the bodies and were trying to ensure that the families did not perform any of the last rites over Satwant Singh or Kehar Singh. After much continuous efforts, the families were allowed to immerse their ashes in the Ganges at Hardwar (Sikhs traditionally immerse the ashes of loved ones at Kiratpur Sahib, Anandpur or at Goindval, but the families had to immerse the ashes in the Ganges as the authorities would only allow them to do so here).

Bhai Beant Singh and Satwant Singh foiled Indira's plans for Operation Shanti, but the bloodthirsty mobs across India still hunted and killed Sikhs for the next three days.

However, instead of a death toll in the hundreds of thousands, the loss was not on as grand a scale as was intended.

Operation Shanti was scheduled to proceed on November 8, 1984, when Sikhs had gathered to celebrate Guru Nanak Dev Jee's Gurpurab. According to Sangat Singh, *"large scale skirmishes virtually amounting to a war were to take place all along the India-Pakistan borders. And it was to be given out that the Sikhs had risen in revolt in Punjab and joined hands with the Pakistani armed forces which had made considerable advances into the Indian territory"* (The Sikhs in History, Sangat Singh, 415).

Sikhs were to be bombarded from the air and slaughtered by the army. India-wide attacks on the "collaborator" Sikhs would also occur. The assassination of Indira Gandhi stopped such a wide-spread assault against the Sikhs.

The Sikh Auschwitz
No one could have predicted that after the death of Indira Gandhi, the rule of law would be ignored to openly murder, torture, abuse and rape Sikhs across India. At the death of his mother, Rajiv Gandhi went on national television to say that, *'when a big tree falls the earth shakes,'* this statement was the precursor to the anti-Sikh riots and genocide of the Sikhs across India.

The death of Indira Gandhi accelerated the Congress party plans *'to teach the Sikhs a lesson.'* The death of Indira Gandhi at the hands of Sikh bodyguards was used as an empty excuse to go out and kill Sikhs with impunity. All the evidence points to the facts that the anti-Sikh riots which lasted a few days from the 31st August – 2nd November 1984 were planned, aided, and abetted by the Congress government. Mobs roamed the streets of Delhi,

Kanpur and other parts of India attacking, abusing, torturing, murdering Sikhs and looting, burning their homes. Homes of Sikhs in Delhi were spray painted before the organised mobs arrived (to clearly demarcate the homes of Sikhs), thus electoral registers were used to plan ahead and the police and army were nowhere to be seen.

Sikhs were openly burnt alive. Tyres were put around their necks, kerosene was poured over them, women were raped and even children were not spared. All this happened in the country that is commonly known as the *'world's biggest democracy,'* Hitler had killed the Jews in gas chambers and had tried to conceal this genocide, yet India took no shame in killing Sikhs openly on the streets, whilst the world sat back and took no notice.

I remember watching the funeral of Indira Gandhi where world leaders such as Ronald Reagan and Margaret Thatcher attended, yet no-one raised an eyebrow to the mass killings of Sikhs only a few days earlier. When Mahatma Gandhi had been assassinated by a radical Hindu, India or Indians did not react by going out and killing members of the RSS, the party that the killer was a member of. Yet when two Sikh bodyguards kill Indira Gandhi, innocent Sikhs who had nothing to do with her killing are murdered, displaced from their homes and abused, made refugees in their so called 'homeland.' To see photos and Sikhtoons about the atrocities please see pages 143 – 144.

The Indian press was also deaf to the atrocities meted out to the Sikh masses, which were also openly killed on trains heading for Punjab; memories of the partition chaos were once again ignited in the minds of Sikhs. In the partition of India and Pakistan many Sikhs arrived dead on trains to what had become India Punjab, due to communal violence flaring up between Muslims, Hindus and Sikhs. Yet now in India the supposed 'homeland of Sikhs' Sikhs were being treated worse than a foreign enemy, being killed without even being allowed to defend themselves and fight an open battle.

On the 20th anniversary (2004) of the government organised carnage against the Sikhs, the Times of India, Indian Express and the BBC ran some news stories of some of the victims of the carnage. Sakhi Arora of the Times of India reported that, out of the 450 Gurdwaras in Delhi, about three-quarters were damaged or destroyed and now most have fortified fences and manned gates. The Gurdwaras became the first targets of the mobs but were also the last refuge of most Sikhs who survived. Many had to return to the Gurdwaras to get support from fellow Sikhs as their homes were looted and burnt and they were made homeless. Many did not want to and could not return to homes where their loved ones had been either beaten to death, burnt alive or they themselves had been sexually abused; many were gang raped.

Sakshi Arora reports that Ravel Kaur, a victim states that:

"I just managed to save my 10-year-old son by removing his turban, braiding his hair and making him wear a girl's dress," Kaur sobbed in her ramshackle glass shop ..."I lost seven people, my husband, two sons, a daughter, a daughter-in-law and two grand-children on that day. But until today, we've got no justice. The people who killed my family still haven't been punished."

About 800 Sikh women were widowed in Delhi alone, and I personally have heard of stories of one extended family having 23 widows. This was the calamitous effect upon Sikh families in Delhi. The widows either seethe with anger or just accept their lot and carry on the best they can. Sakshi Arora reports:

"Nobody cared to listen to the cries of widows. We were almost treated like whores," screamed Jaissi Bai, a grey-haired woman on crutches who lost her husband and son in the riots. *"Our children are treated like criminals."*

The online BBC website reported case studies of different victims. I will quote the responses of the victims:

"Life has been hard. I could hardly afford to care for my children. I could not even give them milk when they were young so I gave them tea. It was that bad." (Harjit Kaur)

This example of Harjit Kaur displays the economic disadvantage that such Sikhs had to undergo, the drinking of milk during childhood is accepted as a given for many throughout the world, but these Sikhs were deprived of this basic nutrition.

"My children implored with my husband's killers to let him go. When they set him on fire, they kept saying, 'Oh God, punish these people!' I kept crying. But they didn't listen and set him on fire. He was left dead on the doorstep, half burnt. There was no dignity in death. I went door to door in my neighbourhood to raise money and gave him a proper cremation. Then I left home. Forever." (Kuldip Kaur)

The strength of Kuldip Kaur is exemplary. Even if the mobs and the support of the India Government had reduced the death of her husband to that of no dignity, she still fought on to ensure that he got the funeral he deserved. She did not let them win and in the end she would only allow a befitting send off for her husband even if his death had been unjust and unwarranted.

"I saw my neighbour's body on the street devoured by dogs after the mobs roasted him. So many relatives of the riot victims just died lamenting for their loved ones." (Nanaki Kaur)

Many family members of victims, mostly women, children and the elderly, developed psychological problems. Some simply became vagrants due to the mental imbalance created by the things they had witnessed and experienced. Others would die lamenting the loss of their loved ones. Others would never be able to form sustainable relationships and many of the offspring of the widows became social outcasts, criminals, or joined the Sikh freedom movement to reap revenge. None of these individuals or families asked for these life choices and circumstances to be forced upon them. They had to react in whatever way they could. This was a man-made problem, that of the Indian Government and ruling Congress Party.

Tavleen Singh, who was one of the journalists who was clearly against any sort of Sikh separatist movement, laments the events that preceded the assassination of Indira Gandhi, (A flashback to the 1984 riots Indian Express, 31st October 1984)

"It's the one event that even the most ardent secularists choose to forget which a constant puzzle is for me. In the many years I have spent reporting wars, riots, caste killings and other violent events on our sub-continent, I can remember nothing that matches the horror of those first 3 days after Mrs. Gandhi was killed ... Nobody bothered to pick up the dead because there was no room left in the

morgues and one of the images that continues to haunt me is of a dog eating a human arm in a Delhi street ... More than 3000 Sikhs were killed in two days, but all the violence was bought to a sudden halt in a couple of hours. All it took to stop the carnage and savagery was a handful of soldiers with orders to shoot at sight. The mobs dispersed as they would have done on day one had the government wanted them to."

Sheila Barse of the Indian Express on the 29th October 2004 reports how many Sikhs were made refugees in their so called 'homeland':

"A 12 year old boy sat alone apart from his kin, on a large stone, brooding, head held firm on a straight spine. The knot of his Kesh had been lopped off but the remaining hair, glued spiny stiff and erect in a bunch, proclaimed his continued identity. 'He's not spoken a word since he saw his father and uncle being burnt to death and flung down from the first floor,' a relative informs."

Not all Sikhs became victims. Those that did have arms tried their best to put up resistance, but many were stripped of their Kirpans and firearms by the police in affected areas, only to leave them open to attack and death. In some cases Sikhs did successfully rebuff attacks, but these were few and far between. One such case is that of some Sikhs in a Delhi Gurdwara - it is taken from www.panthkhalsa.com/naamnet,

A sevadar from a Nanaksar Gurdwara told this story:

"During the anti-Sikh riots, I was living in the Gurdwara Nanaksar, Haryana; there were 7 other sevadars in the Gurdwara. Trouble started brewing early in the morning, we noticed about 50 young men gathering outside a few hundred metres away from the Gurdwara, we didn't really pay much attention to them.

By noon the crowd became rowdy and had increased to about 300 hooligans, we became quite concerned at this point, but could not do anything, as the telephone line had been cut, but we were still in Chardi Kala. At about 3pm a truck driven by a Singh was driving by when the crowd attacked it. The Singh got out of the truck and ran to the Gurdwara. Some yobs injured him in pursuit, but he being a strong man, managed to escape. He was quite bloody when he came in, him joining us increased our number to 9, the number outside had increased to about 500 by evening; they were very loud and obnoxious by now.

At 7.30pm it was very dark and the rabble outside became so bold that they put the Gurdwara's gate on fire. The seriousness of the situation dawned on us and that we may be killed. Our Jathedar gathered us and said,

"Khalsa Jee, the Khalsa has faced worse situations than this, the Khalsa has gone through two holocausts but the Khalsa lives and will live on in freedom forever. Khalsa Jee, the Khalsa has never given up and will never give up. The enemy stands outside, there are 500, we are 9 but remember Sri Guru Gobind Singh Jee has made us equivalent to 125,000 (Sava Lakh) mortals. Khalsa Jee get prepared to fight!

He said this with so much courage and bravery, that our bodily hairs stood on their ends. Even though I had been seriously ill for 3 months, I was ready to fight. The Jathedar then told us, we must make two groups. The first group of five will go out first and fight the enemy, the other four will go later. The Jathedar then chose four other

Pyaras to go out and face the yobs, I wasn't chosen, most probably due to my illness.

The five Singhs put on the uniform of the Khalsa, and then the Jathedar did an Ardas to Sri Guru Gobind Singh Jee:

"Dear Father we are coming to your land,
please prepare for us."

Then the five took out their Kirpans and with, ' *Bole So Nihal, Sat Sri Akaal'* filling the air, came out to face the enemy. It was unbelievable what then transpired, seeing the five Khalsa in the uniform of Sri Guru Gobind Singh Jee, the rabble of 500 ran for their lives. It was as if five Lions were chasing 500 hyenas away. One of the Singh's managed to cut off a running man's ear off. The Khalsa's victory was sweet."

There are other stories of handfuls of Sikhs rebuffing attacks upon Gurdwaras by mobs by the use of their Kirpans.

The actual figures of the dead and affected will never be known. Estimates vary widely. The Government official death figure is 2,733 dead nationwide. Human rights activists say there were at least 4,000 people murdered. A modest estimate would be to say that at least 10,000 Sikhs were directly affected by the violence.

Only about 10 people have been convicted of murder in the cases against the guilty, but these people are not the real culprits for orchestrating and directing the violence. Those indicted by the evidence of victims and investigations of Sikh activists and Human Rights campaigners all point repeatedly to a few key individuals who were leading embers of the Congress Party. L K Bhagat (now deceased),

1984 HALLOWEEN

Narisima Rao (a former Indian Prime Minister), Sajjan Kumar and Jagdish Tytler. The real culprits have got away with their heinous crimes for over 20 years and justice does not seem to be in sight at all.

Many cases of arson, rape and murder were closed by the Police, citing lack of evidence. The most recent enquiry into the carnage was the Nanavati Commission. Its findings were dismissed by the Congress Party and the case closed - so they thought anyway. The repeated dismissal of claims of victims and the lack of justice led to protests throughout India and the globe by irate Sikhs. The Congress Party were made to readdress the situation, as the political opponents of the Congress Party walked out of the Raj Sabha (Indian Parliament).

Compensation to affected victims of up to 1 Lakh Rupees (100,000 RS) has been mooted and the government has vowed to develop a truth commission and take action against the culprits, but I would not hold your breath as you may have to wait another 20 years, by which time all the orchestrators of the violence will most likely be dead. Although acceding to public and political pressure the Congress Party did remove Jagdish Tytler and Sajjan Kumar from their ministerial positions. The party did clarify that this is not an admission of guilt, rather they wanted to neutralise the situation, and in light of this, felt it better that they were not represented in the government in these roles. To date both of these individuals receive government patronage and massive expense is made to protect these two individuals by the provision of government security personnel.

A farcical example of Indian justice was displayed by a story in the Punjabi Tribune of 22nd November 2004, when a Perneet Singh reported that an "'84 riot victim awaits cheque for 18 years." An octogenarian Gehal Singh has been running from pillar to post to for the last 18 years recover a cheque of RS 1 Lakh that was issued to him on 8 February 1986, for grievous injuries that he received to his hands and legs from the mob violence. He has not received the cheque to date. The injustices against the victims continue and it has got to the stage where widows of the carnage are attempting self-immolation to protest against the injustices they have suffered over the last 31years.

6. Sikh Insurgency 1984 – 1992

The beginning of the armed resistance

The calamitous events of Operation Blue Star and the Delhi Riots/anti-Sikh carnage, left a lot of Sikhs completely alienated. Many Sikhs took up arms to break the bonds of injustice and achieve an independent Sikh state. The movement for Punjab to become an independent state or Khalistan (land of the pure, Sikh homeland) was widely supported by the people of Punjab, due to the discrimination against Punjabis by the central government. The support for this independent state, was so widespread that Sikhs fighting for independence asked the central government to organise a plebiscite (a referendum of those living in Punjab) to find out the real opinion of the Punjab public, but this was never fulfilled by the government, partly for fear of the results & partly because they knew that the Sikhs in Punjab would have overwhelmingly supported this idea in the years between 1985 – 1991.

A lot of the Sikhs who entered the armed struggle were victims of circumstance and were not necessarily ideologically disciplined in the need for a Sikh state. There were a few leaders that were ideologically well grounded in the needs of a separate state and made good in roads in spreading the message. But for many, it was just to break free from state repression, in the hope that a better alternative would arise, as they were pained by what they had to endure both physically and mentally.

A mass armed struggle arose in which many groups practising guerrilla warfare against the state would arise and fall. In all, Punjab became a battle ground from 1984-1993 and to date is still officially declared a disturbed area by the government.

Due to the rise of militancy and the fear of being alienated by the government, the Akalis started their underhand game of politics, once again. They would make compromises to hurt the psyche of Sikhs and were trying to negotiate peace, even though very few militant groups took them seriously.

Akali Surrenders

The Akalis all sold out and came out of the attack on Harmander Sahib unscathed, they looked after their own political interests over those of the Sikhs, that they supposedly represented. To add salt to the fresh wounds of the Sikhs Sant Harchand Singh Longowal compromised and signed the infamous Rajiv/Longowal Accord. This accord was supposed to usher in peace; fulfil broken promises and steer towards justice for the Sikhs. Sant Bhindranvale had made it clear in a number of speeches that nothing short of acceding to all the demands of the Anandpur Sahib Resolution would be acceptable to the Sikhs, but Longowal sold out. Here are some of the agreements made;

Rajiv Gandhi – Longowal Accord (Times of India, 25 July 1985), points from the accord are numbered and italicised, my comments follow each point that needs to be noted:

2. *Army Recruitment*
2.1 *All citizens of the country have the right to enrol in the army and merit will remain the criterion for selection.*

The Sikhs had asked for a minimum quota of Sikhs to be recruited to the army, this was both to protect their martial tradition that the British had maintained and also to protect their economic vibrance as a minority in India. This demand was also partly demanded as the army was the only civil service that looked favourably upon Sikhs, in most other government departments Sikhs were discriminated against.

3.0   Enquiry into November 1984 incidents
3.1   Enquiry of Mr Mishra into Delhi riots to be extended to cover Bokaro and Kanpur.

The Mishra enquiry had been the first enquiry into the carnage against the Sikhs and the findings were expected to be non-conclusive or unfavourable to the Sikhs, so extending the enquiry did not hold out for much hope.

4.0   Rehabilitation of those discharged from the army – efforts will be made to rehabilitate and provide gainful employment.

Many Sikh soldiers absconded or quit their posts, when they learnt of the attack on the Golden Temple. These Sikh soldiers were arrested and imprisoned for absconding and lost their income. The rehabilitation promised was way off the mark, as hundreds of Sikhs who were ex-army personnel were languishing in prisons throughout India and the words *'efforts will be made to rehabilitate and provide gainful employment'* sum up the intent of the government, *"efforts will be made"*, the question is what would one define as an effort?

7.0   Territorial Claims, Chandigarh will be returned to Punjab by 26th January 1986.

This promise was made but to date has not been fulfilled.

8.0   Centre – state relations, will refer the proposals of the Anandpur Sahib resolution to the Sarkaria

Commission and make decision upon the findings of the Commission.

This was a clear tool to delay further any critical decisions and many Sikhs had, had enough of waiting for things to happen.

9.0   *Sharing River waters*
        Water sharing will stay the same as under the Ravi/Beas system as on 1.7.85. Quantum usage will be decided by a tribunal by a Supreme Court Judge. Satluj Yamuna Link (SYL) canal will continue to be built and will be completed by 15th August 1986."

This resolution was the real nail in the coffin for Longowal and the most controversial. The Sikhs could have accepted a little compromise possibly, but acceding to the loss of river waters was simply surrendering the crux of the demands. One has to note that this demand of river water cross cuts all divisions of Punjabis and it would not have been just the Sikhs who would have been dismayed at the approval of this clause but all Punjabis as it was accepting further discrimination against Punjab and depriving it, of it's only natural resource. If the demand had been acceded with some monetary benefit to Punjabis this may have eased the loss, but this spelt downright incompetence and surrender by Longowal. The building of the SYL canal would be central to the Punjab problems for years to come and to date the central government has not been able to implement its plans of completing the canal. Whenever the SYL canal work begins, the labour gets assassinated by Punjabi's who are against its implementation.

Sant Longowal fell to the bullets of disgruntled Sikhs, who could not believe that he had compromised on everything that they had been fighting for. In the atmosphere of revenge and vengeance, he paid the ultimately price for being one who failed the Sikhs by compromising. Even though, paradoxically, he was the one to initiate the Dharam Yudh Morcha and in Sant Bhindranvale's own words he was the dictator of the Morcha. He fell from stardom to being a failed Sikh leader, initially there were those who protested his assassination but the majority have come around to agree that the assassination was called for. In the politically charged atmosphere that existed he should have not agreed to such terms.

Panthic Committees & Declaration of Khalistan

1st Panthic Committee

A Sarbat Khalsa (gathering of the Sikh Nation) was called on January 26, 1986 in which a Panthic Committee was announced. This Panthic Committee was declared as the supreme authority for Sikhs on all matters of polity, the five members announced were Baba Gurbachan Singh Manochahal, Wassan Singh Zaffarwal, Bhai Dhanna Singh, Bhai Aroor Singh and Bhai Gurdev Singh (to see photos of the Sarbat Khalsa & Panthic Committee please see page 145). Bhai Jasbir Singh Rode was announced as the Akaal Takhat Jathedar (political leader of Sikhs) but he was in prison and due to this Bhai Gurdev Singh Kaunke was appointed acting Jathedar of Sri Akaal Takhat Sahib. The Sarkar Takhat (government funded replacement of the destroyed Sri Akaal Takhat Sahib) that was built by the Indian Government was also ordered to be demolished. The Kar Seva of the new Akaal Takhat building began that day. On this historic day it was declared that the Shiromani Gurdwara Parbandhak Committee will be disbanded and instead the Panthic Committee will lead the administration of Gurdwaras.

Many thousands of Sikhs attended this Sarbat Khalsa, and it was heavily controlled by the Damdami Taksal and the appointments made were all in line with their preference. Certain groups were not taken into confidence and many power struggles would follow, with numerous Panthic Committees being declared. But to its credit this Sarbat Khalsa and declaration of a Panthic Committee had shown a strategic vision, to move forward the freedom struggle in an organised manner and strengthened the armed struggle.

On April 29, 1986 the Panthic Committee called a press conference at Sri Harmander Sahib and made the declaration of an independent Sikh nation, Khalistan. All members of the Panthic Committee escaped from the Complex after making the declaration, but Bhai Gurdev Singh Kaunke the Akaal Takhat Jathedar did not leave, as he felt he needed to be in the vicinity of the Akaal Takhat as the Jathedar. Subsequently Bhai Gurdev Singh Kaunke was the only Singh of significance that the authorities could lay their hands on after the declaration of Khalistan, thus he was arrested in what many refer to as a mini Operation Blue Star or the first Operation Black Thunder. The police and army surrounded the complex and arrested Bhai Gurdev Singh Kaunke and he had to undergo inhumane torture.

Whilst Bhai Gurdev Singh Kaunke was imprisoned Professor Darshan Singh was appointed Acting Akaal Takhat Jathedar. He was forced to leave the Akaal Takhat by hardliners who thought he was taking a soft stand and subsequently Baba Gurbachan Singh Manochahal was appointed Acting Akaal Takhat Jathedar. Afterwards it was always hard to keep up with who was the real Akaal Takhat Jathedar, as Bhai Gurdev Singh Kaunke remained to be the Acting Akaal Takhat Jathedar as did Baba Manochahal and then Bhai Jasbir Singh Rode when out of jail was known as the Akaal Takhat Jathedar. So it was very confusing, but this was partly to do with the lack of unity.

On the 9th March 1988 Bhai Jasbir Singh Rode was released from jail and all Jathebandhis presented him with Siropas (robes of honour) and unanimously agreed that he was the real Jathedar. The government approached Jasbir Singh and tried to make some ground in halting the rampant militant movement, they said that we will hand over the Punjab Assembly for you and the Singhs to administrate, Jasbir Singh said he will discuss it with the militant groups. Some militants agreed to this compromise which would lead to a political gain but not an all out rule of Khalistan as it would still be under the legislative framework of India, Dr Sohan Singh flatly refused to negotiate a truce on such terms. Thus this attempt faltered and after this, many started questioning the loyalty of Jasbir Singh and it led to accusations and counter-accusations between the different groups, both political and militant ones.

2nd Panthic Committee

Dr Sohan Singh (KCF representative), Satinderpal Singh Gill (KLF), Sukhdev Singh Babbar and Daljit Singh Bittu (AISSF) made up the rival panthic committee that was set up. In 1987 at Anandpur Sahib on Vaisakhi, they called a convention and declared a new Panthic Committee and declared Pooran Azaadi (Complete freedom from India).

Following the above two Panthic Committees many other Panthic Committees arose in different shapes and forms, as there were many power struggles ongoing between the different factions of political and organised guerrilla outfits. The power base of the guerrilla warfare and armed struggle was mostly headed by Sohan Singh's patronage and the groups that were aligned to his patronage were Babbar Khalsa, Khalistan Liberation Force, Khalistan Commando Force (Panjwar), Bhindranvale Tiger Force of Khalistan and AISSF (Bittu). Today, Sohan Singh lives a normal life in Chandigarh and I have no doubt that he caused the most damage to the armed struggle and he walked scot free from the movement, he was not tortured, or imprisoned at length and he simply walked free. More will be said about his disgraceful role later.

Organised Sikh Freedom Fighters

Babbar Khalsa International (BKI)

Bhai Talvinder Singh Babbar was the founding Jathedar of Babbar Khalsa, an outfit that would be feared and respected throughout the globe (to see photos of the Founders of BKI, Bhai Talvinder Singh & Bhai Sukhdev Singh Babbar please see page 145). The legacy of Babbar Khalsa, lives on today, in the form of Babbar Khalsa International.

Bhai Talvinder Singh Babbar was born in V. Panchhat, Phagwara, Kapurthala and in 1970 he migrated to Canada. After becoming an initiated Sikh, he started missionary activities in Canada these included:

1. Stopping the sale of Sri Guru Granth Sahib as an ordinary book;
2. Eliminating anti-Sikh practices in Gurdwaras;
3. He had to struggle hard to stop people entering Divan Halls of Gurdwaras with their heads uncovered.

After the 1978 Vaisakhi massacre of 13 Sikhs by the Nirankaris, he organized the Sikh youth and started punishing those guilty of blasphemy and sacrilege of Sikh shrines. For years the government had no idea of who was behind these well planned and tactical strikes. It was only in November 1981, 3 years after the use of arms, that Talvinder Singh was identified as one of the leaders of the organization. He escaped arrest and in 1982 he returned to Canada via Nepal and Thailand.

He continued his activities from the West and was arrested on 29 June 1983 when entering Germany. He went on hunger strike in Düsseldorf Jail in Germany to win the right of wearing a turban and being given vegetarian meals. In June 1984 he was unconditionally released, but was then arrested again in Canada in November 1985 in connection with the bombing of the Air India Airliner. He was acquitted on 14 April 1987 and had to undergo hunger strikes here as well, to have the right of vegetarian meals.

After some time, he again left Canada to rejoin the Sikh resistance being fought in India and participated in many actions. In October 1992, he was arrested in Jammu and mercilessly tortured and killed in a fake encounter on 15th October 1992 at V. Kang Arian, Jalandhar.

Two factions of Babbar Khalsa developed, one led by Sukhdev Singh and another by Talvinder Singh, although they did reconcile their differences at different points between 1984 – 1992.

Bhai Sukhdev Singh Babbar

Bhai Sukhdev Singh was a great electrician and used his skill to cause havoc among the Indian army. He was the first militant to use explosives against the army and passed his knowledge to other groups to help in the freedom struggle.

An article in 'India Today' reported Sukhdev Singh, as the *"most prominent militant leader since 1978, who had, over the years, acquired an aura of invincibility. With Sukhdev Singh at its helm Babbar Khalsa had acquired a reputation as the most puritanical, austere and ideologically committed militant organisation."* The faction that was led by Bhai Sukhdev Singh took up the name Babbar Khalsa International & Bhai Talvinder Singh's faction stuck to the original name of Babbar Khalsa. Today only BKI is active.

Bhindranvale Tiger Force of Khalistan (BTKF)

In 1987, Baba Gurbachan Singh Manochahal emerged as head of a new organization: The Bhindranvale Tiger Force for Khalistan (BTFK). Some top lieutenants who worked with Manochahal were Bhai Sukhvinder Singh Sangha, Bhai Satnaam Singh Chheena and Bhai Surjeet Singh Behla. Manochahal's brother Bhai Mohinder Singh was also a leading member of BTKF.

Later on Bhai Sukhvinder Singh Sangha made a break off group of BTKF that ran parallel to Baba Manochahal's BTKF (see page 146 for photos of Manochahal & Sangha).

Khalistan Commando Force (KCF)

The KCF was one of the first militant organisations to be formed soon after Operation Blue Star, it became one of the leading militant outfits and remnants of it still live on today. The 1st Jathedar of KCF was Bhai Manbir Singh Chaheroo AKA Hari Singh (see photo on page 146), 2nd Jathedar was Bhai Sukhdev Singh AKA General Labh Singh, 3rd Jathedar is Paramjit Singh Panjwar – who is allegedly, still alive today.

There were many KCF break off groups, the most powerful KCF group although was and has been the one outlined above. The break off groups had the following leaders, Kanwarjit Singh Sultanwind, Sukhdev Singh Jhamka, Wassan Singh Zaffarwal (still alive today, residing in Zaffarwal, Gurdaspur, having officially retired from the movement).

Khalistan Zindabad Force

A relatively new militant organisation that came to be known in the 1990's, led by Bhai Ranjit Singh Neeta, known for bombings and was recently banned as a terrorist organisation across Europe. Bhai Ranjit Singh Neeta is allegedly still alive, his whereabouts are unknown.

Khalistan Liberation Force (KLF)

The founder of KLF is seen to be Bhai Sukhdev Singh Sakira (see photo on page 146), it was from his group of friends that KLF was born. The ideological founders of KLF are understood to be the brothers Bhai Jasbir Singh Rode (ex-Akaal Takhat Jathedar) & Bhai Lakhbir Singh Rode (International Convener of the International Sikh Youth Federation – ISYF). The 1st Jathedar of KLF was Bhai Aroor Singh, he was heavily tortured and was eventually killed by the authorities. The 2nd Jathedar of KLF was Bhai Avtar Singh Brahma, the 3rd Jathedar was Bhai Gurjant Singh Budhsinghvala and the 4th Jathedar was Dr Pritam Singh Sekhon unknown if he is alive or not, but it is alleged by Wassan Singh Zaffarwal that he has been killed in Pakistan in a feud between Sikh militants (Grewal, 2004). The KLF was seen as one of the most disciplined groups and to date, I have not heard a bad word said about the previous leadership of KLF or in print (this is especially so, up to the leadership of Budhsinghvala).

Khalistan National Army – 1988 to 1989 was the life of this group.

Dashmesh Regiment

An underground militant organisation that made strategic hits, but nobody knew very much about the organisation or its leadership. It was only on the assassination of Bhai Harminder Singh Sandhu that it was openly declared that he was actually the leader of the Regiment and had been operating in two capacities, one as the leader of a militant organisation and the other as a political activist as the General Secretary of the AISSF.

All India Sikh Students Federation (AISSF)

AISSF was the leading student body for Sikhs throughout India until it got factionalised, but from 1982 – 1992 it was very powerful, giving young Sikhs a point of mobilisation for political activism. A lot of the organised freedom fighters outfits, drew their recruits from AISSF. Bhai Amrik Singh a close confidant of Sant Bhindranvale was the leader of AISSF up to 1984 when he was martyred in Operation Blue Star. After Operation Blue Star all the leading lights of the AISSF were arrested and imprisoned for a few years, this group included;

- Bhai Harminder Singh Sandhu (martyred);

- Bhai Manjit Singh, the brother of Bhai Amrik Singh, today he is a Vice President of the Shiromani Akali Dal – Badal;

- Bhai Rajinder Singh Mehta, today an SGPC member, also aligned to Parkash Singh Badal.

The AISSF had a leading role in mediating in disputes between common people and were trusted by the people of Punjab to resolve their issues in a just manner, more so than the state/government administration.

After 1984, the AISSF became factionalised and thus lost it's influence. There was much controversy about the sincerity of Bhai Harminder Singh Sandhu who was assassinated by fellow Sikhs. Sandhu was a leading figure in the AISSF until his death, but those that live on, such as Bhai Manjit Singh and Bhai Rajinder Singh Mehta also have questionable credentials as they are aligned to Parkash Singh Badal. Today there are about 5 different groups of AISSF that continue to operate, none being of much influence or real political influence.

Dal Khalsa

The Dal Khalsa was and is mostly a political group, but it supports the armed struggle. Bhai Gajinder Singh, it's leader for most of the last two decades (until recently when he stepped down), hijacked an Indian Airlines Jet to ensure the freeing of Sant Bhindranvale when he was arrested. For the hijacking, Bhai Gajinder Singh spent a long time imprisoned in Pakistan, he is allegedly alive but his whereabouts are unknown. It is one of the few groups still active in India in an organised and co-ordinated way.

International Sikh Youth Federation (ISYF)

The ISYF was founded by Bhai Jasbir Singh Rode in Walsall, England in 1985; it was a political organisation aiming to get Sikhs' justice through political activism and dialogue. It was the leading organisation outside of India fighting for Sikh rights and was truly international in its nature having branches in up to 30 countries, this was at its peak. The only other organisation that had similar influence outside of India was Babbar Khalsa. The ISYF was factionalised as well and differing groups aligned themselves to different organisations in India, the most notable factions were:

- o Bhai Jasbir Singh Rode faction – aligned to Bhai Jasbir Singh Rode and his brother Bhai Lakhbir Singh Rode (allegedly still alive, his whereabouts are unknown, he was the International Convenor). Links with AISSF (Sandhu Faction), KCF Zaffarwal and KLF.
- o Damdami Taksal Faction – Aligned to KCF Panjwar group, having considerable links with BTKF and Dr Sohan Singh.
- o Satinderpal Singh Gill Faction – This faction operated mostly in Canada and had considerable ties with KLF.
- o Bhai Daljit Singh Bittu Faction – Aligned to Bittu and his faction of AISSF.

The ISYF and Babbar Khalsa were proscribed as terrorist organisations in the UK in 2001 and were subsequently banned in other countries. Thus many of the foreign branches of these two organisations disbanded, the only country of note that they have not been banned in and still operate in, is Germany. In 2015 the ban on the ISYF in the UK was lifted after a legal challenge to the ban had been made by the Sikh Federation UK.

The background and different organisations that were and still are involved, in the Sikh freedom movement, have been outlined. I will now go onto explain specific cases and the experiences of Sikhs involved in the insurgency and the many that lived through it. I will start with examples of childhood, of how normal children were affected and how children of insurgents were brutally murdered. I will also outline the extraordinary and inspirational childhood experiences of some of the Sikh insurgents.

CHILDHOOD

Childhood is a formative time when one learns, plays and is care free to a certain extent. Childhood makes a person who they are and having a good or bad childhood or childhood experiences, have a lasting effect on the life course that one undertakes.

In the modern insurgency for Khalistan there have been countless children who have been butchered by the Indian authorities or brutally abused, physically and mentally. The movie "Hawaiyen" (2003, directed by Ammtoje Mann) highlighted the atrocities Sikhs underwent in the organised carnage after the assassination of Indira Gandhi. Can you imagine watching your mother being gang-raped continuously for hours? Or watching your family being beaten and burnt alive? This is what children in Delhi, Kanpur and other areas affected by the rioting had to undergo. Obviously, these children would be disturbed by these childhood experiences, many who live on simply want to forget the past pain and want to try living normal lives, whereas others cannot simply forgive or forget. Many of these children did subsequently participate in the Sikh insurgency and were forced by their circumstance, to make a critical choice, either vow for vengeance or forget.

Many of these children were orphaned and made refugees in "Mother India," what sort of "Mother" kills its own offspring? These were innocents who had no crime, but by being Sikhs it was viewed as being legitimate by the rioters and authorities, that such action was fit for purpose, punishment for their crime of being Sikhs. Sikh History and that specifically of Sri Guru Gobind Singh Jee's sons gives Sikhs fortitude and courage to continue and strive on. The youngest sons of the Guru were bricked alive and subsequently decapitated at the tender ages of 5 years and 7 years old by the Mughal authorities, for refusing conversion. The brutalities against children are not new but along a continuum of History repeating itself, Sikhs paying the price for being Sikhs.

We have children who were affected by the events of the riots and we have children of Sikh insurgents, where the parents of these children took the step of entering battle with the state, knowing their families would be persecuted. These Sikh militants offered themselves to the insurgency knowing that their families would suffer persecution as a result of their activities, but they saw this as part of the greater good, that they were trying to achieve. Who were these children who suffered due to the prominence of their parents? Firstly, I will give case studies of some victims of State terrorism and then I will refer to children and childhood experiences of freedom fighters.

Childhood Victims

Bibi Preetam Kaur[42]

The wife of Bhai Rashpal Singh (PA to Sant Bhindranvale), Bibi Preetam Kaur had given birth to her child only days before Operation Blue Star began, on 19th May 1984. She was in the complex when the attack broke out and she witnessed the death of her son in her arms. Her son died of a bullet wound that was sustained in the attack and her husband fell to bullets right in front of her. Her husband fell on top of her after receiving the bullet wound and both her husband and son died instantly from their bullet wounds, the bullet that had killed her son had gone through his body and directly into her chest. She had to live with the pain of the bullet wound for some days before being treated for it.

---

[42] Taken from Sikh Virsa, Canada, reprinted in Fatehnama June 2005

She also narrates how other pilgrims, women and children were molested, raped and killed. Children were thrown down to the earth, to kill them or cause serious injury by the army personnel, and many were burnt alive. Others had their hands tied behind their backs and were shot at, in execution style killings. Many women and children were forced to drink the bloodied water from the Sarovar of the Golden Temple to survive, as it was the only water made available to them. They had to walk over dead and mutilated bodies and if they were lucky they lived to tell the tale. Witnessing such horrific events in childhood could only have devastating effects on the children and survivors. Amritsar residents (mostly Hindus) came out and danced and distributed Indian sweets in happiness of the attack on the Golden Temple. To see people celebrating at the end of the death and destruction caused by Operation Blue Star, could only sow the seeds of discontent and vengeance.

Bibi Resham Kaur

The police tortured Bibi Resham Kaur's baby son (Simranjeet Singh) to death. They put the naked child upon an ice block in front of his mother, in an attempt to draw out information about the whereabouts of her husband. The woman did not know the whereabouts of her husband, thus could not give the information to the police that they required, her son subsequently died from exposure to the ice and she was murdered also. Similar to the martyrdom of Baba Banda Singh Bahadur's son in the early 18th Century son, where his son's beating heart was forcefully put in his mouth and his son was killed in front of him. Bibi Resham Kaur had to witness her son literally freeze to death by exposure to the ice. This example shows that atrocities we would think, do not occur in modern civilisation, do occur. One has to question what advances in civil liberties have been made for those persecuted by the state in modern India. To see a photo of this mother and child please see page 280.

Shaheed Bhai Balvinder Singh Jatana's family

On the 29th August 1991 Sikh freedom fighters made an assassination attempt in Chandigarh on the notorious SSP Sumedh Saini (who was well known for his illegal torture and murders of Sikhs and freedom fighters). Saini survived the assassination attempt but his driver and bodyguard fell to the bullets of the Sikhs. Bhai Balvinder Singh Jatana was an activist of BKI and he was under suspicion for being the main culprit for this assassination attempt. The police and Indian security forces wanted to send out a message to all Sikh freedom fighters, so they tracked down Balvinder Singh's family who lived near Chamkaur Sahib and went there with a pre-meditated plan of murdering the whole family. The police party knocked the door of the house and upon the door opening they opened indiscriminate fire upon all members of the family, the victims were Balvinder's grandmother Davarki Kaur (80 years old), Aunt Jasmer Kaur (40 years old), sister Manpreet Kaur (13 years old) and his nephew Simranjeet Singh (5 years old) who was riddled with Polio. What threat could have a 13 year old girl, a 5 year old boy and an 80 year old woman impose to the state? This is just one case of many, and there will have been many more of mistaken identity, where the gung-ho security forces murdered innocent children and families. To see photos of this family please see page 280.

Countless children went missing, who were either arrested by the police or taken into custody, when their parents were murdered and/or tortured. It has never been known what happened to them, just imagine living a life of hope, in the hope that your children may walk through the front

door.   Many parents/grandparents live in this hope,
whereas many have gone insane looking and waiting.

But it is not all gloom and doom, a heart-rending account
of a Sikh comes to mind, where an orphan went to school
and all the children were asked who their parents were.
This orphan did not have an answer and came back to the
orphanage, understandably upset, one of the carer's said to
the child, you do have parents – Your mother is Mata Sahib
Kaur Jee and your Father is Sri Guru Gobind Singh Jee.
The child was overjoyed and started shouting I have a
mommy and daddy – this personifies the Sikh Spirit and
the unending mercy of the Guru to care for one who has
no-one or is facing hardships. Sikhs take strength from the
teachings of the following Shabad (verse);

*When you are confronted with terrible hardships,
and no one offers you any support, when your friends
turn into enemies, and even your relatives have deserted
you, and when all support has given way, and all hope
has been lost -if you then come to remember the Supreme
Lord God, even the hot wind shall not touch you. Our
Lord and Master is the Power of the powerless. He does
not come or go; He is Eternal and Permanent. Through
the Word of the Guru's Shabad, He is known as True.
Pause. If you are weakened by the pains of hunger and
poverty, with no money in your pockets, and no one will
give you any comfort, and no one will satisfy your hopes
and desires, and none of your works is accomplished -if
you then come to remember the Supreme Lord God, you
shall obtain the eternal kingdom.* (Sri Raag, Sri Guru
Arjan Dev Jee, Sri Guru Granth Sahib Jee, Ang/Page 70)

The faith of Sikhs in such Shabads, as above, gives them
fortitude to continue and fight on regardless of the

inhumane circumstances they may have endured. This is the nature of the undying Sikh Spirit.

There are also great Sikh mothers who pray that their children die fighting for their faith, and upholding the freedoms of others. I had the good fortune to meet such a mother and her son, who must have been about 6 years old at the time. She said that when the Sikh insurgency was at its peak she was pregnant and she prayed that she be blessed with the birth of a son, who could join the ranks of the fellow Sikh freedom fighters. This is the in-built Sikh Spirit of sacrifice, to be offering one's child to the service of the Guru and for the protection of others' freedoms, even before giving birth. She had also had the good grace of congregating with gifted souls like Bhai Fauja Singh, martyred in the 1978 Bloody Vaisakhi. She spoke in awe of how she would watch Bhai Fauja Singh and his associates, display their martial skills in organised displays of the Sikh Martial Art – Gatka, this had no doubt had a lasting effect upon her life.

The families of Sikh Freedom Fighters and their children also underwent unique circumstances of living double lives and separate lives, for long periods of time. The children of high ranking Sikh Freedom Fighters had to hide their real identities and could not reveal the identity of their fathers in most cases. These children and their familes had to continually move from pillar to post, to ensure their safety and that their identity was not discovered. There are stories of children of Sikh insurgents being born in other states/countries where the militant leader would send a close associate, to visit his wife and new-born child so a description of what the baby looks like could be conveyed. They would not even leave the battlefield for such an occasion but always put the greater good first. Similarly the 9th Guru, Sri Guru Teg Bahadur Jee met his son Sri

Gobind Rai (later known as Sri Guru Gobind Singh Jee) at the age of 6 years old as He had been propagating the message of God on missionary tours and did not return to His family for a long period of time.

Now, returning to the children of Sikh insurgents. These children knew nothing but the movement, and it is what makes up their childhood experiences. Credit is due to the mothers of such children and the wives of insurgents, who had to live lives of uncertainty and risk, whilst bringing up their children the best they could.

An interview with a person from one of the orphanages that looks after children of martyred freedom fighters reveals the lasting emotional/mental effects upon the children:

Q: Any emotional disturbances among the children?
A: Plenty. Call any child and discuss it, and we will have a tough time consoling them. These kids have seen their father's dragged away by their hair. They often wake in the middle of the night screaming, 'they have killed my father.' They are mere children who have seen raw violence.

There are also orphans who are not told about the deaths of their parents, or more specifically, who their parents were. This is done by many trusts who take in victims/orphans of the insurgency; this is done purposely by the administrators of these initiatives, to try ensuring that the children have a stable childhood and to try avoiding a feeling of revenge towards the culprits

Childhood Martyrs & Childhood Experiences (of freedom fighters)

Satnaam Kaur & Vaaheguroo Kaur

Satnaam Kaur (8 years old) and Vaaheguroo Kaur (6 years old) were both martyred in Operation Blue Star. These two sisters were martyred in very different circumstances to those mentioned previously, they were not martyred as innocent by-standers. On the contrary they contributed all they could in defending the Golden Temple Complex. There are differing accounts of their contribution but one thing is for sure that they were martyred defending the Golden Temple. Their parents Bhai Mohr Singh and Bibi Pritam Kaur also fought valiantly in defending the complex and were martyred. Some argue that the sisters had bombs strapped upon them and these were then detonated when they could make collateral damage upon the opposing forces, others argue they fell to bullets whilst helping the Sikhs defending the complex. To see photos of this extraordinary family see page 281. One of their sister's lives on today and is proud of the history of her family and although she has very little family, she keeps faith in her spiritual parents Sri Guru Gobind Singh and Mata Sahib Kaur.

Shaheed Bhai Ravinder Singh Babbar

Bhai Ravinder Singh was born in village Shatrana, Amritsar. Bhai Ravinder Singh was not an ordinary child. From an early age, his dedication and love for Gursikhi were unparalleled and his family recalls his bravery and courage. Once when he was just four or five years old, Ravinder fell off a wall and broke his arm in two places. His father, Giani Harbhajan Singh spoke to his son as he was being taken to receive medical treatment, "Puraatan (Sikhs of old) Singhs would be cut apart, piece by piece but they would not even make a sound. You too should be brave like them." The two reached the home of the person who set broken bones and showed him the arm. He said that because the bone was broken in two places, he would need to twist the bone back into place. Giani Jee had bought some grapes for little Ravinder Singh and told him that while his arm was being set, he could eat them. As the man twisted the boy's arm, Ravinder calmly ate the grapes and did not make a sound. Only those who are gifted by God can undergo such pain with ease, and that is how they go on to become role models for generations to come. They have developed their Sikh Spirit and tendency to undergo pain through meditations in past lives, and they continue to have rising spirits so their spirituality is forever growing. To see a photo of Bhai Ravinder Singh Babbar please see page 282.

Shaheed Bhai Harvinder Singh 'Ladoo' AKA Bhai Suba Singh

Born in 1970 and the brother of Bhai Sukhvinder Singh Baba (KLF). From birth Harvinder was very intelligent and had a calm persona. From childhood he developed the habit of reciting prayers and going to the Gurdwara. He was only 2 years old when he got a small stool and placed a sheet over it, put a small cushion onto the stool and placed a Hazooria around his neck, placed a small keski on his head and would meditate on Satnaam/Vaaheguroo all day long; this was one of his childhood games. From childhood he had a saintly personality and would remain engrossed in prayers all day long. He did a lot of Seva in Kar Seva (construction and restoration of Gurdwaras) when he was older and was respected by various Kar Seva Saints.

When he was 18/19 years old he attained Shaheedi. The notorious Gobind Ram tortured him to death in 1989, but he did not relent under torture and did not reveal the whereabouts of any Singhs he knew. About 50-60 Akhand Paths were performed by different Kar Seva Saints that he did Seva with, he was respected by many due to his saintly qualities. To see a photo of Ladoo please see page 282.

Generation X

Generation X – is a generation of Sikh Youth who have simply "disappeared". We can attempt to give reasons for their disappearances but they are no longer here to testify or verify their own accounts of what occurred. Between 1981 and 1993, Sikhs (mostly males) between the ages of 14-35 years old were systematically targeted by the authorities, being a Sikh and being of this age was co-terminus with being a terrorist. Wearing of the orange/saffron turban was seen especially as a colour of revolt by the authorities and youth wearing this colour would be targeted more so, than others. Sikh Youth underwent indiscriminate harassment, they would be regularly arrested, tortured and/or humiliated by the Indian Police (especially so in Punjab and adjoining areas). This treatment led to the youth responding in most cases to one of the following routes of action:

1) Seeking vengeance/revenge – taking up arms and joining the Sikh insurgency;
2) Political action – rebellion and protest in peaceful ways, this was usually through the All India Sikh Students Federation;
3) Becoming an informer for the authorities or joining them, becoming employed in their staff, ensuring their own safety from torture & harassment from the state;
4) Fleeing persecution, migrating to other Indian states or to a foreign country. This option would involve economic burden in the immediate future, with the hope of alleviating it, in the long term. As loans to

fund the migration would be undertaken and/or the sale of land/property.

The majority of the youth undertook one of the first two options presented and joined the array of militant outfits or the competing factions of the All Sikh Students Federation. It has to be acknowledged that some of these would then go onto the third option presented and become informants or join the Black Cats of the Police to commit extra-judicial killings. The ones who undertook this route, was mostly due to them being weak in character and not being able to take torture or the constant threat of death. The Black Cats were paid assassins who played duplicit roles of joining or being members of Sikh freedom fighters and working for the authorities, it has to be acknowledged that they were very successful and they were a key factor in ending the Sikh armed resistance.

Conversely the insurgency for many young Sikhs led to a realisation of faith and identity, which was forced upon them, due to the circumstances they lived in and not necessarily due to a longing for faith. Thus this choice was made as a way of surviving in the terrain of Punjab, thus a lot of these Sikhs knew little about their faith and practices, due to their relative inexperience of practice. One Sikh that I met used to be a member of Khalistan Commando Force when it was under the leadership General Labh Singh, he wanted to withdraw from guerrilla warfare and return to his family life to raise his two children. He was given an ultimatum of staying, or leaving the 30-40 people he would recite Sri Jaap Sahib (the Sikh 2nd daily prayer) to on a daily basis, as he was the only one who knew it off by heart. In the end he decided to stay on and was later caught and severely tortured.

On a more positive note though, there were young Sikhs who had firm faith and had, had the practices and discipline of faith methodically nurtured, two clear groups who can be cited are students of Damdami Taksal and those that attended the Khalsa training camps organised at the Khalsa Farm by Bhai Fauja Singh (who mostly became the founding members of Babbar Khalsa). These young Sikhs became the leading forces of the insurgents and political organisers. The leading figures of All India Sikh Students Federation were also well-versed in Sikh theology and history, and the AISSF became a force to be reckoned with under the Presidency of Bhai Amrik Singh, but all of its entire executive committee of about 11 members were arrested and imprisoned for about 5 years directly after Operation Blue Star. Thus the AISSF was leaderless for 5 years, crippling its influence.

Most of this Generation X were either martyred whilst being involved in the freedom struggle, or killed as innocents caught in warfare, or they fled Punjab (as did most insurgents after 1992). Those that survived and lived palatial lives are those that became an arm of the state and carved out their future serfdom as state sponsored stooges.

Even today the loss of Generation X can be clearly seen, all you have to do is go to border districts of Punjab such as Gurdaspur and Ferozepur and see how these districts suffered economically in comparison to other districts of Punjab. In these areas you can see a gap in the population, the majority of the population is either young or old, there are very few middle-aged men around (who made up Generation X). Many families have had difficulty marrying their daughters over the last 10-12 years due to a lack of young men.

These youth who underwent hardships, drew strength from Gurbani such as the uttering of Bhagat Fareed Jee:

I am not afraid of losing my youth,
As long as I do not lose the Love of my Husband Lord.
Fareed, so many youths, without His Love,
Have dried up and withered away.
(Ang/Page 1379, Sri Guru Granth Sahib Jee)

Inspiration would have been drawn from such uttering's and the Sikh Youth had to develop a diehard spirit, that they would survive and persevere, no matter what the state machinery threw at them. The weak faltered and went against the very tenets of Sikh philosophy and cowardly died a death of conscience, a famous saying of Sant Bhindranvale comes to mind in relation to such youth:

Death I do not fear,
but a death of conscience is a sure death.

These youths who sold out and aided and abetted the murder, torture and rape of fellow Sikhs will have to carry the burden of their actions to their graves as will those officers in the Indian authorities who committed such heinous crimes.

I will now cite three case studies which will shed further light on Generation X:

Mata Gurjit Kaur Sodhiwal – A mother's suffering
(Source: an interview with the BBC)

Gurjit Kaur makes ends meet by doing odd jobs at Amritsar's Golden Temple. She lost her husband and daughter during operation Blue Star. They had been visiting the shrine, when they were caught in the army assault and were subsequently martyred, like thousands of other pilgrims. Later her oldest son was killed by the police and her two other sons took to arms and were subsequently killed in encounters with the security forces in 1991. Her youngest son was only 14 (Baljinder Singh) when he disappeared after the police took him away.

"Twenty years have gone by but I still cry each day. I cannot forget how my entire family was wiped out. Those who have seen the blood of loved ones spilt will never forget and I will carry my memories with me to my funeral pyre. Today I am all alone. My only surviving child lives with her husband outside Punjab. She does not visit me because the police harass her each time she came here in the past. My only remaining wish is to identify the men who killed Baljinder Singh. He was only an innocent little child. I want to know what kind of men could bring themselves to murdering a child. I want to know if they made my sweetest child suffer. "

"My heart will not stop aching.
Nothing else matters to me now."

Gurjit Kaur has no family to support her and no land or other means of income and was paid a meagre 500 RS (monthly) by the SGPC for her labour; bed and board was included as payment. Today Gurjit Kaur has been relieved of her duties by the SGPC (management committee of Gurdwaras in Punjab) in Amritsar, but she continues to live in SGPC provided accommodation. She breaks down in tears when asked about her anguish and life experiences. She spends her days praying at all times to reduce the burden of her memories.

Bibi Amandeep Kaur
(Source; "Fighting for Faith & Nation – Dialogue with Sikh Militants" Cynthia Mahmood)

Prior to 1988 Bibi Amandeep Kaur (pseudo name used to protect her anonymity) had no interest in politics, but when she saw victims of state brutality, this all changed. One girl called Harjinder Kaur Khalsa had come from Australia to get married in Punjab and on the way back she was arrested at the Delhi airport and martyred. Then there was the captain of the hockey team at college, Gurmukh Singh, who was so badly tortured by the police that he was admitted to hospital and after 5 days of profuse bleeding he succumbed to his injuries.

After our colleague Gurmukh Singh died, some of us went to his house to express our sympathy to his family. We found out that he was the only son, he had four sisters and he was the eldest:

"When I saw those little girls crying. I couldn't understand, why can't the police be held answerable for these atrocities? My mind was in a state of excitement. Why shouldn't it be me, who should ask these police why this innocent boy was killed?"

But Amandeep Kaur knew that asking these questions would lead to one of two consequences:

(i)   That she would be killed in a police encounter;

(ii)   Police will frame her by putting ammunition upon her and she will end up languishing in jail for years on end.

So she decided to not do anything. It was really paining her heart, to see deserving Sikh boys and girls being discriminated against. By divine grace she was asked by a distant relative to ferry some ammunition from one place to another. She accepted to do this as she wanted to know why her colleague, Gurmukh Singh was martyred. She wanted to hold the police to account for their crimes and felt this was the only route for redress; she could not stand the torture and killing of innocent boys.

The climate of terror was so extreme that even the parents of boys/girls killed in police brutality, refused to identify or claim the bodies. If they did claim the bodies the police would compel them to issue press statements that their sons/daughters were terrorists. Even after complying with the police they would still be continually tortured and humiliated by the police, being used as scapegoats for any crimes in the area. For these reasons Amandeep Kaur decided to not get her family involved in the resistance movement and kept her actions secret from them, she did not want to disturb the "peaceful life of my little brothers and parents."

Knowing all this she continued to be involved and committed, and went on to assassinate informants. In her dreams she started getting visions of unidentified bodies at a crossroad and she saw her own body amongst them. She was haunted by these visions and knew it was a known fact of history that brutal governments try to destroy the youth of a nation, so no-one can challenge them.

Eventually she slipped out of the country to the Middle East, her commitment to her family restricting what she could do. Her family never knew what she was involved in and she did not want to bring harm or shame onto them.

"I know that whenever my Sikh Nation will really need my help, however, I am capable of breaking all these shackles that bind me. If need be I will break them. I will be back there in a second with a gun in my hand, and no-one will stop me."

Bibi Preetam Kaur Jee
(Wife of Bhai Rashpal Singh, PA of Sant Bhindranvale)[43]

Bibi Preetam Kaur is a prime example of a survivor of Generation X, but her case shows what the devastating effects of being someone of prominence can be. Even though many would consider that her life has been of much suffering and turmoil, she still holds her head high, is steadfast in her beliefs and has still not faltered in her faith.

Her journey began when she got married to Bhai Rashpal Singh on 20th February 1983, who was the PA of Sant Bhindranvale. From the time she got married she lived in the Golden Temple Complex, initially being housed at Nanak Niwas and later moving near to the Akaal Takhat Sahib (within the complex). Close proximity to Sant Bhindranvale was obviously maintained.

Operation Blue Star broke out and Bhai Rashpal Singh and her young son of a few weeks were both martyred. She was captured in the Golden Temple complex and came under suspicion from the army officers who later learnt of her real identity. From this point on, she was singled out for treacherous treatment by the Indian authorities. The authorities also learnt that General Subegh Singh had referred to her as his own daughter, as he had no daughters himself, which added further fuel to the fire.

---

[43] Taken from Sikh Virsa, Canada, reprinted in Fatehnama June 2005

She was jailed, tortured and abused by the authorities, and in her own words *'I do not have the words to explain what they did to me.'* She was first imprisoned in Ludhiana Jail and then moved to Nabha Jail and subsequently sent to Jodhpur Jail. At Jodhpur she was imprisoned alongside women who were mentally unstable or notorious dacoits, to ensure that she could have the worst possible prison term. She was the only Sikh woman in Jodhpur Jail. She was released on 4th June 1988. She lived at her native village of Bariar, Gurdaspur between 1988 and 1992.

One would assume that she had been harassed enough, but things took a turn for the worst again in 1992. On the 9th December 1992 her three brothers were arrested and 'disappeared.' Her spirit would not allow her to take this lying down so she filed a writ to the Supreme Court in 1993 in search of justice for the deaths/disappearances of her brothers. By doing this she invited police harassment upon herself and was implicated in a false case and was harassed by the police until 1995. It was only from 1995, that she could peacefully settle down again.

She spent 11 years of her life either being persecuted or harassed by the police. Her husband, son, 3 brothers have fell to the bullets of the Indian authorities, but there are many thousands more Preetam Kaurs out there. There are many "Preetam Kaurs" who cannot tell their story either due to fear of continued reprisals or simply because they have *'disappeared'* themselves.

Sikh Women

The role of Sikh women in the insurgency was central to its success. Mothers, wives and daughters were pivotal to the movement's success and were probably abused more so, as they lived at home and were easily accessible to the security forces. They had to endure separation from their husbands and sons, and were left to survive economically in the best way they could. They have had to live with the nightmares of the horrors that they had to endure. Bhai Balpreet Singh http://shaheedkhalsa.com/atrocitieswomen.html) has collated some accounts of certain events, that highlight the atrocities committed against women, firstly the International Women's Day – of 8th March 1991 is mentioned in which Brig. RP Sinha addressing assembled Sikh villagers said:

"If any action occurs in this village, every single male is going to be taken out and shot. Then we're going to take all the women to our camp and there we're going to create a new breed for Punjab."

This was the way International Women's Day was celebrated in Punjab by these heinous individuals. The untold story of the Sikh Resistance Movement is the story of Sikh women. It is a feature of Punjabi culture that atrocities on women are rarely reported and remain hidden. Families feel ashamed to speak of the treatment women received at the hands of Indian Security Forces, but this story must be told.

Many Sikh women participated in the Sikh resistance movement as fighters. Like their sisters from past ages, Sikh women joined their brothers in the fight for freedom. Many brave Singhnees fought side by side with their Singhs and attained Shaheedi. Sikh women often worked as messengers for Sikh Resistance groups, as well as preparing hideouts and serving tired Sikh fighters.

But unfortunately, many Sikh women were also the target of the blood thirsty Indian Security forces. Sikh women were ruthlessly tortured, not only physically but also mentally. They were used as tools to force the surrender of Sikh fighters who were their relatives and also as a means of humiliating families. When Sikh women were arrested with their husbands, the husbands were often forced to watch the rape of their wives. Rape was used as an interrogation tool.

The Indian Forces also began a program of "shudhee karan", which was a code name for the rape of Sikh women. They joked that the offspring of their rapes would change the genetic makeup of the Sikh community and they would kill the Resistance in this way. Many rape victims took their own lives, unable to live with the ongoing humiliation at the hands of the Indian police.

The Story of Bibi Gurmit Kaur

Bibi Gurmit Kaur was a student of the 10th grade at village Lehrkaa near Kathoo Nangal. Bibi Gurmit Kaur and her older sister Bibi Paramjit Kaur had gone to visit their father Swarn Singh and brother Satnaam Singh who were in prison, for giving shelter to Sikh Resistance fighters. They had returned home on the 21st April, 1989 when the Indian police raided their home and arrested Bibi Paramjit Kaur. The police told villagers that the Deputy Commissioner wanted to record her statement. Paramjit was kept in custody one night and then returned home. Next Gurmit Kaur was arrested and kept for two nights. She too was released but threatened with dire circumstances if she told what had happened to her. Gurmit did not remain silent and recounted what had happened to her.

When Gurmit was brought to the police station, she was stripped naked and tortured in the veranda of the police station, in plain view of all the police officers. That night, the police blindfolded her and locked her in a room. In that room, drunken Indian Police officers took turns raping her. Gurmit Kaur fell unconscious and when she woke up the next morning, she found herself covered in blood and stark naked. The next day, Gurmit Kaur was tortured again. The perverse and twisted police officers went so far as to put salt and chilli peppers into Gurmit Kaur's private parts.

On April 24th 1989, when Gurmit Kaur was released, she could not walk. She was taken to hospital for treatment by the villagers. This is just one example of the despicable nature of the Punjab Police.

Another appalling case is that of Bibi Manjit Kaur. Bhai Nirvair Singh was the Granthi of Gurdwara Shaheedaa(n), Amritsar. Bhai Nirvair Singh's younger brother, Bhai Kulwant Singh was a Sikh Resistance Fighter and the police constantly raided their home in search of him. Finally, unable to locate Kulwant Singh, SSP Azhar Alam and his "Black Cats" shot Bhai Nirvair Singh to death. Bhai Nirvair Singh's wife, Bibi Manjit Kaur, was with him at the time and ran to save herself. The police caught Bibi Manjit Kaur and badly beat her with their rifle butts. They let her live, but her ordeal was far from over.

On May 5th 1988, the police again raided the house. Bhai Nirvair Singh's youngest brother, Bhai Dilbagh Singh, a Granthi at Gurdwara Baba Bakala, was home but hid himself, fearing for his life. The police spotted him and without any warning, shot him dead. Bibi Manjit Kaur was still in the house when the police entered and they immediately began to beat her. They grabbed her by her hair and dragged her to the fields where the Indian Police tortured her for an hour and a half. When Bibi Manjit Kaur was almost senseless, they threw her on top of Bhai Dilbagh Singh's dead body and laughed, *"Now get your*

Khalistan...". Bibi Manjit Kaur's feet were so swollen from the torture that she could not walk for days. Her scalp also oozed blood from the repeated blows. Villagers who witnessed this scene were also beaten and told to keep their mouths shut. Harassment of their family and relatives continued. [44]

Another case was that of Bibi Harpreet Kaur Rano who was mercilessly killed by the Police. On the 25th June 1992, 15 year old Harpreet Kaur Rano was stopped while riding her bicycle in Amritsar's butter market (Ghio Mandhi). Harpreet had an avid interest in the Sikh struggle and would keep printed pictures of Shaheed Singhs and their notices of Bhogs (funerals) from newspapers. The police decided to search her purse and they found an excuse to arrest her, the pictures of Singhs.

She was taken directly to the famous torture centre at BR Model School in Amritsar. She was put in the custody of Thanedar Darshan Lal who punished her for her so called *"crime"* of keeping pictures of Sikh Insurgents who had fell to enemy bullets. God only knows what suffering and brutality she underwent.

Despite her family's best efforts to get her released, the newspapers reported that Harpreet Kaur Rano along with 3 other *"terrorists"* had been killed on the 27th June 1992, near Sultanwind, her body was not given to her family. The family went to the cremation grounds at Durgiana Mandir and in one pile of ashes Harpreet's sister recognised a Kara. The two sisters used to wear identical Karas and the ashes were recognised as Harpreet's, no justice was expected for this cold blooded murder. One

---

[44] Based on a post by Bhai Balpreet Singh http://shaheed-khalsa.com/atrocitieswomen.html

cannot begin to imagine identifying a loved one through random ashes. Finding Harpreet's Kara must have confirmed the worse for the family, but they weren't even given the opportunity to perform her last rites or see her face prior to confirmation, which is a common practice for all Sikh funerals. To see a photo of Harpreet Kaur Rano please see page 282.

The case studies cited are merely examples of a few women who underwent torture, rape, harassment and in some cases died at the hands of the authorities. The silent majority whose cases are unknown of, still live on and have to live with their nightmares of what they have undergone, at the hands of the Indian authorities.

7. Fake Encounters

The Punjab Police very rarely entered true encounters with Sikh insurgents, but is famous for its cowardice in committing fake encounters. Fake encounters are 'staged deaths' of people (and Indian Punjab in this case), the police would kill the person(s) in cold blood and then make up a falsified story of the dead person shooting at the police/attacking them, thus the police had to act in self-defence. Fake encounters were staged commonly against innocent people who would later be termed *'terrorists'* even though they had nothing to do with the insurgents, their only crime would be that they had been in the vicinity of where insurgents had stayed or passed by. Please see the Sikhtoons on pages 282-283 which aptly summarise fake encounters and the role of the Punjab Police.

A typical case would be X militant assassinated Y in Ropar. X was pursued by the police and he opened fire on the police, the police returned fire, X escaped, but A & B his two associates were killed in the exchange of fire. A & B's bodies would be quickly disposed of by the police and a vast array of arms would be shown to the media that supposedly belonged to A & B. In reality A & B would be two innocent people who had been nearby, they had simply been assassinated by the police to show that they were making progress in their pursuit of the insurgents. In many cases those that would be killed would be poor labourers, whose families could not raise objections easily, due to their economic situation.

A pathetic case of a fake encounter is that of Beer Singh (30) who according to his father Virsa Singh was killed when he had gone to see a film in Amritsar. He was shot dead on the Sultanwind Road and his body was cremated as unidentified. Many other such cases of innocent people being killed and cremated as unidentified are recorded in detail in "Reduced to Ashes – the Insurgency and Human Rights in Punjab" authored by Ram Narayan Kumar et al (2003), readers can read of more despicable cases in this book.

In other cases where Sikh insurgents were killed by the police and/or Indian authorities, the police would again make up a tale of an encounter between the insurgent and the police, the police being victorious and taking the scalp of the insurgent. In many cases the reality would actually be that through the work of an informant or good intelligence work the insurgent would be either outnumbered or caught with no or little arms and would be killed in cold blood extra-judicially, thus not following legalities of a trial. The police would then make up a story of how they valiantly defeated the militant and brought his demise. Two examples from the findings of the Indian Human Rights Organisation (IHRO) of the martyrdoms of Sukhdev Singh Babbar (Chief BKI) and Gurjant Singh Budhsinghvala (Chief KLF) will be cited.

An IHRO Report - THE KILLING OF GURJANT SINGH BUDHSINGHVALA BY POLICE:

Police could have taken him in custody, but killed him in cold blood for showing bravery. The residents of the locality approached the IHRO, with a different tale, regarding the killing of an unarmed Bhai Gurjant Singh. A four-member investigation team, comprising of the IHRO General Secretary Mohinder Singh Grewal and Secretaries Gurbhajan Singh Gill, Bhupinder Singh Somal and Balbir Singh Sooch, after making on the spot inspection and interviewing more than a dozen persons, reached the following conclusions:

Gurjant Singh was staying with one Kaur Singh, an ex-Havaldar, at his resident in the locality. Kaur Singh testified his good morals and civilised behaviour. Mrs Kaur Singh used to identify him as her cousin. Thus, an uncle-niece relationship had developed between Budhsinghvala and Kaur Singh's three daughters- Kamaljit Kaur, Rajinder Kaur and Harinder Kaur. He had a reciprocal friendship with the local residents with whom he used to play games, when free. Kaur Singh, it is learnt, was accustomed to visit the local Gurdwara in the evening and used to return home before 9pm positively. On the fateful night, he dilly-dallied to leave the place even up to 10pm, when his acquaintances left him at the Gurdwara wherefrom he was escorted by two plain clothed policemen to the police headquarters, after 11pm. At his place, however, another drama was being enacted. At about 10pm, Bhai Budhsinghvala was dressing up his bed in the veranda of the house.

His weapons were still lying inside the room when the house was stealthily encircled by the police. He rushed towards the room but finding its door bolted from inside, ascended the stairs and from the roof jumped into the vacant plot behind. Seeing police officers surrounding the area, he managed to reach the adjoining plot, occupied by some migrant labourers from Uttar Pradesh. A police party happened to pass by that plot. Budhsinghvala being unarmed remained out of their way. When that party returned to the same side, he presumed that the other side was clear of the police. He left his position and came on to the road. At this juncture, he was detected and the police started firing on him from all sides.

As a result of this firing Budhsinghvala was shot, he fell down and succumbed to bullet injuries, just outside the vacant corner plot. The police immediately picked-up two migrants from UP, Bishamber and Chalitter, who were eyewitness to the whole drama, as Budhsinghvala had taken shelter in the plot under their occupation. They were kept in illegal custody for two days. Even when the IHRO team contacted them, they were very reluctant to tell the true story. Moreover, some other residents of the locality, who saw the whole act through their windows etc, were hesitant to disclose their identity and preferred anonymity, for fear of police reprisals. On the other hand, the police have provided permanent security at the residence of Kaur Singh, though he himself is still in police protective custody but other members of his family were released a couple of days after the incident.

According to the IHRO team, the police story about the KLF chief, Bhai Gurjant Singh Budhsinghvala, having been killed in an armed encounter with the police, is totally false and fabricated. In fact, no encounter took place, as Budhsinghvala was unarmed. Moreover, the police did not try to capture him alive in spite of the fact that, in the circumstances, there was no possibility of his breaking the strong police cordon empty-handed. The police has alleged that the "encounter" lasted for about one a half hour and 1056 rounds were fired and those too, mainly in a few minutes around 10.15 PM, whereas four shots were heard at 5 AM next morning. It appears that those were fired by the CRPF, so as to join the action, because according to some eye-witnesses CRPF personnel were not seen at night. The police version about two grenades having been hurled upon them by Gurjant Singh does not hold ground, as nobody in the locality heard any explosion, nor did the IHRO team find signs of any explosion in the area.

The weapons allegedly recovered on and near the body of Budhsinghvala were planted by the over-enthusiastic police officers, after he was killed. The residents of the colony were not allowed to venture out of their houses, right from 10pm to 6am the next morning.

The way an unarmed Gurjant Singh was killed by the police and was later shown to have been killed in an armed encounter, is a clear indication that in the process of eliminating the Sikhs who are nonconformists to the state, the Indian Government can throw to the wind, all Indian as-well-as universal laws and norms.

The Police account is obviously at odds with the IHRO's findings and states that in Ludhiana on August 19th 1992, Gurjant Singh Budhsinghvala, chief of the Khalistan Liberation Force, was killed at about 10pm in a "Police encounter" staged in the Model Town Extension, Ludhiana, while he was staying at 95/A, Model Town Extension, with one Kaur Singh, an ex-Havaldar of the Indian Army. The police version of the "encounter" is narrated in the FIR Number 135 dated 30.7.92. U/s 307 IPC, 25 Indian Arms Act, 4/5 Indian Explosives Act and 3/4/5 of Terrorist and Disruptive Activities (Prevention) Act, registered at the Police Station Civil Lines, Ludhiana at the instance of Mr Balwant Singh Gill, Superintendent Police (Detective) Ludhiana. The FIR describes, inter alia, the event as below:

On the basis of information to SSP Sidharath Chattopadhya that the top leadership of the Khalistan Liberation Force was to meet in Block 'A' of the Model Town Extension colony, in order to chalk out a programme to commit some heinous crime in Ludhiana city. I along with (a list of persons) reached the pointed house and warned the accused to surrender. Instead, they replied in heavy firing. Our party, in order to defend ourselves and to capture the accused, resorted to firing while in crawling position. Meanwhile, a suspect ascended the roof through the staircase and jumped over to the rear of the house. Notwithstanding the danger to our lives, I and the SSP, along with our posse went to the roof and jumped over the suspect. In the meantime, Inspector Manmohan Singh of CIA, along with his force, came to the fore, while crawling. And after encircling the suspect, he started firing. Finding himself trapped, the suspect managed to reach the adjoining vacant plot by scaling the boundary wall and started firing on the SSP and myself (BS Gill). He threw two hand grenades upon us, but in spite of the powerful explosions, we survived.

After removing some bricks from the boundary wall, we fired, through the holes. The firing continued for about one and a half hours. When the firing ceased, we searched the area with the help of a search light and located the dead body of the suspect youth in a corner of the enclosure. One AK-47 rifle No: CC-1 x 17024475, with five live cartridges in the magazine and two empties were lying beside him. 45 live rounds of Dragon rifle were found in the bag hung around his chest. A small diary containing currency notes worth Rs. 150/- was also recovered from his pocket. Bhai Gurjant Singh Budhsinghvala, Chief General of Khalistan Liberation Force, was written on the diary. 70 empties of Ak-47 were lying near the corpse. On house search, we recovered two rocket launchers, along with rockets, 5 Kg explosive material and 3 live detonators with wire on the roof, and 35 empties of AK-47 from the courtyard. In all 951 rounds were fired by the police, the break-up being; SSP-60, SP(D)-50, DSP Narinder Pal Singh-150,DSP Nachhattar Singh-135, DSP Gurmail Singh-175, Inspector Manmohan Singh-160, SSP's party-145, SP's party-72 and CRPF-4. As the accused had fired upon the police party with the intention to kill them, he committed offence under section 307- IPC, 25/27 Arms Act, 4/5 Explosives Act and

3/4/5 of TADA (P) Act and this document is sent to the
police station for registration of the case.
Signed/
Balwant Singh Gill SP (D), 30.7.92 at 3 AM

One can draw conclusions of whose version, one wants to
believe. Another investigation of IHRO will be cited, the
next case study is that of Bhai Sukhdev Singh Babbar.

SUKHDEV SINGH 'BABBAR' KILLED IN A FAKE ENCOUNTER

Bhai Sukhdev Singh 'Babbar', the chief of Babbar
Khalsa International was announced by the police to have
been killed in an encounter with the police on the
Sahnewal-Dehlon Road in Ludhiana district at 5am on 9th
August 1992, but contrary to the police claim, all other
reports indicated that Sukhdev Singh was already in police
custody. It was in these circumstances that IHRO
appointed a four-member team comprising of its General
Secretary Mohinder Singh Grewal and Secretaries
Gurbhajan Singh Gill, Bhupinder Singh Somal and
Harchand Singh Gill to investigate the incident.

The Fabricated Police Version
According to FIR Number: 63 dated 9.8.92 u/s 307/34 IPC,
25/27 Indian Arms Act and 3/4/5 TADA (P) Act of Police
Station Sahnewal, "SSP Sidharath Chattopadhya instructed
that various militant organisations, especially the Babbar
Khalsa International are likely to execute a big action in
connection with the Bhog ceremony of the Khalistan
Liberation Force Chief, General Gurjant Singh
Budhsinghvala, so nakabandis (police check points) were
done around Ludhiana. I along with Shiv Kumar-DSP (D),
Narinder Pal Singh-DSP, PP Sabharwal-SP (O), Ganesh-
SI (CRPF) and their parties was present at the Dharaur
Culvert in the revenue estate of village Nandpur when at 5

AM, a Maruti Car No: CH-01-F/1607 arrived from Dehlon side. Two Sikhs were sitting on the front seats. We signalled them through torchlight to stop but they left the car and after taking positions on the canal bank, started firing in order to kill the police party, but we in self-defence replied the firing and I informed the police control room through wireless. From the nearby check-post, the SSP along with his party came to our help. The firing ensued from both sides with automatic weapons. The militants made me a special target. I used my Self Loading Rifle (SLR) but the firing from their side was very heavy. Not afraid of losing my life, I continued to fire. When the firing ceased, we found a dead body there. The other man had escaped. One AK-47 rifle with six live rounds was found on the body, while 32 empties were lying nearby. A small dairy bearing the name of Sukhdev Singh, Head Sevadar, Babbar Khalsa International was recovered from his person. The escapee had left seven empties of .30 mossier behind. The police fired a total of 203 rounds during the hour long encounter whereas, the militants fired 39 rounds".

(SD) BS GILL SP (D), 9.8.92 at Nandpur at 7.30 AM

Miraculously both Sukhdev Singh Babbar and Gurjant Singh Budhsinghvala had diaries from which they could be identified. These claims make a mockery of both the Punjab Police and the insurgents, these were two of the leading figures of the insurgency who had gone undetected for years. To believe that they would be as simplistic as to carry diaries with identifying features, beggars belief and at the same time for the Punjab Police to make such stupendous claims, shows their arrogance in their injustice.

FAKE ENCOUNTERS

The IHRO Findings

   According to the findings of the IHRO team, Bhai Sukhdev Singh was living at house number 20, Urban Estate, Patiala in the garb of a contractor as Jasmer Singh Sandhu (this was the alias that he had lived under for many years and fooled the security forces, by leading a double life). On the night of August 8th 1992, the Ludhiana SP(D) , Balwant Singh Gill, on receiving cue from Chandigarh went to Patiala with a selected police force and rang the call bell of the said house and also gave the 'code word' which was known to a top notch of the Babbar Khalsa and a very few other associates[45]. When the Babbar Khalsa chief descended from the upper storey of the house and opened the gate, the police immediately pounced upon him. After a short scuffle, the Babbar fell down and was over-powered. He was then taken to Ludhiana along with his Maruti Car (CH-01-F/1607). At Ludhiana, he was interrogated and tortured by the CIA staff at the Focal Point police station. In the early hours of August 9th 1992, when he was almost dead due to severe torture, he was put in his car and taken to the Dharaur village culvert on the Sahnewal-Dehlon road. At about 5am, while he was still seated in the car, he was shot dead and his body was thrown out of the car. Later the police made up the story that the Babbar was shot dead in an armed encounter, in order to project the 'bravery' of certain police officials like SSP Chattopadhya, SP(D), B. S. Gill, DSP(D), Shiv Kumar, DSP, Narinder Pal Singh, SP(O), P. P. Shabharwal and Inspector Gurjit Singh in anticipation of rewards and promotions.

---

[45] This has been one of the contentious points of the movement, people were accused of being informants and for informing and identifying Bhai Sukhdev Singh Babbar, but to date no conclusive evidence as who actually informed has been presented or found. It is clear although that only an informant could have led to the arrest of Bhai Sukhdev Singh and who knows he or she, is probably still in our midst.

Another fabricated case of a death in custody of an insurgent is that of *Bhai Joginder Singh AKA Joga Singh* V.Folreevaal, Jalandhar. He was arrested on 13th March 1992, at 3am from V. Pragpur, from then on he was in police remand until 27th March 1992. Police made up a story of him escaping from custody, when on the way to make a court appearance, but this was not possible as:

1) He could not walk due to his arms and legs being swollen, from continuous torture;
2) It was part of an agreed court order that he would be handcuffed and cuffed at the ankles at all times, when making court appearances.

Thus he would have had to first break free of his hand and ankle cuffs, and make a miraculous recovery from his injuries to make a rapid escape. His body was not recovered.

The case of Bhai Jaswant Singh Khalra, is of an activist who fought tirelessly to get justice for those who died in fake encounters, but in the end he became a statistic himself.

Jaswant Singh Khalra

"Jaswant Singh Khalra of the Human Rights Organisation worked tirelessly to expose the truth about mass cremations and extra-judicial killings by the Indian security forces. He tells his own story below of how he started out on a road that led to startling discoveries:

On the 19th February 1993, after a 50 hour encounter (the police say it was a 50 hour encounter), Baba Gurbachan Singh Manochahal attained martyrdom. His last rites became a point of contention, as for the first time Sikhs

*fighting against persecution asked for the body of Baba
Manochahal, so that they could perform his funeral and the
government was in a fix over this. Usually the police
would argue that they had to complete the funerals of Sikh
insurgents as no-one would come forward to claim the
body, if they did come forward the police would persecute
them. But the tyrants quickly performed Baba
Manochahal's cremation at the Tarn Taran Municipal
Cremation grounds, so that they wouldn't have to hand
over the body for a proper funeral. When we investigated
what happened we learnt that the police had cremated his
body as unidentified. From this a question arose – How
many other Sikhs were cremated by categorising their
bodies as unidentified?*

*Prior to this I was already searching for families of two of
my friends. I was suspicious that the police had killed the
families and disposed of the bodies. One of these was
Amrik Singh Matheval who was a director at the Amritsar
Central Bank and the second was also a director. With
them, when they went missing, was Darshan Singh, who
was the brother in law of Sital Singh Matheval. The police
had arrested them from their home but was not telling us
what had been done to them or giving any information on
where they were. After what happened to Baba
Manochahal I got the suspicion that I could find their
bodies in a cremation ground, being disposed of as
unidentified bodies. In the end I found their bodies in the
cremation grounds of the Durgiana Mandir, Amritsar. In
1992 alone the police had cremated 300 bodies as
unidentified. I started searching for further missing
persons and got assistance and enquiries from over 2000
families to search for their family members (who were
mostly young men) who had been taken away by police but
had not been seen since.*

FAKE ENCOUNTERS

We made a press release of these findings (Human Rights Wing – SAD) about the missing bodies of these 2000 people that we had created case files for. The police Chief KPS Gill thinking he could dismiss it like other human rights reports, challenged our findings saying they were not based upon fact and that our report was aimed at denting the morale of the police and increasing the support for Sikh insurgents. He even went onto say that the missing Sikhs were in foreign countries, working and earning a living.

We took on his challenge to prove him wrong with credible evidence; we immediately started collating evidence to bolster our case. We made contact with other human rights activists and organisations, researching the numbers of people reported missing and collated press reports of people who have gone 'missing.' From this Amnesty International collated a report and asked the Indian government to answer what had happened to 200 specific cases of missing persons.

We only had information of about 2000 missing people in Amritsar but we were shocked to learn that in the cremation grounds of the Amritsar District, in the 3 City Municipal Cremation grounds, the number of bodies cremated as unidentified was 6017. In the whole of Punjab the number of bodies disposed of an unidentified was over 25,000 (this relates to the period between 1984-1994 and these are only the cases that are recorded whereby the police handed over bodies to the Municipal Cremation grounds, thus the real figure which will never be known is actually much higher than this, there were thousands of bodies disposed of illegally which were mostly thrown into canals and rivers).

FAKE ENCOUNTERS

In accordance with the law, the Municipal Committees have to pay for the cremation of the unidentified bodies found in their city but a police investigation into the identity of the body and a post-mortem are mandatory. The medical staffs who conduct the post-mortem have to keep photos of the body and proof of DNA and note any distinguishing features, all this information is to be kept safely to assist in the identification of the dead person later on. The police are then supposed to advertise the cremation of the unidentified bodies with photos on posters, in the hope that someone will identify the body. But the police had illegally arrested, detained and murdered thousands of Sikhs, whose bodies were then dumped on mass in the Municipal Cremation grounds. To complete the formalities a false First Information Report (FIR, this is what starts a legal proceeding in India) would be made, but the case would not be pursued. Some bodies were officially identified this was so police officers could collect the bounties on offer for the death of Sikh insurgents, this was the exception to the rule and would number less than 100 across Punjab.

In our investigations we learnt that the Municipal Committees had not treated these unidentified bodies any better than the police had, for example the paperwork for a mass cremation may say that 3 tonnes of fire-wood was used to perform the cremation where in actual fact only 2 tonnes was used and the staff would illegally sell on the other tonne of fire-wood and fraudulently benefit financially. This would lead to bodies being half-burnt and bodily parts would then be disposed of by the staff in the drains of the canals. The most disturbing fact we learnt of was that where the cremation grounds were on the outskirts of a city, dogs were seen dragging about and devouring legs, arms and bodily parts of bodies that hadn't been disposed of properly and the local residents would then collect what bodily parts they could and cremate them themselves. If a family would approach the staff of a cremation ground for the ashes of a loved one the staff would say that they have already immersed the ashes at Hardwar, but the staff told us that in reality in the main the ashes were thrown into the drains of the cities."[46]

All of this was done due to haste in destroying evidence and due to the high turnover of bodies that the Indian security forces were creating, as they were murdering so many Sikhs. These illegal practices led to many families never knowing what happened to their loved ones. Jaswant Singh Khalra went on to fight the cause to prove these illegal cremations, which had to be authorised by police officers, the offending police officers used to sign off the bodies at the cremation grounds and they would illegally ensure that no distinguishing marks/evidence of who these bodies are, would be kept. This was in direct conflict with the law and was discovered by Jaswant Singh Khalra who then went on to get justice through the courts as the appropriate judicial processes had not been followed.

Jaswant Singh Khalra started receiving death threats from the police and received threats directly from KPS Gill the Chief of Punjab Police, Gill now had his tail between his legs and was running scared as the evidence he had challenged Khalra to produce, had been brought into the public domain. Khalra said that he would not falter from his mission and would fight for justice to his last breath. He said he would accept God's will for when his death came, but he did emphasise that if his death should come by illegal means, then the Sikhs should hold KPS Gill and Chief Minister Beant Singh as personally responsible. Gill even said to Khalra that where 25,000 bodies have

---

[46] Article translated from 'Fatehnama', February 2005

disappeared, do you think an extra one going missing will make any difference.

SSP Ajit Singh Sandhu of Tarn Taran was notorious for his illegal methods used against Sikhs and Sikh insurgents. Khalra found an extensive list of illegal cremations that had been personally authorised by Sandhu in the Tarn Taran area and Sandhu was caught red-handed and due process by judicial means had started. Subsequently Jaswant Singh Khalra became another statistic and went missing on 6th September 1995, from his residence of 8 Kabir Park, Amritsar, never to return home. God only knows what they did to him before murdering him, but the son of Sri Guru Gobind Singh did not falter one iota in his aim and was victorious even in his death. SSP Sandhu was going mad, worrying about the pending cases of the illegal cremations and was found dead on rail tracks in Tarn Taran in May 1998, it looked like a clear case of suicide but others have their suspicions as it had been said that Sandhu was going to declare that he only authorised the cremations on the orders of KPS Gill. The poison that Sandhu sowed was in the end the cause of his death, regardless of whether it was suicide or a murder. There are other conspiracy theories regards the actual whereabouts of Sandhu as the body that was cremated at his funeral was unidentifiable and there were reported sightings of him in Halifax, Canada some years ago. So this murderer may actually have done a deal with the state and slipped out of India and be living under a false identity.

Progress of Jaswant Singh Khalra's cause is steadily progressing, the National Human Rights Commission in July 2004, admitted and published details of 2097 persons cremated as unidentified killed in encounters by the Punjab Police and security forces in Punjab between June 1984 to December 1994. Four full page advertisements in national and regional newspapers listing those who had died and inviting compensation claims, had vindicated the exposure made by Jaswant Singh Khalra and was a leap towards justice.

Paramjit Kaur Khalra the wife of Jaswant Singh Khalra, has valiantly carried on with the fight for justice and on the 9th September 1995 and the 11th November 1995, she had moved the Supreme Court to investigate the disappearance of her husband. The Supreme Court ordered the CBI to investigate the case. Her efforts bore fruit after 10 years when on the 18th November 2005, six police officers were convicted for the killing of Jaswant Singh.

Two of the officers found guilty DSP Jaspal Singh and SHO Satnaam Singh were previously awarded the President's medal for fighting militancy in Punjab. This exemplifies what sort of atrocities would have been common amongst the rank and file of Police who were rewarded for the fight against the Sikh insurgents.

DSP Jaspal Singh and ASI Amarjit Singh were sentenced to life imprisonment and four others were imprisoned for seven years. The crucial evidence was given by SPO Kuldip Singh who had been the gunman of SHO Satnaam Singh at the time of Khalra's disappearance. Both the police and Paramjit Kaur Khalra are appealing against the sentences to the High Court, the police officers are appealing against the length of the sentences and Paramjit Kaur is appealing to increase the severity of the sentences, she would like capital punishment for those found guilty of the murder.

The Punjab Police has not mended its ways with the Punjab Human Rights Commission declaring that as many as 90% of the cases registered with it were against police personnel (reported in December 2004). One only has to read the Punjabi dailies to see cases of human rights abuses occurring, this is common practice with the law enforcement agencies against people arrested rightly, or wrongly.

8. Warrior Saints

SEVA

Fruitful and rewarding is that selfless service,
Which is pleasing to the Guru's Mind.
When the Mind of the True Guru is pleased,
Then sins and misdeeds run away.
The Sikh intuitively listens like a student
To the Teachings imparted by the True Guru.
Those who surrender to the True Guru's Will
Are imbued with the immense Love of the Lord.
This is the unique and distinct life-style of the Gurmukhs:
Listening to the Guru's Teachings,
Their minds are imbued with the teachings.
(Sri Guru Amar Das Jee – Gauree, Ang 314 Sri Guru
Granth Sahib Jee)

In Sikhi - Seva (selfless service, voluntary work), is a core tenant of faith and practice. The countless Sikhs who sacrificed their lives in the Khalistan movement to date, have done so in the name of Seva and not for the ulterior motive of power as has been argued by Manraj Grewal in "Dreams After Darkness" (2004). The underlying argument of this polemic book is that all the Sikhs case studied by Grewal, were led by power; I disagree and argue that the majority of the Sikhs who led the insurgency/freedom struggle were led by a passion for freedom and not for a passion to gain power. One has to highlight that these Sikhs who put their heads on their palms and played the game of love as dictated by the Guru, had to undergo:

   o   Living travellers lives of continuous movement, not
        having a fixed abode;

- o The risk of coming under attack at any time (in most cases having poor artillery in comparison to the armed forces of the Indian authorities);
- o The fact that their families would be persecuted (including rape, torture, harassment, and/or being murdered);
- o Close friends and family being martyred (watching, seeing loved ones die).

Three great Sikhs who led lives of Seva will be cited, concentrating specifically on their Seva:

Bhai Fauja Singh – he was the first prominent Sikh to openly welcome Western Sikhs in India and raise their profile, alongside Yogi Harbhajan Singh who had been doing so for some time. He was forever in the service of fellow Sikhs and the Guru, if a Sikh would comment on his clothes being nice, he would immediately remove the garment being referred to and offer it to the Sikh giving the compliment. In the complex of Sri Darbar Sahib he would remove the faeces from the toilets with his bare hands as many did not how to use the toilets and they had a poor flush system on them, which invariably would not work, this was in the 1970's. He would say the house of the Guru is my house I cannot let it be defiled, such was his passion and fervour to do Seva. The Guru always came first, regardless of the circumstances.

Another famous Sikh insurgent whose whole life exemplifies Seva is **Shaheed Bhai Kulwant Singh Jee Babbar - A.K.A. Bhai Mehnga Singh Jee.** A short biography of Kulwant Singh translated from the diary of Shaheed Bhai Anokh Singh Jee is quoted,

"Satguru (true Guru) may my body be blessed at your glorious feet, Oh Father whilst in the battlefield may I

never turn my back to the enemy, may I become Shaheed in the battlefield putting tyrants to justice. Oh Father have pity on me, please ensure that I will always take the brunt of the enemy face on, so that I do not get struck down - with my back to the enemy. Satguru do not look at my faults, bless me in the presence of your feet." This was Kulwant Singh's daily Ardas (supplication) at the feet of Guru Sahib.

When the time comes for a Sikh to offer his/her head in the defence of righteousness, the Sikh becomes excited. The Sikh believes it to be a great honour to offer his/her head in the defence of Sikh principles. A Sikh does not enter any sort of plea bargain, the Sikh cannot be bribed and the Sikh is unshakeable in his/her faith when the time of self-sacrifice (Shaheedi) comes and the enemy cannot scare the Sikh, one iota. Through the great teachings of Sikhi the Sikh enters opposition against tyranny and fights for righteousness, this person is referred to as a Shaheed. The only desire of these self-sacrificing Gursikhs is that their head may be offered for upholding Dharam (righteous principles).

On the 1st June 1984 the ungrateful Indian Empire decided to attack Sikhs and Gurdwara's, and specifically to attack the House of God - Sri Harmander Sahib/Golden Temple. Bhai Mehnga Singh Jee gained martyrdom in the attack whilst defending the sanctity of the shrine and complex. He gained the great honour of becoming the first Shaheed of the army assault and thus gained much respect.

Bhai Kulwant Singh Jee was born at Yamnanagar, Jagadhri in 1957 to Sardar Partaap Singh at Vishkarma Nagar. He was educated at Yamnanagar until his 9th Grade, after which he was inducted into I.T.I. and he undertook a one-year building course. Upon completion of his studies

Kulwant Singh began working in a shop. The bloody Vaisakhi of 1978, had an immense effect upon the soft-heart of Kulwant Singh. Kulwant Singh began attending Kirtan Smagams and started praying day and night for the blessing of Amrit (initiation of nectar). With the great grace of the Guru, Kulwant Singh took Amrit at the Hola Mohalla Smagam (Sri Anandpur Sahib) in 1979. He would read Sikh History frequently and would discuss the lessons learnt from history with others. He was constantly persevering to mould his lifestyle and mannerisms to assimilate the Great Sikhs of the past. He used to eagerly discuss the meting out of punishments to those who had disrespected or murdered Sikhs. Once there was a gathering of the Fake Nirankaris at Jagadhri, so Kulwant Singh and his associates attacked these tyrants, the tyrants made quick their escape, as they could not take the roars and attacks of the valiant sons of Sri Guru Gobind Singh Jee. Soon after this, the police made a list of charges against Kulwant Singh and his associates, and they started to pursue the Singhs. He did not create a defence against the charges, on the contrary Kulwant Singh said, *"I do not believe in this false governance, so why should I go to their courts?"* His colleagues did create a defence against the charges and in the end, all charges were dropped against all the Singhs. With thoughts of serving the Panth and joy in his mind, he went to live with Bibi Amarjit Kaur (the wife of Shaheed Bhai Fauja Singh Jee) in Amritsar. Here Kulwant Singh joined a group of roaming Sikhs - who used to make their way around Sri Harmander Sahib Complex, performing various tasks, as Seva. He did Seva with his mind, body and soul, he was so imbued in Seva that his own clothes would become tattered and torn, but he would not spend even a paisa (a penny) from the Dasvand (tithe) of others for himself. As part of this group of roaming Sikhs, he would do Seva at Sri Harmander Sahib, assist in the Ishnaan of Sri Akaal Takhat Sahib, and knead the chapatti flour in the Sri Guru Ramdas Langar Hall, cook chapattis and serving Langar, were all daily acts of Kulwant Singh. He used to passionately serve Bibi Amarjit Kaur and Mata (mother) Joginder Kaur (mother of Shaheed Bhai Fauja Singh Jee), he used to see this as a great honour as he was being blessed with the Seva of the family of a great Shaheed. Mata Joginder Kaur's affection for Kulwant Singh was similar to the love of a mother, for a son.

In September 1979 a camp was held on the farm of Shaheed Bhai Fauja Singh Jee – at which, Gurmat and arms training were given. Kulwant Singh attended the camp with the ambition of learning about weaponry. At this camp he met Shaheed Jathedar Bhai Sukhdev Singh Jee Babbar, Shaheed Bhai Kulwant Singh Jee Nagoke, Shaheed Bhai Sulakhan Singh Jee Babbar, Bhai Balvinder Singh Jee, Bhai Vadhava Singh Jee, Shaheed Bhai Anokh Singh Jee Babbar, Shaheed Bhai Manmohan Singh Jee Babbar and many other great Sikhs. The Singhs who gave the weapons training developed affection for Kulwant Singh due to his gifted characteristics of a great Gursikh. Many other camps were held at Sapravan and Goindval, in turn the Singhs who attended these camps developed a love for one another and a common thinking and they began to congregate as a formalised group. The aim of all the Singhs was the same - to put the tyrants and oppressors to justice. The authorities had no idea who was meting out punishments to the tyrants and it was the thinking of common people that it was Shaheed Armies[47] who were doing this Seva. The author can humbly assert that it was only with the support of the Armies of Shaheeds that such actions were completed. During this period this great

---

[47] These are armies of Shaheeds who exist in the afterlife but who assist great Sikhs in their actions in this world

Warrior took part in many actions with the Jathebandi, he did Seva day and night, to break the chains of slavery for the Sikhs.

In 1982 Sarpanch Surjan Singh Nagoke informed the authorities of the activities of Bhai Kulwant Singh Jee Nagoke and he gave a full report of the activities of all the Singhs. In turn Bhai Kulwant Singh Jee Nagoke was arrested and tortured to death by the authorities and was declared dead, in a fake encounter. Bounties were placed upon the heads of the other Singhs and the rewards of information leading to the arrests of the Singhs were widely advertised. Bhai Kulwant Singh also had a bounty placed upon his head. All the Singhs who were advertised with bounties upon their heads had to go underground and the authorities commenced huge operations to track down the Singhs. Only a few days had passed since going underground when Kulwant Singh went for Ishnaan in Sri Guru Ramdas Sarovar and to be in the presence of the Guru, he said that *"even in dire circumstances and even in the most dangerous circumstances the great Gursikhs of the past would still go to Sri Harmander Sahib for Ishnaan and to be in the presence of the Guru."* The daily routine of Kulwant Singh was to rise at Amrit-Vela, do Ishnaan (bathe) in the Sarovar, do his Nitnem (daily prayers) and sit in Sri Harmander Sahib to listen to Sri Asa Dee Var Kirtan. He would then serve the Singhs Langar, dust the shoes of Gursikhs and arrange the supply of arms for the Jathebandi/Babbar Khalsa.

At about 12pm on the 1st June 1984 the Central Reserve Police Force (CRPF) and Border Security Force (BSF) opened indiscriminate fire upon the Sri Harmander Sahib Complex, in accordance with the government programme of eradicating Sikhs. Kulwant Singh was positioned at Gurdwara Baba Atal Sahib, from where he put 3 soldiers to justice, filled with passion and emotion he raced to the top floor of Baba Atal Sahib. The enemy had become aware of Kulwant Singhs whereabouts and when he became visible they opened automatic fire on him and he was shot in the forehead, he fell to the ground. **A nearby Singh shouted,** ***"Bhai Mehnga Singh - how are you?"*** **He replied,** ***"Chardi Kala!" (In high spirits).***

As soon as the Singhs learnt of what had happened Bhai Manmohan Singh Jee Fauji sent 2 Singhs to go and fetch the injured Bhai Mehnga Singh. The Singhs brought him down from the top floor of Baba Atal Sahib to Guru Nanak Nivas; this was whilst they were under fire from the enemy. No doctor or professional treatment could be arranged, but the Singhs cleaned the wound and applied a bandage. Gurbani was read in the presence of Kulwant Singh and upon the completion of Sukhmani Sahib he entered the abode of the glorious feet of the Guru, for eternity. On one hand many Singhs were busy in battle with the enemy and on the other, many Singhs were busy in looking after the body of Kulwant Singh, Jathedar Sukhdev Singh ordered the Singhs to read Gurbani continuously in the presence of Bhai Mehnga Singh Jee.

On the evening of the 1st June 1984 when the firing had ceased a message was sent to the parents of this great warrior. On 2nd June 1984 just after midday, Kulwant Singh's parents arrived at Guru Nanak Nivas from Yamnanagar under very difficult circumstances whilst the curfew was still in place. Upon seeing the body of Kulwant Singh his mother affectionately said, ***"Son, you have accomplished your ultimate aim. When you left home to do Seva of the Quam (Sikh nation) your only desire from the Guru was that you could become a Shaheed, you have accomplished your aim and in turn you have blessed me for giving birth to a Shaheed."***

All the Jathebandhis within the complex that heard of the Shaheedi of Kulwant Singh sent their representatives for the last rites of this warrior; they all spoke of the courage and valour of Kulwant Singh. The Guru does reward those who endeavour with a true heart. We are a sacrifice to this warrior, who was a truly gifted soul, who was the first Shaheed of the army assault on Sri Harmander Sahib Complex. Kulwant Singh was cremated close to Sri Manji Sahib and was the first person in many years, who was blessed with the honour of being cremated here.

Jathedar Sukhdev Singh Babbar and his colleagues performed Ishnaan of Kulwant Singh with devotion, they dressed him in his 5 K's, a Chola (Sikh warrior attire) and a Dumala (traditional turban). His body was carried to near Sri Manji Sahib and a large number of people followed to see the last rites performed. Sant Jarnail Singh Jee Bhindra Vale sent Bhai Sujaan Singh Jee to the final rites and he placed a sheet over Kulwant Singh's body, many others placed sheets and flowers over Kulwant Singh's body. Each and every Gursikh congregated at the funeral of Kulwant Singh, felt pangs of separation. The funeral was performed according to Gur-Maryada (Sikh Code of Conduct) and Kulwant Singh's father set the funeral pyre alight. The flames of the funeral pyre gave each Sikh congregated, the teaching to die in the battlefield, whilst defending the sanctity of Dharam.

Kulwant Singh was a truly enlightened soul, whose self-sacrifice gave all Jathebandhis and Sikhs the courage to continue the fight for justice." To see photos of this Great Sikh please see page 284.

True Encounters

There were also true encounters between the police/security forces and Sikh insurgents but these were far and few between, when they did take place the Indian security forces always outnumbered the insurgents by at least 10 to 1 and in many cases it would spiral upwards into the 100's to 1. The security personnel and the Punjab Police were scared to put their lives on the line. In most cases the Police would turn a blind eye to known insurgents as they did not want to enter combat and risk losing their lives.

Bhai Amarjit Singh Daheru

The first documented true encounter between the security forces and Sikh insurgents was that of Amarjit Singh Daheru of Babbar Khalsa in 1983. Amarjit Singh was wanted by the police, his house was surrounded and an encounter started. Amarjit Singh fell to the bullets of the police quite quickly but his wife continued in combat against the police for a total of 48 hours and she was also eventually martyred. To see photo, please see page 286.

Bhai Surjeet Singh Behla

In 1991 – during the Congress rule of Chief Minister Beant Singh in Punjab, Surjeet Singh Behla made a secret bunker in an empty building in his village, and lived there with one companion. The mason who helped construct this bunker informed the police. The Tarn Taran SSP Ajit Sandhu, SP Operations - Khoobee Ram, DSP Gurjit and other well known police officers led a group of soldiers and police to the bunker. This was on 7th June, 1992. The Police believed that this hidden bunker only had weapons in it and not Behla himself. But Behla and the other Singh were present in the bunker along with another Singh who supplied them food. The terrified police officers took the Village Head and other innocent villagers as shields and entered the building to search it. The mason began to break the bunker and Behla and his companions heard this and realised what was going on. These beloveds Tigers of the Guru performed an Ardas (prayer of supplication) and decided to fight to the death. They took their weapons and opened the inner door of the bunker. When they stepped out, they immediately let out a burst of bullets and the searching police team ran away. The officers went on the highest roof of the building and once the encounter began, were stranded there.

After the Police had run away, Behla and his companions searched the ground floor of the building, where they found the Village Head. Behla was shocked to find him here and asked why he had come. The Head and others explained how the police had brought them as shields. Behla told them he would give them cover fire and help them escape the building. Before helping the Village Head leave, he gave him a final letter for his family which had three main messages:

1) Tell my father not to leave Behla village;
2) Tell my wife to obey my mother and father;
3) At a certain place, I have put Rs. 20,000 and tell my father to take that money and arrange Akhand Paaths for us.

After giving this message, Surjeet Singh Behla gave the innocent villagers cover-fire and sent them out. Taking inspiration from the Chamkaur Sahib battle, a unique type of fight began. At the start of the encounter, the Punjab Police took innocent villagers as human shields and fired a shower of bullets towards the building. The villagers still become emotional when they tell how the security forces made the villagers stand around the building and the police fired between their legs.

They also tell us how Behla in a thundering voice was yelling Jakaras (war cries) and also curses, saying *"Fight us straight! Why are you putting innocent people in front of you?"* But these insults could not make the *"brave"* Punjab Police feel any shame.

The villagers smile and tell us how Behla's bullets avoided the villagers but kept hitting the police officers (this was the skill and tact of some of the insurgents). The police brought bullet proof tractors to the place of the ensuing encounter. These were a new invention of the Punjab Police that were introduced by the Beant & KPS Gill Coalition, they created these fortified tractors as then they would not have to get armoured vehicles such as tanks and avoid having to call in the army. The two hungry and tired Singhs fought this force for 36 hours and were finally martyred. The building which held the bunker is still standing today, it is in ruins, reminding people of the heavy fire and bombardment that took place.

When the Security Forces saw that only two Singhs had fought them, they took 6 innocent villagers who had been wounded and killed them and told the press that 9 militants had been killed. The slaughter of these innocents led to the police being heavily criticized and the bravery of Surjeet Singh Behla was discussed in every village of Punjab. Baba Gurbachan Singh Manochahal heard about Bhai Behla's martyrdom and said *"Today my right arm has been broken."* He wrote an emotional poem on the martyrdom of Bhai Behla, and when reciting it, he would begin to cry. Perhaps today no one speaks about the martyrdom of these Singhs openly, due to fear, but that time will come when ballads of their bravery will again be openly sung on stages.[48]   To see photos of this encounter please see page 285.

Baba Gurbachan Singh Manochahal

Baba Gurbachan Singh Manochahal had a number of true encounters with the security forces.   Once he was surrounded by the police, but the police were too scared to approach the hut he was in, so the police brought the Sarpanch (village head) and when the Sarpanch went to speak with Baba Gurbachan Singh, he tried to explain that the hut was completely surrounded. The Police again demanded that Manochahal open the door. The Sarpanch was asked to stand aside. Manochahal then yelled from inside,

"Give me a flashlight!"

The police were confused and asked,

"Why do you need it?"

Manochahal replied,

"We've locked the door from the inside and need it so we can see the lock!"

The police passed a torch through the space under the door. Manochahal and his brother loaded their assault rifles and set them on "burst". Manochahal opened the door and began to fire. The CRPF officer at the door fell immediately and the others also came under fire. The

---

[48] Baljit Singh Khalsa, translated from Khandydhar magazine, translation courtesy of https://www.1984tribute.com/shaheed-bhai-surjeet-singh-behla/

Bihari officers began to run in all directions, screaming *"Run! They're going to kill us!"*

Manochahal and his brother jumped over the officers who were still lying in their positions. A Punjab Police officer tried to tackle Manochahal as he was running but failed in his attempt. Manochahal had wreaked havoc on the police and escaped. One officer thought Manochahal was chasing him and he ran for a number of kilometres in front of Baba Jee. Baba Gurbachan Singh did not harm the poor police officer and let him go.

One of the most famous battles in the history of the modern Sikh Movement took place in village Rataul where Manochahal and some of his companions were staying. The village was cordoned off by the police as they had learnt of the presence of the Singhs in the village. One Singh was resting in a house, different from the one being used by Baba Manochahal, when the police entered the house the Singh entered an underground bunker. The police became suspicious as a set of muddy foot prints could be seen leading to a corner and then mysteriously disappearing. When they went to the corner and moved a drum of flour, the entrance to the bunker became visible. Right away, the Singh inside the bunker opened fire and dropped the entire group. The cowardly Indians began to run in different directions and the Singh managed to escape from that house. Word was sent to Baba Manochahal that the village was surrounded and he should escape. Manochahal along with his body guard broke the cordon and escaped. To see a photo of Baba Manochahal please see page 286.

Inside the village, 5 Singhs gathered at a house where they had made a concrete bunker. They had decided to show the police what a real encounter was like. The army along with police divisions from Amritsar, Gurdaspur, Tarn Taran and Batala surrounded the area. The Singhs were well armed and had sniper rifles as well.

A DIG of the police was trying to lead his men and give them courage to fight when the Singhs shot him dead. The loss of such a high ranking officer demoralized the already scared troops. The Singhs continued to bellow Jakaras (cries of victory) from inside the bunker as they fought. Police officers attempted to pick up the body, but each time were forced to retreat, under heavy fire. The body lying there continued to demoralize them.

The Singhs fought for a total of 72 hours. The Security forces had lost so many men that they could no longer stand to fight anymore. They ordered a helicopter to open fire and had the bunker bombed. The five Singhs inside were all martyred but they showed the world that Guru Gobind Singh's words that he will get a Sikh to fight an army of 125,000 by him/herself are still true.[49]

Another case of a true encounter is that of Bhai Jagroop Singh Kalak & Bhai Jangjeet Singh Dhaka, where the effectiveness and cunningness of police informants and agents is displayed. Bhai Jagroop Singh was born at V. Kathavi, Ludhiana (this was his maternal grand-parents village) his actual village was Kalak, Ludhiana. He was an insurgent and a member of the KLF during the reign of Bhai Gurjant Singh Budhsinghvala. He was drugged in his tea by hosts at a house but his friend who was with him at the time, did not drink the tea, thus he did not fall unconscious. Police immediately surrounded the house, as the Singhs had been entrapped and his friend Bhai Jangjeet Singh Dhaka started an encounter with police. Bhai

---

[49] Based upon accounts authored by Amardeep Singh Amar

Jagroop Singh regained consciousness after a while, but by then they were entrenched in and the police had brought out their bullet proof tractors. Both the Singhs fought bravely for 10 hours and attained Shaheedi.

These are merely a few examples of true encounters between the security forces and Sikh insurgents, many true encounters took place, but very few are documented. Many Sikhs who took part in encounters still live on, but keep quiet about what they did or witnessed, as they will welcome the attention of the police and/or criminal charges by retelling their history.

Bravery

In the lives of insurgents, examples of their courage and bravery shine through. Here I will document some examples of bravery from a selection of Sikh insurgents.

Bhai Mathra Singh

Sant Jarnail Singh was preaching to Sikhs when a Sikh woman made a request that he should accept her son in his Jatha (organisation), Sant replied that anyone can join the Jatha and do Seva and learn about Sikhi. The woman went on to request that Sant accepts her son in his permanent Jatha, i.e. to stay with Sant at all times, Sant replied that only those Singhs are allowed to stay in this permanent Jatha who go out and disarm the CRPF of a gun and come and present it here. The woman quietly sat down when she heard this condition.

Harvinder Singh who was about 18 years old at the time heard the request of Sant Bhindranvale and he quietly walked out of the congregation. He left the Golden Temple complex through the Clock Tower entrance and went straight up to a CRPF officer, pulled the Sten Gun off the officer and kicked him with all his might and made quick his escape. He went straight to Sant Bhindranvale and presented the gun, the Singhs present, shouted Jakaras.

Harvinder Singh became initiated as a Sikh at the next available Amrit Sanchar (Initiation Ceremony to become a practicing Sikh) and he was renamed Mathra Singh. He went on to became an infamous Sikh insurgent who worked alongside Bhai Harjinder Singh Jinda and Bhai Sukhdev Singh Sukha and was wanted by the police. In 1987the bounty on his head was 14 Lakh RS (1,400,000 RS),[50] to see his photo please see page 286.

Bhai Talvinder Singh Babbar
Bhai Talvinder Singh Babbar was the founder of Babbar Khalsa and a much feared insurgent, who had a die-hard spirit (photo on page 286). He is spoken of highly by all that knew him, two people who knew him well, recall their memories of his bravery,

A: If there were 15 soldiers outside the house all armed with AK47's and I asked Talvinder Singh to go out and take them on, he would not even flinch and would go straight outside to take them on.

B: In 1992 when all the leaders of the top militant outfits were getting eliminated and Talvinder Singh had little support from other militant groups, we asked that he did not return to India as the climate was ripe for him to also get assassinated. He did not heed our requests to just hold out a little longer before returning to India, but instead chose to enter India at the time that was most likely to lead to his martyrdom. He did not have an ounce of fear and was a true warrior.

---

[50] Jujharoo Yode, Maninder Singh Baja

Baba Manochahal

Even before the 1984 attack, Manochahal was a wanted man. The security forces knew he was close to Sant Jarnail Singh Bhindranvale and committed to the Sikh nation. As early as 1980 the police had once surrounded Gurdwara Baba Dhanna Singh in Naushera Panooaa(n) where Manochahal was doing Seva and ordered him to surrender. Manochahal told the police party that he would change his clothes first. He went inside his room and came out with a big Kirpan. Taking it out of its sheath, Baba Jee bellowed, *"Whoever has got the courage can come and arrest me..."* The police party were terrified and no one approached him. By this time villagers had also assembled at the Gurdwara and the Police were forced to return to their stations empty-handed.

In 1992, when most of the leaders of the Sikh insurgent outfits had been martyred, all efforts became fixed on eliminating Baba Manochahal.   Manochahal challenged the Chief of Police KPS Gill to open combat, he said let us agree a time and venue and let us have a true encounter and see who succeeds. KPS Gill did not rise to the challenge.

Shaheed Bhai Ranjit Singh Babbar, Amritsar

Azhar Alam (a Punjab Police officer notorious for torturing Sikhs) asked Ranjit Singh whilst in custody,

Alam:	*Where is your Jathedar?*
R Singh:	*We have many Jathedars, which one?*
Alam:	*Sukhdev Singh*
R Singh:	*I have a meeting with Jathedar Sukhdev Singh at a set time and location. I challenge*

*you to try and get this information from me.
I am a Sikh of the True Guru, Emperor of
the Universe. You are a disciple of Delhi -
let's see who will be victorious?*

Ranjit Singh was tortured continuously for 36 hours, during which time he gave no information to the tyrants and attained martyrdom after succumbing to his injuries.[51]

Shaheed Bhai Ravinder Singh Babbar

Once, Bhai Ravinder Singh and a companion were taking arms to their fellow insurgents. They performed an Ardas for the success of their mission and left. They had packed the guns and ammunition in a bundle of sugarcane and placed it on the back of their motorcycle. On the way, they saw that at a distance there was a major Police checkpoint (naka). The Singh accompanying Ravinder suggested they turn around. Ravinder Singh replied that they had done Ardas and they should now have faith. The police motioned for the motorcycle to slow down. Bhai Ravinder Singh slowed the motorcycle's speed, making it seem as though he was pulling over but all of a sudden he pressed the gas and drove through. The police opened fire and began to chase, but the Singhs entered the village streets and threw the police off their trail. Ravinder had full faith that Guru Sahib would himself help them in their cause.

Finally, when crossing the border into Pakistan, he would never wait for our 'all-clear' signal. He used to say that life and death are in Guru Sahib's hands and when it was time for him to die, nothing could save him.[52]

---

[51] https://www.1984tribute.com/shaheed-bhai-ravinder-singh-bagga/

[52] ibid

Shaheed Bhai Kulwant Singh Gumti (**Dec 1963 – 14 March 1992**)

In 1983 Bhai Kulwant Singh Gumti was initiated as a Sikh and he became close to Bhai Amrik Singh and was the Bathinda lead for AISSF. Gumti worked very hard in all AISSF programmes and he received the backing of students across Bathinda. When the railway stations were burnt in 1984, a case was registered against him. In May 1984 he was charged under the National Security Act (NSA), he was the first person in Bathinda to be charged under the NSA. In jail, Gumti continued studying and passed the Giani exams and completed his BA whilst in Bathinda jail.

The Barnala Government was formed in Punjab and Gumti was released as he was under 20 years of age. Only a few days after his release a new accusation of murder by the Police was fabricated and Gumti decided to go underground. A few days later outside S.D. College Barnala, he was surrounded and arrested by police. The party that arrested him included Police from Barnala, Jail Wardens of Sangrur Jail and CRPF from the area.

Gumti started a hands-on fight with the police, when they surrounded him. Anyone who approached him ended up on their back on a nearby jeep, after being tossed over by Gumti. He shouted to onlookers and passersby:

"I am Kulwant Singh Gumti and the police are going to arrest me."

All the onlookers were amused by the spectacle of the police officers being thrown about like rag dolls and were astonished at the strength and bravery of Bhai Kulwant Singh Gumti. Gumti was about to run away and make good his escape when another police party with the DSP of Barnala arrived. In protest of his arrest the whole of Barnala was closed and a curfew was imposed by AISSF.

Whilst in custody Gumti was tortured, his thighs were ripped open and his nails were pulled out by the Barnala police yet he still did not divulge any information to them. Bhai Sahib was produced in Court two days later and then different police forces came in with requests for his custody. To see a photo of Gumti please see page 287.

Shaheed Bhai Surinder Singh 'Baba' AKA Bhai Gurcharan Singh Jee (12.12.65 - 5.10.88)

Another front runner of AISSF, "Baba" had much affection for Sant Bhindranvale, whom he met on many occasions. He went to jail 3 times as part of the Dharam Yudh Morcha. He did Seva in Amrit Sanchars (initiation ceremonies) after Operation Blue Star.

A police informant told of Baba's whereabouts and police knew that he was unarmed, 2 police officers tried grabbing hold of him and he pushed them both away. He jumped over the boundary wall of the house where they were trying to arrest him and ran for 6km. He had been shot in the back and due to the wound, he took a rest in a field near V. Jora(n). As the police had received reliable information that it was definitely Baba they had shot, they remained in pursuit. The police knew he was inside the field, yet they stayed outside of it, as they were too scared to get near him. More reinforcements were called and Baba was eventually arrested. The police questioned,

Police: *What shall we now do with you?*

Baba: *What can you do apart from kill me, you can't even get me to admit my name.*

Due to Baba being a member of the 5 man ad-hoc Committee/Panthic Committee he was mercilessly tortured by Gobind Ram and Azhar Alam's forces in Jalandhar. To see a photo of Bhai Surinder Singh Baba & Bhai Anokh Singh Babbar please see page 208.

Shaheed Bhai Anokh Singh Babbar

Bhai Anokh Singh was tortured beyond belief. His nails and eyes were pulled out. During torture a police officer asked again and again about where the other Singhs were? Anokh Singh had remained silent throughout his torture, he spoke and said,

"If you were now to bring a cup of tea for me, and if I were to drink it right in front of you. If you were then to ask me whether I had drunk that cup of tea, your torture would not make me even tell you that much."

The Silent Majority & Silent Army

Many people who fought and/or assisted in the Sikh insurgency will never be known for their service, the reasons for this are varied, but I felt it pertinent to mention the tireless work of both the silent majority and the silent army.

The silent majority refers to the many Sikhs in Punjab, across India and across the globe that assisted the insurgents and insurgency in any manner that they could. In Punjab this was the many families who gave food and shelter to the insurgents, but it was also the numerous Sikhs who carried intelligence reports and ferried arms for the insurgents.

This silent majority crossed all boundaries of age, occupation, gender and caste, which usually interfere with

Punjabis working together. The Sikhs and Punjabis in general, accepted the insurgency and were committed to getting their just rights, thus for 8 years between 1984 and 1992, they worked as a cohesive force.

The silent army refers to those Sikhs who were involved in armed combat against the state, again many who were involved were never discovered or they moved to different states or went abroad to escape being caught. This silent army diligently worked against the state and the true levels of support will never be ascertained.

Sikhs across the globe were involved in both forming part of the silent majority and the silent army, they funded much of the insurgency but were also hand in glove with the array of Sikh insurgent militant outfits that existed. Fighters from abroad were martyred but many who supported the movement in whatever manner they could, still live on.

Silent army of married couples

There were many married couples who worked hand in glove with one another in fighting in the Sikh insurgency and many lived normal lives, but when the opportunity arose they would become involved in armed actions. One such couple used to go on assassination trips on their scooter and they would get through police check-points without any hassle as the police would never suspect that a man would put his wife at risk in such actions. The police would assume this, as they knew that if they caught the man and wife together they would torture and rape the wife in front of her husband. But some couples threw the consequences to the wind and did what they thought was called for.

In many cases women would be left to rear children and would have to move from pillar to post to avoid persecution. These women bore the brunt of the fact that their husbands were fighting for the wider good and many supported their husbands in their endeavours.

Marriage & Married Couples

Many Sikhs got married whilst they were involved in the insurgency and married couples then went on to support and be involved in the movement. I will go onto narrate some examples of Sikh married couples and their unique relationships. Firstly let us start with *Shaheed Bhai Raminderjeet Singh Jee Tainee & Shaheed Bibi Manjeet Kaur Jee* (photo on page 288).

Out of the thousands of Shaheeds who have fought for the independence of Sikhs, one such Saint-Soldier who lived according to Banee[53] and Bana[54] was Babbar Bhai Raminderjeet Singh Jee Tainee. Tainee was born in October 1965 in Jalandhar. His mother was Bibi Sharanjeet Kaur Jee and his father was Master Amrik Singh Jee.

He went to the Phagwara Ramgharia College and the SukhChain College (Phagwara) to get educated. He got involved in the Sikh cause while he was at college, he developed a close relationship with Shaheed Paramjit Singh "Gadassa" who assassinated the Shiv Sena President Rama Kanth in Jatala. Many other Gursikhs were in contact with Tainee during this period and he developed an extensive network. In 1984 after Operation Blue Star, Tainee was arrested under false charges, mercilessly tortured and sent to Jalandhar Jail. More false charges

---

[53] Gurbani - the utterances of the Gurus
[54] Performing actions according to the teachings of the Guru's

were added to the charge sheet and Tainee was sent to Nabha High Security Prison. After 2 years in jail, he was released and returned home. After coming out of jail he was not at peace with living at home. He was always thinking about how to make the Sikh cause more successful.

In 1987, in Jalandhar, Tainee assassinated a police informant, after which he left home and started putting the aggressors to justice. Tainee now worked with Bhai Avtar Singh Pehlvaan, Bhai Manjeet Singh Babbar and other famous Babbars. After a while Tainee was arrested by Jalandhar Police, this was with the help of a police informant. The police used their most wretched methods of torture, but he remained in a peaceful state of mind and took all the atrocities that the authorities could dish out to him. He was then again charged and placed in Nabha High Security Prison. In this period he met Bhai Harmeet Singh Babbar Paooval, Bhai Charanjeet Singh Chana Babbar and many others. Tainees affection of Bhai Harmeet Singh Paooval was more than that of brothers, which was sustained until his last breath.

After spending a long period of time in jail, in 1989, Tainee was released and he returned home. He only spent a short period of time at home as he was eager to serve the Panth once again, he again left the comforts of a homely life and became heavily involved in the Jathebandi (Babbar Khalsa). He never considered returning home to live a normal family life. In July 1990 Black Cats[55] attacked Tainee's father, who was seriously injured in this attack, Bhai Sahib accepted this treatment meted out to his father as the will of God. Tainee then assassinated a whole group

---

[55] A sub-group of the Police whom operate like a law onto themselves, trained to kill and infiltrate the Sikhs – trained assassins.

of Police Black Cats who were popularly known as the Indian Lions. These Indian Lions fell one by one to the Lion of the Guru, Bhai Raminderjeet Singh Tainee. Out of the utmost respect of Tainee's Seva, Bhai Sukhdev Singh Babbar appointed Bhai Sahib the Regional Commander for the Jalandhar district.

After a while Tainee along with his close associates, moved their base to Ropar district. With the co-operation of Bhai Harmeet Singh Paooval, Bhai Balvinder Singh Jatana, Bhai Charanjeet Singh Babbar and many other Singhs, numerous evil-doers were put to justice throughout Malva district and outside of Punjab.

On the evening of 28th February 1991, Tainee along with Bhai Nirmal Singh Babbar Geegemajara and Bhai Harpal Singh Babbar were in a Maruti van, near Geegemajara (Chandigarh). Somebody informed the police of the whereabouts of the Singhs, the police surrounded the van that they were travelling in. Bhai Geegemajara swallowed a cyanide tablet instantly and was thus martyred but Tainee and Bhai Harpal Singh were arrested by the Chandigarh police. They were both severely tortured by the Chandigarh S.S.P. Sumedh Saini. This tyrant thrashed the Singhs with hot metal rods and inflicted burn marks all over their bodies. Tainee was steadfast in his stand and conviction, he did not reveal any information nor did he beg for mercy, but accepted the torture as the will of God. Upon hearing of the arrest of Tainee, his colleagues kidnapped the relatives of the Cabinet Minister Boota Singh and demanded the release of Bhai Sahib from the police. Police officials from Jalandhar and Ludhiana went to Chandigarh especially, to further torture Tainee. The S.S.P. of Jalandhar made a scheme to take Tainee from Chandigarh to Jalandhar and eliminate him in a fake encounter, as Bhai Sahib had put many Police Black Cats of this S.S.P. to justice. But the Chandigarh police did not give Tainee police remand, so his evil scheme could not take place as Bhai Sahib remained under the supervision of the Chandigarh Police. But the S.S.P. did not give up easily, he returned after about a week, but he had to go away empty-handed again, as Tainee was again refused police bail from Burail Prison (Chandigarh). On numerous occasions the Jalandhar police attempted to get his custody on police remand so they could carry out their evil scheme of elimination. They made another plan to capture Tainee, this time they decided to capture him whilst he was under the supervision of the prison authorities.

According to pre-arranged plans Tainee was taken for a medical check-up to the P.G.I.[56] in Chandigarh on 25th February 1992. The Singhs ambushed the police forces and got Bhai Sahib freed, during this encounter 1 inspector was killed and a number of officers were injured.

Taineee once again, immediately resumed doing underground Seva for the Sikh cause. The Punjab Government placed a bounty of RS 1,500,000 upon the head of Tainee. Bhai Sahib got married in Ropar district in village Gango Radhram to Bibi Manjeet Kaur, who was a true Gursikh. Bhai Harmeet Singh Paooval performed the marriage ceremony and Bibi Manjeet Kaur was handed a handgun to protect herself throughout the ceremony. The wedding was carried out in secret and they could have come under attack at any time. Even after getting married there was no reduction in the level of commitment to the Sikh cause by Tainee, on the contrary Bhai Sahib's Singhnee (wife) played her part in various actions and she did Seva of the Panth on an equal footing as Bhai Raminderjeet Singh.

---

[56] Hospital

In the Sikh Nation countless warriors have been born, but the number of traitors is on a par to this. A traitor informed the police of the whereabouts of our glorious warrior on the 5th March 1993. Tainee was travelling on a bus from Patiala to Ludhiana, when someone revealed his whereabouts to the S.S.P. of Khanna. The S.S.P. got the bus stopped and surrounded it with his forces, Bibi Manjeet Kaur was also travelling with Bhai Sahib at the time. The police were unsure of what Tainee looked like, they had received a rough description and were unsure of who their prey was, thus they ordered off all the young men who fitted the description. They then went on to kill all the young men who could be Bhai Raminderjeet Singh, one young man was pleading for his life and was claiming to be the son of a Congress Party member, but the police party carried on with their evil scheme as they wanted to make sure they killed Tainee. Bibi Manjeet Kaur was also subsequently assassinated by the police as they learnt she was travelling with Bhai Sahib.

Due to his younger brother and father being in jail, only Tainee's mother saw her son and daughter-in-law for the final time at their funeral, which took place under the supervision of the Khanna police. Until his last breath Bhai Sahib fought like a tiger and went to the abode of the Guru along with his Singhnee. The Quam will respect such Shaheeds forever.

Jathedar Sukhdev Singh Babbar & Bibi Jawahar Kaur
Bhai Sukhdev Singh Babbar led Babbar Khalsa for many years and did so with much diligence. This was largely down to the fact that he successfully started to live a double-life. Even before Operation Blue Star he was wanted by the Punjab Police, but after it he rose to more

fame and the government were desperate to get hold of him. Babbar Khalsa had become one of the leading militant groups and was a force to be reckoned with.

Sukhdev Singh set up an elaborate double life of a contractor building roads. He got married to Jawahar Kaur who was the sister and daughter respectively of the women who used to make up the Nabha women's Dhahdi Jatha (group singing ballads about Sikh History, to inspire Sikhs). Sukhdev Singh lived under the pseudo-identity of Jasmer Singh and only a few high ranking individuals of Babbar Khalsa knew of this double-identity, many thought he was just extraordinarily talented in changing his identity to suit his environments, but contrary to belief he actually roamed freely under his pseudo-identity and socialised with the wealthy and powerful.

This double-life allowed him to fund the movement and get access to information that would have been virtually impossible to access. He got married to Jawahar Kaur and she bore him a child. She has done a great service to the Sikh nation, as she had to live this life of secrecy and had to always be alert to others finding out the true identity of her husband.

Many Sikhs were shocked when they learnt of Sukhdev Singh's double life, but this was the greatness of his ways, that even those that had known him, could not believe that he had been so expert in setting up his double-life. He was already married prior to going underground after 1984, but he started a completely new life after the 1984 attack and the climate of militancy called for such drastic actions to be taken.

Bhai Satwant Singh & Bibi Surinder Kaur

Satwant Singh had got engaged to Surinder Kaur prior to his visit to the Golden Temple Complex, after which he decided to assassinate Indira Gandhi. When Surinder Kaur visited him for the first time after being incarcerated, Satwant Singh advised her to get married to someone else, as it was clear that he would receive capital punishment. She refused this advice and instead said that she had vowed to be his wife and would see herself as such, until her dying days. Surinder Kaur had been allowed to visit Satwant Singh as the family had told the prison authorities that she was his wife. The prison authorities learnt that she was not his wife but his fiancée and they said that she could not visit him anymore, as she was not actually married to him. They did this to cause as much discomfort to Satwant Singh and his family as possible.

At the Sarbat Khalsa of 26th January 1986, Satwant Singh was awarded the title of "Living Martyr" (Jinda Shaheed) and his mother – Pyar Kaur was given the Shaheed Sukha Singh and Shaheed Mehtab Singh[57] Gold Medal.

Surinder Kaur then took the brave decision of getting married to Satwant Singh, and this wedding would take place in the absence of Satwant Singh, but it would be a unique wedding that would make history. She decided to display her conviction and commitment to her fiancée by getting married to his photograph, this wedding had two motives, firstly to display that she was committed to her pledge to Satwant Singh and secondly wanted to continue to meet Satwant Singh in jail as she would become his wife. The wedding took place on the 2nd May 1988, but

---

[57] Sukha Singh & Mehtab Singh beheaded Massa Rangar in the 19th Century for desecrating the Golden Temple Complex.

became public knowledge through the media on the 30th May 1988.

Both the families of Satwant Singh and Surinder's tried to convince her not to go through with her plans to marry Satwant Singh. They argued that she would have to live with the decision for the rest of her life and capital punishment for Satwant Singh was inevitable, they also knew that the death sentence was approaching and could be declared anytime. She was stubborn in her conviction and would not budge, she was determined to get married to Satwant Singh and refused to change her plans. The wedding took place as a normal Sikh wedding, with both families in presence, the only difference was that a photograph of Satwant Singh enacted his role, in his physical absence, but Satwant Singh was happy that his wedding took place like this. Satwant Singh later distributed sweets to his fellow inmates, celebrating his wedding. To see photos of this historic wedding please see page 288.

On the 18th June 1988 Surinder Kaur went to visit Satwant Singh in Tihar Jail, Delhi, she was convinced that she would now be allowed to visit her husband. The prison officials still refused her entry and said that they could only allow her to visit when they had received documentation from the District SSP (police officer) stating that she had actually got married to Satwant Singh. Tarlok Singh, Satwant Singh's father pleaded with the prison officials to allow Surinder Kaur to visit Satwant and he argued that their claims of not knowing about their marriage were spurious as their marriage had been well documented in the media. In the end Satwant Singh's parents visited him whilst Surinder Kaur waited outside. On a later date they returned with proof from the SSP that the wedding had taken place and the prison officials after seeing the proof said that they had to get approval from their superiors to allow Surinder Kaur visit and they again refused her entry. Surinder Kaur was never granted her wish of meeting her husband.

In December 1988 the government had made all necessary preparations to hang Satwant Singh and Kehar Singh,[58] on the 6th January 1988 at 8am they were both hanged to death. Even on the final family visit of 5th January 1988, Surinder Kaur was not allowed to visit Satwant Singh.

Surinder Kaur remained true to her promises of lifelong commitment to Satwant Singh, after his martyrdom she carried on living with Satwant Singh's family. She contracted cancer and died on 26th December 2000. She said she is going to the next world and will be united with her husband. Surinder Kaur will be remembered the world over as the wife who got married to her husband's photo, yet never even met her husband when once married. Surinder Kaur's and Satwant Singh's story is one of true love and of the commitment of a wife, which is one in a million.

God's Army

The Khalsa is described by Sri Guru Gobind Singh Jee as the army of the Timeless Lord, thus the Khalsa will fight for all just causes and see this as servitude to God. I will give examples of this exemplary trait of being such selfless warriors and those that are truly gifted with this

---

[58] Kehar Singh was arrested and charged in the assassination of Indira Gandhi, he was charged with conspiracy charges and aiding and abetting, Satwant Singh and Beant Singh. There was no concrete evidence on Kehar Singh, only circumstantial evidence was available and the basic prosecution case was that he was ideologically responsible for getting Satwant Singh and Beant Singh to assassinate Indira Gandhi.

extraordinary talent of wielding weapons, yet being very pious. Let us first start with Bhai Jugraj Singh the Tornado,

Shaheed Bhai Jugraj Singh Jee A.K.A. Toofan - K.L.F.[59]
(Translated from notes from the diary of Shaheed Bhai Bagel Singh Jee - K.C.F.[60] and an article written by Kamal Jeet Singh Choorchak Preet).

Shaheed Bhai Jugraj Singh Jee "Toofan" (the Tornado) was born at village Cheema Kudi, District Batala, Punjab - in the house of the virtuous and hardworking, Sardar Mohinder Singh and Mata Harbans Kaur Jee, he was born in 1971. Toofan was an only son and had 5 sisters. He was only 6 years old when he took Amrit and he regularly meditated, prayed and read about Sikh History from this young age. He was softly spoken and well-mannered.

Toofan was about 14 years old at the time of Operation Blue Star, he could not stand to see these attacks on the faith and nation of Sikhs and he was deeply moved. These events gave birth to thoughts of fighting against tyranny and oppression and he decided that he would revenge these sacrileges. Toofan was very close to Bhai Dharam Singh Jee Babbar Kanshtheevaal, with whom many actions were carried out.

From 1984 to April 1990 Bhai Jugraj Singh continuously fought in the battle against oppression, fighting for justice. According to the wishes of Guru Kalgidar (the 10th Guru), Toofan kept arms as a Saint-Soldier, became a Khalsa and stayed within the disciplines of Gursikhi. Toofan punished

---

[59] Khalistan Liberation Force
[60] Khalistan Commando Force

countless enemies of the Panth and he looked after the poor and powerless. The Sikh Panth is a Panth of Shaheeds, Sri Guru Gobind Singh Jee revealed the Khalsa and made them Saint-Soldiers, due to the peaceful martyrdom's given earlier. Shaheedi is a priceless gift but it should be pure:

'The death of brave heroes is blessed,
if it is approved by God.'
(Sri Guru Granth Sahib Jee Ang 579)

Shaheedi according to the wishes of Guru Kalgidhar Jee is the accepted Shaheedi, a true Shaheed according to the Khalsa tradition is one who is sacrificed for the welfare of faith or one that becomes Shaheed whilst fighting oppressors.

Bhai Jugraj Singh Jee Toofan did not kill innocent people, loot, steal, or bully anyone into anything. He made his Shaheedi with no given reward in mind, nor did he perform Seva with any reward in mind. He cleared his locality of thieves and criminals, he put many thieves to justice. Those Hindu families who had fled from their villages, out of fear of communal tensions, were reinstated into their original homes and Toofan ensured that they were safely resettled[61]. This is why Toofan was respected and loved by all, in his locality he was referred to as a *'freedom fighter'* *whom reinstated their freedoms in many ways.*

Toofan was arrested and he spent some time in Sangrur and Hoshiarpur jails, even whilst in jail, he inspired others. Whilst in jail he taught others about Sikhi and even made friends and supporters of the movement whilst in jail. Toofan played his role in many important actions for the

---

[61] Some Hindus fled Punjab in fear of reprisals from Sikhs as the government was trying to stir communal tensions between the two communities

Sikh Cause and his main aim was to eliminate the oppressors. S.S.P. Gobind Ram was a notorious enemy of the Sikhs, he falsely arrested and tortured and murdered countless Sikhs. He was famous for saying to Sikhs under torture "that you have had the Amrit of Guru Gobind Singh but now take the Amrit of Gobind Ram," he was of such a disgraceful nature. Toofan along with his colleagues and Jathedar Bhai Gurjant Singh Budhsinghvala made plans to eliminate this tyrant; to eliminate such a person was no easy task. He and his colleagues thought up a very daring plan in which they would explode a bomb in Gobind Ram's office. The bombing went to plan and Gobind Ram was blown to smithereens, not even a limb of Gobind Ram was recoverable and the police had to make an effigy of Gobind Ram to perform the funeral.

On the 8ᵗʰ April 1990 Bhai Jugraj Singh Jee Toofan was martyred. The B.S.F. and police took his body away immediately. In protest to his martyrdom 20,000 people surrounded the police headquarters of Hargobindpur on the day of his Shaheedi and demanded that his body be released from government control. Again new records were set on the day of Bhai Jugraj Singh's funeral when 200,000 to 300,000 people attended the funeral at village Cheema Kudi. Such large gatherings are rare in the history of Shaheeds. The gathering of 200,000 - 300,000 people blessed Bhai Jugraj Singh Toofan with the title of Amar Shaheed/Immortal Martyr.

Everyone knows that the ages of 14-15 years are one of lack of experiences/knowledge and teenage passions. For a teenage boy to have the great thoughts of Panthic Seva and Shaheedi, can only occur with the great grace of God. If we ignore the families of the Guru's for one moment, we will find very few examples of such an honourable and exemplary Shaheed. Bhai Jugraj Singh's love for Sikhi, selflessness and steadfastness can only be referred to as the blessings of the Almighty. Bhai Sahib is an exemplary role model of the modern era, whom fought and died in the battlefield fighting for the freedoms of all and everyone, his life gives us much inspiration and the power to persevere. Bhai Jugraj Singh was referred to as *'Baba Jee'(term of respect used for elders and the wise)* by people of his locality due to him being of high morality and a truthful character. He was very benevolent and merciful, he personally used to fund the weddings of the poor and spend thousands of Rupees on their weddings.

Bhai Jugraj Singh's Shaheedi teaches all Sikh youth to follow his exemplary traits, if we put the success of the movement first and make those who steal, murder or harass the innocent our targets; and if we stay within the limits of Sikhi when doing this; then all people of the world will support the Sikh cause. The dislike of the Khalistan movement will be eradicated and we will gain success in a shorter and quicker period.

Sikhs are only to fight against tyranny and oppressors, no Sikh warrior should instigate fear into anyone. Sikhs are to make themselves successful by earning the respect and love of all; they should be shining examples of *"The Khalsa is The Timeless Lord's Army"* as was Bhai Jugraj Singh Jee. To see a photo of this inspirational warrior please see page 288.

Shaheed Bhai Gurjant Singh Budhsinghvala, Chief of Khalistan Liberation Force (KLF)
Bhai Gurjant Singh was born in 1964 to Sardar Nashatar Singh & Mata Surjeet Kaur, in Faridkoth District, near Baghapurana, village Budhsinghvala. Bhai Gurjant Singh was martyred in Ludhiana, model town extension when he was 28 years old on 29th September 1992.

His father – Jathedar Nashatar Singh had a common farmer's living. Sikhi was flourishing in the family for generations. Gurjant Singh had three brothers and a sister. He was the third-eldest out of the sons. He only studied to the 5th grade and he had to leave his studies, as his family needed him to work, as they were not that well off. Budhsinghvala was religious from a young age and met Sant Jarnail Singh Jee Khalsa Bhindra Vale on numerous occasions. He started helping around the house and started farming along with his brothers on the family farm. He never tired doing work and never lost faith whilst the family went through hardships, but was always in Chardi Kala (high spirits).

The government's carnage reached the Moga area and the Bibi Kahn Kaur Gurdwara was surrounded by armed police, indiscriminate firing was opened on the congregation and many were drenched in blood and attained Shaheedi. Budhsinghvala's paternal grandfather Bhai Kehar Singh was one of the Shaheeds of this incident, he had much affection for his grandfather. The Shaheedi of his grandfather had a deep effect upon his tender heart at the age of 18 years.

The government tyranny making its way throughout the Moga area, arrived at Bhai Sahib's village. Budhsinghvala was arrested and imprisoned in Ferozepur jail for one and a half years. He had just been released from jail when the police re-arrested him and his brother, Bhai Jagroop Singh for murder. In the ensuing interrogations of the police both Bhai Gurjant Singh and his brother were tortured severely. When they were released after 8 days of torture, they both could not walk and got home in the evening. On the same night the police re-entered their house and took their father, brother and paternal uncle into custody.

Budhsinghvala after undergoing all this oppression and torture, decided to live the life of serving the Panth and left his home, to protect and fight for the rights of the people of Punjab. A tornado of fighting for justice was invested within him by the authorities, due to their torture and oppression across Punjab. From the outset Budh Singh worked alongside Bhai Varyam Singh Khapia Vale - after his Shaheedi he worked under the leadership of Bhai Aroor Singh of K.L.F. Slowly, slowly his fame grew due to the missions he completed and the enemy started to fear for their safety. When the enemy used to hear the name of Budhsinghvala they used to shiver with fear. Bhai Gurjant Singh became the Chief of the Khalistan Liberation Force (K.L.F.), after the Shaheedi of Bhai Avtar Singh Brahma in 1987. Under his leadership K.L.F completed numerous successful missions and became one of the leading freedom fighting outfits. He was respected as a mastermind and one of the most intelligent Sikh freedom fighters.

A Nihang Sikh, who used to live in the same village as Bhai Gurjant Singh informed the police on numerous occasions of Bhai Sahibs actions and whereabouts. This informant helped the police arrest and torture Budhsinghvala on a number of occasions. Bhai Gurjant Singh was arrested and sent to Faridkoth jail on one of these occasions. Upon release from jail - on bail, instead of going home, he went directly to Shaheed Bhai Varyam Singh 'Khapia Vale' and became once again engrossed in Seva. He caught the Nihang informant and poured petrol over him and burnt him alive in the middle of the village. People of the surrounding area were happy and ecstatic at the elimination of this Nihang, who caused much distress to the inhabitants of the locality.

He started bringing many oppressors to justice and the police started to repeatedly harass the family of Budhsinghvala. His brothers were severely tortured and subsequently jailed. Bhai Sahib's sister's (Bibi Gurcharan Kaur's) family were tortured and harassed on a number of occasions. To try to detract Budhsinghvala from his Seva – the authorities used oppressive tactics of the worst kind. His paternal Uncle Chand Singh and paternal cousin Bhai Joga Singh were martyred in a fake police encounter. His mother, father, and brothers were also terrorised. But, Budhsinghvala was steadfast and did not retract an inch from his resolve.

After seeing the effectiveness of Budhsinghvala, the Punjab Director General of Police Ribeiro, got the most brutal Station House Officer (S.H.O) Mith Singh appointed at the Baga Purana Police station, which was adjoining to Budh Singh village in Thana Baga. The S.H.O made Bhai Gurjant Singh's family his target for meting out police brutality and this brute got the front iron gate from Bhai Sahib's house removed and placed it at the police station. He humiliated Bhai Gurjant Singh's father by dragging him by the hair, in the heat of the Punjabi summer in front of the police station and made a public display of torturing him. He challenged Budhsinghvala's father to *"go get your tiger of a son to come and face me, face to face."*

Budhsinghvala learnt of the atrocities meted out to his family, and after a while he made plans to avenge these evil actions. He along with his 3 associates Bhai Lakhvinder Singh Lakha village Dhole Ke, Ajmer Singh Lodhivaal and Bhai Darshan Singh Tarkhanbad, exterminated the S.H.O at the police station whilst he was under the guard of his bodyguards. After removing the S.H.O, Budhsinghvala and his associates fired at the police in the police station, but they locked themselves in, out of fear and did not dare to return fire. Bhai Gurjant Singh and his associates left the police station at 7.30am with such calmness and braveness, no police official had the courage to even follow the Singh's after they left. The newly appointed S.H.O got the very same iron-gate reinstated at Bhai Gurjant Singh's house.

He put many oppressors to justice and worked with Bhai Jarnail Singh Halvara (Sant Longowal assassin), Varinder Singh Daka, Amar Singh Maan, Binderjeet Singh Dune ke, Manjeet Singh Mini Baba Moga, Amrik Singh Dune Ke, Kulwant Singh Kukrana, Gurmit Singh Machaki, Manohar Singh Teera, whilst completing his missions. Budh Singh Vala and his associates eliminated the following oppressors: S.S.P Gobind Ram, S.S.P A.S.Brar - Patiala, S.P. Patiala - R.S Gill, S.P. Detective R.S.Tiwara, D.S.P Tara Chand Jagroan and in turn avenged the deaths of many Shaheeds.

Budhsinghvala also seriously injured the following oppressors: D.G.P Mangat, S.S.P Sumedh Saini, S.P Kehar Singh. Other prominent successes of Bhai Sahib were the Punjab Congress Vice President Lala Bagvan Das who was eliminated along with his bodyguards at Jaito, ex-treasurer Balwant Singh was eliminated in Chandigarh, Magistrate Goyal Moga was eliminated after getting his armed guards to surrender. The son of the S.S.P Des Raaj Sharma of Tarn Taran was kidnapped in order to get Budhsinghvala's associates freed from the police, this was the first time a hostage was taken for political demands in Punjab and Bhai Sahib's friends were freed.

There was a bounty/reward of 400,000RS upon his head. Budhsinghvala was one of the most wanted Sikh freedom fighters and he was believed to be the mastermind of many successful actions against the authorities. The Ludhiana police had received confirmed intelligence reports that Budhsinghvala and other freedom fighters were holding a meeting at Model town extension – in house no. 95. The police along with the assistance of the army at about 10pm surrounded the house and ordered the inhabitants of the house to open the gate, but the house owner replied that he had dignitaries in attendance. According to the police the Singh's tried to escape through the back of the house, but the police had already surrounded the house and opened fire on the Singhs, one Singh got injured in the firing. Budhsinghvala did once again try escaping but due to the heavy fire he was martyred. The police claimed in their press release that Bhai Sahib was martyred within the house but all other accounts of eyewitnesses said that Budhsinghvala was martyred about 50 meters from the house in an alleyway.

This police operation was carried out by the S.S.P of Ludhiana 'Chotpadhiea' & D.S.P D.S.Gill. There were large engravements made upon the grass around the house – where the police had entrenched themselves. The police did not return Bhai Sahibs body to his relatives.

Budhsinghvala was a freedom loving spirit who did not enter controversies with others and all Sikh Jathebandhis/Organisations respected him. He used to speak very little, due to which he was able to command K.L.F for a relatively long time (not giving vital intelligence away). Budhsinghvala was said to be wanted for 37 accomplished actions by the police.

The people began to admire and respect Bhai Gurjant Singh more and more as time went by, as he was extremely against thieves and robbery and he put numerous such thieves to justice. He attained Shaheedi on 29th July 1992 at the age of 28 years. The Panth will never forget the

service he rendered.   See page 288 for photos of
Budhsinghvala and his brothers who were martyred.

Sant Bhindranvale

Sant Jarnail Singh Bhindranvale is portrayed by the
Indian Government as the terrorist who started the Sikh
insurgency, yet the Sikhs have awarded him with the title
of the Greatest Sikh of the 20th Century.   I will quote
directly from a speech made by Sant Bhindranvale which
portrays his saintly qualities;

*"I have no enmity with the Hindus as such.   If I were their
enemy, why would I rescue the daughter of a Hindu from
Jalalabad.   A Hindu young man forcibly kidnapped the
daughter of Hukam Chand, a Hindu.   In an assembly of ten
thousand people, coming to the stage he started crying and
said,*

*"Sant Ji, you are the sevadar (servant) of Damdami
Taksal.   In old times, Sikhs used to rescue the daughters of
Hindus. A Hindu has kidnapped my young unmarried
daughter."*

If I discriminated (against Hindus), I would have said,
"Get off this stage. Go and tell the Hindus (to help you)."

*But no, the duty of a Guru's Sikh is expressed by the
phrase, "Nanak says, Through God's Name one is in high
spirits (Chardi Kala); there is good for all in accepting
your will." We have always followed this.   It was about 12
noon when I told him from the stage in Jalalabad, which is
near Fazilka, that by 5 o'clock his daughter would reach
his home, if his statements were true and there was no
other confusion.   I assigned this task to Mohinder Singh
Sahianwala.   Khalsa Ji, the girl was brought and handed
over to the   Hindu by quarter to five.*

Kailash Chandar owns a retail shop here. His shop was burnt down. The Retail Merchants Union asked him, "Name Bhindranvala." He did not do so. The Hindu along with two Sikhs, the three of them, came to see me in my room. He came and started to cry, I asked him, "What is the matter? Why are you crying?" He said, "My shop has been burnt down." I asked him what he wanted from me, he said, "If you give me about a hundred rupees, it will give me the excuse for making a collection." I gave him five hundred rupees.

In Kapurthala, a copy of Ramayana (a Hindu holy scripture) was burnt. The leaders of that place know about this. The Jatha (Bhindranvale's organisation) spent 5,000 rupees in litigation over that (to get the culprits punished).

On the 4th (April 1983), two Hindus were martyred in connection with the "Stop the Traffic" Campaign (part of the Dharam Yudh Morcha). Shiromani Akali Dal and the Shiromani Gurdwara Parbandhak Committee paid (their families) 10,000 rupees each and the Jatha gave another 5,000 to each family.... (extracts from a speech delivered at the Annual Conference of the AISSF, 20th September 1983, translated by Ranbir Singh Sandhu).

All the above is the antithesis of how the Indian government portrayed and still attempt to portray Sant Bhindranvale. To see photos of Sant Jee & Bhai Surinder Singh Sodhi, please see page 289.

Bhai Surinder Singh "Sodhi"

Sant Bhindranvale declared that his right arm had been chopped off on the day that Bhai Surinder Singh Sodhi was assassinated. Sodhi was a very close confidant of Sant Bhindranvale and he was wanted by the authorities prior to Operation Blue Star. He was assassinated by a man and a woman who had been sent by the Akalis, and he fell to their bullets on 14th April 1984. He was a very talented man who had completed many secret missions for Sant Bhindranvale.

Once he had been on a mission for Sant and the location he was in, got surrounded by police. The police cordoned off the area so that he could not escape. He had a motorbike but could not advance, due to the police presence, so he scoured the area for alternative routes and he found a railway line. The only way he could escape would be by riding his motorbike very skilfully along a single beam on the rail track, he did this and he escaped unscathed. This trick of Sodhi became folklore in Punjab, of how such Singhs were talented and endowed with extraordinary skills.

He was also very skilful in using an array of weapons and vehicles, it is stated that he could drive anything with wheels and he could even pilot aircraft. He was the only Singh prior to Operation Blue Star who could fire anti-tank missiles, thus his loss just before the attack was critical as the Singhs did have anti-tank missiles but they could not use them as no-one else knew how to fire them adeptly.

Shaheed Bhai Davinder Singh "Baba"

Bhai Davinder Singh was born in Village Chabeval, near Singpur Village, Hoshiarpur. His involvement in the insurgency started when he joined AISSF, he then went on to join the BTF (Sangha group), he was jailed numerous times and he escaped to Germany to get away from police persecution. He went back to India and began supplying arms to Singhs of various militant outfits, especially those aligned to the Sohan Singh Panthic Committee. He was captured by the police and he allegedly took cyanide, this is according to Police sources. The police said his martyrdom would be a massive blow to KCF (Panjwar), KLF, BTF. The greatness of Bhai Davinder Singh was his hunger for the freedom of the Sikhs, he left Germany where he could have easily settled but he chose to return and re-enter the battlefield. He was a resource to a number of militant outfits and was respected by one and all. Please see photo at page 289. (Translated from an article by Bhai Ranvir Singh – Southampton, UK)

Shaheed Bhai Amarjit Singh "Billa" (6.11.67 – 29.6.93)
Bhai Amarjit Singh was born in Village Begowal, Kapurthala. He got involved in the insurgency by first joining the AISSF he then went on to become a member KCF (Panjwar). He had the chance to escape from India as he had two brothers in USA, his family pressured him to leave India, and thus he went to Nepal in preparation to leave India. But he could not leave, his heart was really in staying and he returned to Punjab. He had a 5 Lakh (500,000 Rs) reward on his head and on the 29th June 1993 near Sri Hargobindpur he had an encounter with the Police and attained martyrdom. Like Bhai Davinder Singh Baba, Billa had the chance to have a settled life abroad but his commitment to the freedoms of Sikhs could not deter him. He knew of the risks of staying and in the end, he did not falter in his principles and stayed true to his true love – to fight and die for the upholding righteousness and freedom.

Shaheed Bhai Gurdev Singh Debu
Bhai Gurdev Singh Debu was born in Village Dheerpur, Jalandhar. He attended a Gurmat Camp organised by Sant Bhindranvale & Bhai Amrik Singh that was held in Darbar Sahib from 26th - 31st Dec 1983, where the attendants were educated on Sikh History, Sikh way of Life and the teachings of Gurbani. He went on to join the AISSF and enthusiastically took part in the activities of

AISSF. On the 2nd March 1984 at the conference of AISSF of District Jalandhar, which was held at Mata Gujri Gurdwara, Debu was appointed the President of the Kartarpur zone of AISSF. After this he never returned home again, due to his prominence in AISSF, his family was continually harassed, persecuted and tortured by the Police, he would have been an easy catch if he were to return home.

Sant Bhindranvale appointed him the Seva of collating old and worn Sri Guru Granth Sahib Saroops to take to Goindval Sahib, to get there cremations performed. Whilst doing this Seva, Operation Blue Star occurred. He participated in the co-ordinated attacks on train stations where a number of train stations had fires started to disrupt the state owned train services and he showed that the Sikhs are by no means finished, but are still as defiant as before. He escaped to Pakistan and upon his return his photo and his colleagues' photos, were broadcast on TV showing them as dangerous terrorists, wanted by the state. He was a member of KCF, which was then under the leadership of Manbir Singh Chaheru.

He was appointed the Doaba Zone Commander (Hoshiarpur, Kapurthala, Jalandhar) of KCF. He had countless police encounters and he played cat and mouse with the security forces on a number of occasions, and escaped safely from each encounter. He was drugged by a friend's family, they drugged his milk which made him unconscious and subsequently he was brutally killed by the police. Ordinary people gathered in trolleys, tractors, buses outside the police station, demanding Debu's body. His body was handed over due to the protests – but when it was handed over it wore horrific scars that proved Debu had been horrendously tortured; he had been boiled alive. His thighs were cut open in many places and had been filled with chillis. One eye had also been removed. All who saw the body were shocked to see the effects of the inhumane torture and could not comprehend how other human beings could commit such heinous torture. Such tortures are heard of in medieval times but this torture and martyrdom, shows how backward the so-called biggest democracy in the world can be. To see photos of Bhai Gurdev Singh Debu & his torture, see page 289.

Shaheed Bhai Ravinder Singh Babbar

Bhai Ravinder Singh was an active member of Babbar Khalsa and had exemplary traits, those families that Bhai Ravinder Singh stayed with (whilst underground), all say that he did not come and stay as a guest or issue orders, he became like a member of the family and even helped around the house. For a period of two months, he was told to stay in Gurdaspur amongst the relatives of a Singh in the Babbar Khalsa high command. The families were not Gursikhs and the men were drunks and gamblers. It was because of this that the families would not be suspected and could hide Bhai Ravinder Singh. It seemed like a difficult task for a Gursikh to live in such an environment, but Bhai Ravinder Singh did not complain. He continued with his meditations as normal and his humble personality drew everyone close to him. Bhai Ravinder Singh left such an impression on the families, that they all became initiated at the next Amrit Sanchar (Sikh initiation ceremony) and became practising Sikhs. The Singh in the high command of Babbar Khalsa was humoured by this and said that he had not been able to influence his relatives all his life, not due to a lack of effort, yet Bhai Ravinder Singh had transformed them in just two months. (https://www.1984tribute.com/shaheed-bhai-ravinder-singh-bagga/)

Shaheed Bhai Kulwant Singh Gumti

Bhai Kulwant Singh Gumti was an insurgent loved and respected by many Sikh militant groups and those fighting for freedoms through political means. He was a leading member of the AISSF and did Seva in a number of militant outfits. He masterminded the kidnapping of a Romanian Diplomat to free some of his colleagues who were imprisoned. The diplomat once freed said that he was treated very well and that he respected their cause, although many argue that the kidnapping was not successful in achieving its aim of getting the Singhs freed, it did have a wider strategic impact, which was to raise the international coverage of the Sikh insurgency and raise the issues of the freedom struggle to a wider audience. I will now give a few examples of incidences in the life of Gumti which will inspire readers and display the true nature of such gifted souls.

Dirty songs in Bus

A brother and sister from Phool used to go to College together. One day both of them and other female students were travelling in a private bus to college. The driver started playing songs which contained lewd lyrics and the brother got up and asked the driver to turn the music off and show some respect to the sisters on board. The driver became confrontational and slapped the brother and the conductor tried throwing him off the bus.

The boy got off the bus at College and went straight up to Bhai Kulwant Singh Gumti who was weight-lifting at the time. Gumti went with the brother and set up a checkpoint, on the road, outside the college. Every bus that passed that was owned by the same bus-company was halted and the driver and conductors were locked in a room in the college. At about 4pm the bus upon which the incident had occurred showed up, similarly the bus was emptied and driver and conductor locked up. The female students made a positive identification of the bus driver and conductor. By now, in all, 9 buses had been halted. The culprits were given a rewarding beating and the other drivers/conductors were released and were told to send the owners of the bus company to the college.

The Principal, staff and students of the college were determined to get justice, the SDM Phool and DSP Phool were present and were trying to negotiate the release of the buses and driver and conductor. In response Gumti asked those trying to negotiate, *"Would you accept the disrespect of your sisters in a similar fashion?"* The police officers were silenced by this question.

At about 6pm the owner of the bus company arrived at the College, he made an apology for the insult caused by his staff and immediately terminated the employment of the bus driver and conductor. Bhai Kulwant Singh Gumti said, "We have already punished the drivers and you have apologised for playing such songs in your buses. It is not necessary to terminate their employment and put their livelihood in jeopardy, just change the bus route that they work on." Gumti was firm and fair, reflecting true Sikh principles.

Opportunity Knocks
        Bhai Kulwant Singh Gumti was arrested and the authorities started taking him to Dayalpura, which was renowned for torturing prisoners, by chance the van in which he was being transported had an accident. One of the officers died on the scene and another officer was injured but fortunately Gumti did not receive a single scar. The Thanedar's (officers) legs were broken and he pleaded, *"I'll open your handcuffs, please help me and don't run away."* Gumti replied, "The Guru's Sikhs always help the

needy and never run away from those in need, like cowards, like you."

Gumti then ripped all of his clothes up to make bandages to cover the wounds of the officers. He gathered their weapons and stopped the next bus that went by and took it to the Phool Courts where he was going to be presented in Court. He placed all the weapons of the officers in front of the judge and he told the judge about the injured officers. He also donated his own blood in the same hospital where the officers were admitted.

In 1989, Gumti came out of jail on bail and was appointed the leader of the AISSF after the assassination of Harminder Singh Sandhu. He went underground and did Seva in Saffron Tigers of Khalistan and then became a General in the Khalistan National Army. He founded a new Jathebandi in 1991, with a press release dated 5th Oct 1991 which was called the Liberation Tigers of Khalistan. In the press release it was stated that full support would be given to the Sikh Students Federation Presidium for its programmes of political and religious reforms.

Gumti was upset by needless killings and on the 5th November 1991 he made a press statement that his militant brothers should take the battle out of the villages and take it straight to Delhi (i.e. to the Central Government). Within a week he took responsibility for the kidnapping of the Romanian diplomat Radu.

He was martyred on the night of 12/13th March 1992 after a 6 hour encounter with the Police/Security Forces. 15,000 people managed to attend the funeral, even though the Police set up road blocks in many places. Gumti's mother was given a golden medal on behalf of the Liberation Tigers of Khalistan. Babbar Khalsa gave her a gold medal at Vaisakhi. Many Bhogs were held in foreign countries on the 22nd March 1992. ISYF UK did 11 Akhand Paths continuously and the Bhog was on 2nd May 1992 in London.

Shaheed Bhai Davinder Singh "Baba" AKA Bhai Gurcharan Singh Jee

Bhai Surinder Singh was a leading member of the AISSF and he later became actively involved in KLF. He was seen to be the right hand man of Bhai Gurjant Singh Budhsinghvala. In Village Bahla, Hoshiarpur a 101ft high Nishan Sahib has been erected in memory of Baba.

Torture - When he was captured by the police, he just kept on reciting Sri Japji Sahib whilst being tortured and the Police were getting increasingly frustrated. He kept on reciting prayers out loud, yet would not answer anything when questioned. He remained true to his word and did not answer any of their questions and attained martyrdom on the 5th October 1988 and the police fabricated a story about a fake encounter in Village Beeka, Jalandhar.

Protests - Protests against this merciless killing were held across Punjab, many schools and colleges closed for 3 days and exams were boycotted. Many Jathebandhis gave statements in favour of Baba and criticised the manner in which he was executed in a fake encounter, these included AISSF, Ad-hoc Committee, BKI, KCF and KLF. To see a photo of Baba, please see page 289.

Shaheed Bhai Anokh Singh Babbar

After the 1978 massacre, Nirankaris were punished in Patti & Tarn Taran in which the name of Anokh Singh began to be mentioned.

Bravery

Bhai Anokh Singh was told by Singhs close to him that he should leave Punjab as the police knew what he looked like. He refused and was martyred within a year. He was caught and tortured to death. Facing up to the daily reality of being caught and killed, takes bravery, especially when one has access to escape routes and decides rather to face death head on, not shying away from it.

Spiritual Prowess

One could raise the sleeve of Anokh Singh, put their ear on his arm and hear the word "Vaaheguroo" (wonderful enlightener) vibrating. Before going underground Bhai Surinder Singh Nagoke had an Akhand Paath (recital of Sri Guru Granth Sahib) at home, Anokh Singh sat through the 48 hours of the Paath from start to end in one position.

On one occasion, Anokh Singh & some other Singhs were being pursued by the police and therefore split up. Bhai Amarjit Singh went onto his roof to see what was happening, the police had surrounded the village and started conducting searches. Amarjit Singh went up on to the rooftop again 2 hours later and saw Anokh Singh sitting cross-legged in a field of wheat immersed in Simran (meditation), police got closer and closer, they were 5 feet away from Anokh Singh but could not see him. Amarjit Singh was sure that Anokh Singh could see the police but he did not flinch. He could not believe his eyes, he could see Anokh Singh from his rooftop through the darkness of the night but the police could not see him from only 5 feet away. Amarjit Singh was subsequently arrested by the police. Some days later they met up and Anokh Singh refused to discuss the matter and just replied that it is in Satguru's will, we cannot comprehend His wondrous ways.

A group of Singhs were travelling with Anokh Singh and police were in pursuit of them. They got to the river bank and could not cross it as it was flooded with excess water. Anokh Singh performed an Ardas (supplication prayer) and after the Ardas the water level lowered to their knees and they crossed the river with ease.

Panth's money

Anokh Singh's brother had a son and Anokh Singh gave him 2 Rupees as a present and his sister-in-law was annoyed and said: *"Brother Anokh Singh, you are such an infamous militant and at the birth of your brother's son, all you are giving is 2 Rupees?"* Anokh Singh saw the annoyance of his sister-in-law and replied, *"Even this money seems a too much to me. These 2 Rupees are the Panth's property and I don't want that my family's newborn should use any of the Panth's money."*

Rehras Sahib & Torture

Anokh Singh was finally arrested by Jalandhar police, whilst riding his bike. He was brought to Vairoval Police Station (Amritsar) and brutally tortured, his hip was broken and using a bayonet his eyes were plucked out.

After being tortured Anokh Singh was lying semi-consciously on the floor, quietly recuperating, when he asked one of the guards what time it was. The guard replied it is 7.15pm, Anokh Singh replied, *"It is then time for Rehras Sahib,"* and he immediately began his daily evening recital. He sung it in a sweet voice and conducted his Ardas whilst on the floor (due to the torture[62]), he could not see, as his eyes had been removed by this point. He ended his Ardas with a roaring Jakara (war cry) that echoed

---

[62] The Ardas is conducted in a standing position, Anokh Singh had to conduct his Ardas from the floor as he could not stand due to the severe torture he had undergone.

throughout the police station, showing that no matter what the odds the Khalsa is never down and out. To the contrary the Khalsa is always ideologically victorious regardless of the circumstances, this never die spirit was infused by the 10th Guru in 1699 and the conflagration of this flame burns on forever and grows stronger by the blood of new Shaheeds/Martyrs.

The police officer who had told Anokh Singh the time, watched all this in amazement and immediately tendered his resignation. He said to the SSP on duty, *'I can't do this job that forces people to kill Saints ... I can't ... I can't'* He kept on repeating. The SSP cursed, *'They are all magicians ... another one of our officers has left the service because of this Paath.'*

Torture & Shaheedi

Whilst meditating, Anokh Singh's tongue was cut off with a metal saw, the blood streamed over his handsome face and through his beard. Metal bars that were 2 feet in length were heated and then hammered from the souls of his feet, up to his knees. The heated rods were then poked through his chest and one was put through his skull. Anokh Singh withstanding all this torture, only had one Ardas which was that he did not falter/compromise his principles, this Ardas was fulfilled and in the end the torturers shot him dead. His body was thrown into the River Beas and the torture was overseen by SSP Azhar Alam. (https://www.1984tribute.com/shaheed-bhai-anokh-singh-babbar/ & "So Kaheeat Hai Soora" – Sept 2004)

Bhai Palvinder Singh Boorevaal
AKA Bhai Bhupinder Singh Bhinda (4.6.67 – 1.6.90)

Bhai Palvinder Singh Booreval was one of the leading members of the AISSF in Kapurthala. He was the President of the AISSF at the Randhir College, Kapurthala.

On the 29th January 1987 Booreval, his brother and a friend were all travelling to College when they were stopped and searched by the Police & CRPF, who tried to then arrest them. Booreval pushed off the CRPF officers and made a run for it. The Police opened fire and started to pursue him. He got to the State Gurdwara Sahib and the Police surrounded the Gurdwara, the news of this, spread like wildfire across the city. AISSF organised immediate demonstrations and got all the schools and colleges in the locality shut down, out of protest. The protestors also started shouting anti-police slogans. Under the command of DSP Shabra the Kapurthala police entered the Gurdwara with their shoes on and fired 30/40 shots inside.

The police arrested Bhai Palvinder Singh and took him to the Sadar Police station Kapurthala, where he was mercilessly tortured, his only crime being that he was a lead member of the AISSF. AISSF Kapurthala/Jalandhar zone then organised demonstrations for the next few days and caused traffic jams in protest. Booreval was produced in court a few days later and fabricated charges were made and he was sent to Kapurthala Jail. Booreval went onto join KCF Panjwar and finally joined Babbar Khalsa and attained Shaheedi on the 1st June 1990 when he was shot down in public, by the police in the Chandigarh Rose Garden. He did not return fire when shot at by the police, as an informant had informed the police of Booreval visiting the Rose Garden thus the Police who were in civilian clothes mercilessly shot down Bhai Palvinder Singh in cold blood and a premeditated manner. In short, he was murdered. The Punjab Police murdered thousands of Sikh Youth in a similar cold blooded manner and did not undergo any criminal investigations, regardless of the anguish raised by families of victims and human rights agencies across the globe.

Baba Manochahal

In the early days of the movement, Baba Gurbachan Singh kept a hideout in the swamps of the Mand area. Here he set up some huts for habitation and also a separate hut for Guru Granth Sahib, a Gurdwara. Manochahal would sleep on the floor and every day wake up at Amrit vela and do two hours of naam abhyaas (meditation). After which he would complete his very long Nitnem (daily prayers) and recite from Guru Granth Sahib. Manochahal daily completed five Sukhmani Sahibs even in the thick of battle. Baba Jee even held Amrit Sanchars at this small dera for those who wanted to become initiated as Khalsa. (Amardeep Singh Amar)

Bhai Gurdev Singh Usman Vala

The police who tortured Usman Vala to death were shocked by his spiritual prowess, they tortured him inhumanely, yet he would not reveal any information. When the torture got so bad that Usman Vala fell unconscious and was nearly dead, the custody officers report that they could hear Mool Mantar (meditation of the first verse of Sri Guru Granth Sahib) vibrating from his bodily hairs and they report that he attained martyrdom in this state and they could hear the Mool Mantar until he breathed his last.

From Muslim to Babbar ; Bhai Lachman Singh Babbar

(Based on an article by Amardeep Singh Amar, Fatehnama May 2005, translated by Balpreet Singh (https://saintsoldiers.net/bhai-lachman-singh-babbar/ and https://www.1984tribute.com/shaheed-bhai-lachman-singh-babbar/)

Conversion

DSP Sukhdev Chahal of Mansa Police, entrusted his personal bodyguard Bashir Mohammed to infiltrate the

Babbars as they were causing havoc in the Mansa area. He was used as an infiltrator as the DSP thought he would definitely not have any sympathy for the Sikh resistance movement, as he was Muslim.

Bashir started spending time with Singhs, although at first he would send regular reports to the police, after a while he started to develop a deep respect for the Singhs. The Singhs would rise at Amrit Vela (before dawn), meditate and do Nitnem together, their love in reciting Banee (scriptures) and their faith in Vaaheguroo impressed Bashir. The Singhs had complete love and respect for one another and were willing to sacrifice their all, for their brothers.

Bashir Mohammed spent time with Bhai Rashpal Singh, Bhai Gurmel Singh and came into contact with Bhai Dharam Singh Kashteevaal and Bhai Vadhava Singh. Bashir had taken the Sikh identity to infiltrate the group, but was now beginning to feel Sikhi in his heart. He felt he was a traitor to his own conscience by being an informant. After being troubled for some time, despite the risk of death, Bashir told Bhai Gurmel Singh that he was an informant of the Punjab Police and a Muslim. Bashir explained that he could no longer continue the act of informing and wanted to dedicate his life to Sikhi and fight for Sikh Liberation.

He was given time to reconsider and think through his decision, subsequently he took Amrit and became Bhai Lachman Singh Babbar. After participating in the movement he moved to Calcutta with his wife Bibi Rani Kaur. On May 17 1993, Bhai Lachman Singh & Bibi Rani Kaur were martyred. The Police party led by DSP Chahal opened indiscriminate fire for 15 minutes on their apartment and both of them were martyred; Bibi Rani Kaur was pregnant at the time.

9. Mission Impossible

Mission Impossible is Possible

The word impossible does not exist in the Sikh dictionary. Baba Deep Singh proved this when in 1757 AD he valiantly fought on in battle whilst being decapitated, some may question this feat and indeed they do. But the Sikhs have a firm belief that spiritual prowess can defy science and the laws of nature, for example Sri Guru Arjan Dev Jee states:

The True Guru can kill and revive the dead
(Ang 1142 SGGSJ)

If we are to believe that the Guru can revive the dead, surely, He can keep Baba Deep Singh alive for a little longer, so he fulfils his vow to free the Golden Temple from the control of Ahmed Shah Abdalis forces and remain in battle until he reaches the Golden Temple. Similarly many said that the Sikhs would not be able to bring about the death of Indira Gandhi but her Sikh bodyguards caused her eventual demise. Similarly one of the army generals who were in charge of Operation Blue Star, General Vaidiya was assassinated by two Sikhs. I will now concentrate on telling their story.

Bhai Harjinder Singh "Jinda" and Bhai Sukhdev Singh "Sukha" got revenge for the attack on the Golden Temple by assassinating General Vaidiya, he was one of the 3 Indian Army Generals who co-ordinated the army assault. Sukha & Jinda were first actively involved in the AISSF and their close associates included Shaheed Bhai Mathra Singh, Bhai Nirmal Singh (still alive) and Bhai Daljit Singh Bittu (still alive and active in Punjab Politics).

Sukha and Jinda had made their way to Pune, as they had learnt that General Vaidiya had retired there. They found the address of the General but when they went to the house, the General had moved to another house, the Singh's then asked one of the servants at the house, of the new address and they found out where he had moved to.

On the 19th August, 1986 at around 11am, they saw Vaidiya's wife come out with an umbrella and the General followed. Vaidiya himself was driving the car. He went to the bazaar and bought some household commodities. Sukha and Jinda were on a motorcycle following them. When Vaidiya was returning home after shopping, Jinda pulled the motorcycle beside the car and Sukha began to shoot. Vaidiya's head hit the wheel and his head was bleeding. The Singh's shouted Jakaras and made their getaway. The Singh's had also wanted to kill General Dayal another officer responsible for the attack, but decided now was not the time, he later died of natural causes but died a long protracted death and was riddled by disease, so he suffered for his deeds. They returned to the house they had rented, changed clothes and took a bus to Bombay. From there, they went to Durg and then Calcutta by train. Sukha & Jinda had a motorcycle that only started with a push-start, thus they had limited resources, but still, they bravely took the risk of assassinating the General. This motorbike was used in the Vaidiya's assassination also. They never lost hope and made the best of the resources they had. This truly exemplified their Chardi Kala (rising spirits).

On September 17, 1986, Sukha returned to Pune to get weapons that were left there. He along with another Singh got into an accident with a truck and they were arrested. They were tortured for five months, and were kept in leg irons for eighteen months.

While Jinda played cat and mouse with the police for a year. There was much media coverage of his near misses with the police, he was hunted all over India, yet would manage to escape from the clutches of the police. A year later (in 1987), Jinda and Bhai Satnaam Singh "Bawa" were arrested from Delhi at Gurdwara Majnoo Daa Tilla. Jinda was shot in the legs so he could not walk. The police tried to cut his leg off but a Bengali doctor refused to allow this. Jinda was tortured for four months and then taken to Pune. Bawa was handed over to the Punjab Police, who went on to kill him.

In Pune, Sukha and the other Singhs had finished doing Ardas after Rehras Sahib, and then shouted Jakaras. Jinda was in a nearby cell and also shouted Jakaras. Jinda had recognized Sukha's voice. Finally the two had been reunited. They stayed together from there on and will also be remembered in history together. They were subsequently martyred by being hanged to death.

I will now give examples from the letters of Sukha and Jinda which exemplify their extraordinary characteristics.

Fear of Singhs
Letter by Jinda, 27th October, 1989:

The day of the 21st October, 1989 was a day of great happiness for Khalistan. On that day, at 11 o'clock, we were taken from the jail to the courthouse. When we arrived at the courts, we were still in the car when the police came and told us that we would have to take our shoes off before entering the courthouse. We refused to take off our shoes. The judge was thinking that we might beat him to death with our shoes. We sent the judge a message that we would never do such a lowly thing and that if he had any doubts, he could have us handcuffed, but we would never remove our shoes. The judge agreed to what we said and did not even have us handcuffed.

Said no to reduction in sentence – happy at death sentence

We were presented in the courthouse. The judge came and met us especially, with folded hands. Right upon sitting down, the judge announced his not-guilty verdict for brother Nirmal Singh (he is still alive today and is currently employed by the SGPC as a bus driver in Amritsar). Then the judge said to us that we were guilty in the General Vaidiya case. The judge asked our lawyers about a reduced sentence but we had already forbidden them, that they should not negotiate anything. Then the lawyers came to us and asked if they could ask the judge to reduce our sentences. We said that they should not and that we ourselves would talk to him about it.

Jakaras at pronunciation of death sentence

The judge returned at 2.05pm and began to read the sentencing. At 2.17pm, Brother Sukhdev Singh was called to the stand and was awarded the death sentence. He accepted this award with Jakaras and slogans for Khalistan. Then Nirmal Singh was called to the stand and pronounced not guilty.

When the judge was reading his sentencing, his voice was shaking and his hands were trembling. He was having trouble speaking. The judge then called me to the stand. He also gave me the award of death. Just like brother Sukhdev, I too shouted Jakaras in happiness and shouted slogans for Khalistan and Sant Jarnail Singh Bhindranvale. We also thanked him for sending us to the gallows.

MISSION IMPOSSIBLE

Celebrating with eating sweets
We were then taken back to jail. We came back and began to distribute barfee (milk based sweets). When the people in the jail found out we had been sentenced to death, they did **not** eat them. So we ate them ourselves.

Judge troubled by sentencing;
"I did not want to sentence them to death. I had no choice. I have affection for them (Jinda and Sukha) from my heart. I have never met such people before. They are very good people. I will put up their photos in my house."

Self-realisation/true consciousness
How long can someone run along a wall? Its end will eventually come. Like this, life's limited breaths also finish. Whatever we see in the world, besides God, is transitory. The eternal and life-giving naam-nectar is pouring down everywhere, though. But it only falls in the mouths of those who are sanmukh (those continuously prostrating) to their Guru. Those who have attached their consciousness to the Guru's Banee (scriptures), their lives become sacred. They are accepted before God.

Self-conviction – admittance
Jinda also notes how their conviction was based on their own admissions. Of the 170 witnesses presented against them, only one managed to recognize Sukha. The rest were proven to be fakes and liars. The government's case was a total disaster.

Happiness at Hanging - 2ⁿᵈ October, 1992
That blessed hour which we were awaiting impatiently, for such a long time, will come at 4am on the 9ᵗʰ October, 1992. God has been very merciful to us. We consider ourselves very lucky. The preparations for your

249

brothers' weddings are complete but the world does not know about it (Singhs see Shaheedi as a wedding to death). Look at the fear of these rulers!

Audacity in Jail

Many times they tried to force us to wear prisoner uniforms, but we refused. We said, *"We don't accept your laws, so why should we wear prisoner's uniforms?"* We used to grab the Jail DIG and Superintendent by the neck and ripped many uniforms and slapped some other officials. We roughed them up with resolution. We humiliated them in every way. We have pushed them so far, that they start to shake just thinking about coming into our yard. (This is how caged tigers become, the Singhs of Guru Gobind Singh).

Gun in Jail & Bravery

Brothers, On the 22nd September 1992, our jail was turned into a police cantonment. On all four sides, commandos surrounded us. Our yard itself was surrounded by more than 100 commandos. At that time we were doing paath when suddenly they pounced. The jail DIG, IG (jail), Commissioner of Police Pune, three DSPs and many other officials came. They came to us and said that we should be handcuffed because they wanted to search our cells. We grabbed the DIG and the Superintendent by their necks and began to beat them all. We refused to be handcuffed and said they could search the place but could not touch anything. We would show them ourselves. We said, *"If you try to use force, until we have breath in our bodies we will not let you enter our rooms. If you have the strength to take us, come on."*

But they quickly accepted our conditions and said that we could show them everything. We knew why they had come. That police officer from whom we had asked for a weapon had been caught because of his misdeeds a couple days ago. The weapon had reached him, but for some reasons he could not get it to us. After the confirmation of the Vaidiya case in the Supreme Court, the jail had become very strict and because of this, he was afraid and his intentions changed. If he wanted, despite the strictness, he could have given it to us. No one comes to our yard and if someone does come, he is searched. But when we are in front of the guard room, the person on duty does not have the courage to search anyone. We used to give the prisoner that cleaned up our yard, letters we wanted taken out. That officer had the job of pressing clothes and we used to send that prisoner to him, to find out about the weapon. The prisoner knew everything and was even ready to bring it to us because we had given him some money. But we have found out the truth now, about why the police officer was not giving the weapon to us. He had given the weapon to some thug who began to commit robberies with it and when he was caught, he spilled everything. That police officer is now in remand. He has turned in four others from the jail that are also in remand. The newspapers were telling this story with extra zest and were saying that if Sukha and Jinda got the weapon, they would have escaped from jail. But this is not the case. We had a big tyrant in our sights and we think we would have been successful. If we weren't, the jail's DIG, Superintendent along with the deputy and senior jailer weren't going anywhere. We could have punished them any time we wanted.

3rd October, 1992

We don't know why the jailers have taken a hating to our clothes. Today, they came again with 20 or 25 police officers along with the jail's DIG. We were stubborn and said "Who's going to come forward first?" They want that we should be hung while wearing prisoner's uniforms. But we will try to go while wearing kesri dastaars, cholas and kachheras. We have full faith in Satguru Jee that our wish will be certainly fulfilled. (Baba Thakhur Singh Jee the former acting Jathedar of Damdami Taksal provided the clothes for the hanging of the Singh's, the Singh's wore these clothes from Baba Jee as they had much love and respect for him. After being hanged, when they were bathed for their funerals, clothes from both the families of the Singh's were put on for their final rites)

Inspiration – Karas
Today the police DSP came and asked for a Kara as a memento. We said, *"We'll give you the Kara, but then you're going to have to do good things with your hands."* He replied, *"I already do good things."* Two inspectors also took Karas.

Power to punish a tyrant
4ᵗʰ October, 1992
> *"For our principles, we must fight a war that has a high character. For those who travel this path, it is essential that they have a very high character. The right to punish a tyrant only goes to that Gurmukh (Guru Centred/orientated person) whose own life and character is much higher than that tyrant. Only by travelling on these lines will Satguru Jee have mercy on us. We have no strength of our own. Akaal Purakh will only give us power and strength if we stay within the divine principles [of Sikhi].*

Inspiration, Influence & Bravery
October 6, 1992
> The IG said, *"You are brave. Even after being so close to death, there is no sign of fear on your faces. There is in fact a glow."* I laughed and said, *"Otherwise you call us extremists and terrorists, and today you are calling us brave?"* The IG then replied, *"You two have some reason*

for which you are going to the gallows with laughter. We can say whatever we want about you, you are still lions." When leaving, he spoke very warmly and said, *"I will pray for you."* I said, *"Don't pray just for us, pray for the well being of everyone."* A lot of things were said, but because I don't have enough paper, I can't write them down.

High Spirits – Chardi Kala

Now let me tell you something funny. Yesterday or the day before, the jailer came and asked in a quiet voice, *"What is your final wish?"* I replied with a laugh, *"Hang the Superintendent in my place".* He laughed very hard. I told two jokes to the IG as well. One was the Superintendent one and the other was this: someone sentenced to hang is asked his final wish and he says, *"I want to eat a cantaloupe."* They reply, *"It's not the season for cantaloupes..."* The prisoner then says, *"That's ok, I can wait..."*

Celebration of Shaheedi/Martyrdom
6ᵗʰ October, 1992

No one should feel sad at our Shaheedi. This is a happy moment for all of us and we've prepared boondee [sweets] to distribute in celebration. We've always got so much love from all of you. It is because of all your Ardas's that today we are in total Chardi Kala.

Gidda before execution

Sukha's mother asked the girl family members who came to the hanging to do gidhaa - a traditional dance, performed usually at weddings and other happy occasions, as her son was going to be married tomorrow. Sukha & Jinda's mothers started the gidhaa first and others then joined them. These are inspirational Sikh women who dance and are in joy at the martyrdom of their sons, this takes real fortitude - Sikh fortitude. Before leaving, Jinda's mother took her son's face in her hands and said, *"Wherever you go, be happy. And know that I am proud of you."* She did not cry. Her face was red with emotion. I recently met Bhai Harjinder Singh Jinda's mother and when we met her and started talking, one of the first things she said was Singh's who were like diamonds were sacrificed in the insurgency. She did not give priority to mentioning her own son, but on the contrary, she was very complimentary of all Singh's who were martyred. She said that when Jinda left home to become an insurgent he only came home on one occasion and that was only for a few minutes, he never visited home again.

Day of Shaheedi -Thanks to Jailers
They dressed in white cholas (Sikh robe) with saffron dastaars (turbans) and kamarkassas (waistbands). Jinda shook hands with the jail officials and thanked them for keeping himself and Sukha for 5 years ... The two Singhs climbed the gallows with smiles. They had wanted to bring sweets for the executioners, but perhaps they were not allowed. They kissed their nooses and even though they wanted to put them around their own necks, were not allowed to do so. The time had come and according to Bhai Nirmal Singh, Jinda shouted loudly to Sukha, "Veer Sukhiaa! Roar a Fateh!" He then heard Jakaras. And then they stopped.[63] To see photos of Sukha & Jinda, please see page 290.

Spectacular End
In 1992 the Congress Party won the Punjab elections, Beant Singh was appointed the Congress Party Chief Minister. The combination of KPS Gill and Beant

---

[63] Based on the letters of Bhai Harjinder Singh Jinda and Bhai Sukhdev Singh Sukha, based upon translations by admin of www.tapoban.org

Singh created havoc among Punjabis; they are both accused by Human Rights Activists of violating basic human rights and making a lawless extermination of anyone suspected of being supportive of Sikh insurgents. The election success was partly down to the fact that the majority of the Sikh insurgents chose not to participate in the elections and sent out appeals to the masses to not vote, as they were arguing that they did not recognise the Indian state. This had disastrous effects on the insurgency with all leaders of all militant organisations being martyred by the end of 1993 (barring Daljit Singh Bittu who was imprisoned).

Beant Singh and KPS Gill were very proud of their new mantle of crushing the Sikh Insurgency. They thought they were invincible and had no idea that the Sikh Insurgents could still plan and deliver a strategic hit. On the 31st August 1995, Beant Singh was exploded along with 11 others, by Bhai Dilawar Singh (a human bomb). The bombing occurred in Chandigarh outside the Punjab and Haryana Secretariat. Bhai Dilawar Singh was a Punjab Police constable who had diligently acted out the role of a double agent and had successfully completed his mission of assassinating the Chief Minister.

The bombing sent out a clear signal that Sikhs were down but not out. It displayed that the Sikh insurgents may not be seen (openly) but they were definitely heard on the 31st August 1995. The bombing though did signal a return to peace for Punjab as it ended the days of terror that had been implemented by the coalition of Beant Singh and KPS Gill. It meant that Punjabis were no longer being ruled over by an iron fist and tyrannical policing reduced.

Much has been said about the bombing and the trial continues, 13 Sikhs were named as suspects 9 have been arrested they are Jagtar Singh Hawara, Jagtar Singh Tara, Paramjit Singh Bheora, Balwant Singh Rajoana, Gurmit Singh, Nasib Singh, Lakhwinder Singh, Navjot Singh, Shamsher Singh, 3 are absconding they are Vadhava Singh (current Chief of BKI), Mehal Singh (older brother of previous BKI Chief, Bhai Sukhdev Singh Babbar) and Jagroop Singh and the final suspect was Dilawar Singh who was martyred on the spot (to see an artist's impression of the bombing and photo of Dilawar Singh please see page 290). Some of the accused are alleged to be BKI operatives, whilst others are allegedly KLF members.

On the 19th March 2006 in the Special Court of the Burail Jail Chandigarh, Balwant Singh Rajoana admitted to being responsible for the assassination, he said Dilawar Singh was also guilty, but he argued that the other suspects had been falsely implicated. When making his statement in court he waved a flag of Khalistan, afterwards he handed over the flag and his written statement. The authorities are investigating how Rajoana managed to smuggle the flag into the prison and court.

The Great Escape
On the 22nd January 2004, a great escape from jail was made by three of the accused of the assassination of Beant Singh (Chief Minister). This great escape is something one hears of in Bollywood and Hollywood, and it still defies belief. Jagtar Singh Hawara, Paramjit Singh Bheora and Jagtar Singh Tara were lodged in the high security Burail Jail, Chandigarh, yet they managed to burrow their way up to the boundary wall and scaled it, to reach an awaiting vehicle. The tunnel was 14 feet deep and 94 feet long. One of the biggest manhunts of modern India was launched when the police learnt of the escape, to date two of the accused have been caught; they are Jagtar Singh

Hawara and Paramjit Singh Bheora. Jagtar Singh Tara is still at large.

It was later learnt that other tunnels had been started, but had not been continued by the accused. The Singh's were able to make their escape due to meticulous planning, but also due to the fear of prison officials, who were too scared of them to maintain discipline, which led to them being awarded certain freedoms whilst inside. It has been alleged the Singh's had TV's and very lax checking of the cells, thus making it easy to smuggle things in and out of prison.

This escape again highlighted the diligence of the Sikh Insurgents, but also displays that they still have the networks and intelligence to pull off such unbelievable feats. The lion may be in a slumber but when it roars everyone takes note.

10. Down Not Out

The Sikh insurgency talked about in the preceding chapters was bought to a swift end in military terms by the end of 1992. All major leaders of the various militant outfits had either been martyred by the authorities or had fled from India. The leaders that were martyred in 1992 included Bhai Sukhdev Singh Babbar, Bhai Talvinder Singh Babbar and Bhai Gurjant Singh Budhsinghvala. Bhai Paramjit Singh Panjwar and Bhai Vadhava Singh Babbar allegedly escaped from India in 1992, whereas Bhai Daljit Singh Bittu was arrested and Baba Gurbachan Singh Manochahal was martyred towards the end of 1993. Thus the military leads for the Khalistan Commando Force, Khalistan Liberation Force, Babbar Khalsa International, Babbar Khalsa, AISSF and BTFK were martyred, arrested or had to flee to survive.

What led to this abrupt end was the culmination of two key factors; first the political and militant leadership of Dr Sohan Singh was a destructive force that sowed the poison. Secondly, the state leadership of Beant Singh and KPS Gill (Police Chief), that leashed a lawless extermination of Sikhs. I will first talk of Dr Sohan Singh's role and how he effectively poisoned the insurgency.

Dr Sohan Singh was an educated and well respected Sikh. It is argued by some that he even had a direct hand in the first Panthic Committee of 1986[64] and that even this Panthic Committee was his brainchild. The second Panthic Committee is commonly referred to as the Dr Sohan Singh Panthic Committee and this was when his name was openly declared and known in the media. He was seen and

---

[64] A leadership committee of 5 individuals appointed to lead the Sikh Insurgency

respected by the leading militant organisations, as the leader of the insurgency and even today many defend him and argue that he did not play a duplicit role (but the evidence is clearly in conflict with this conjecture). When key strategic targets were eliminated, press releases were signed under the leadership of Dr Sohan Singh, this was especially so with the Babbar Khalsa International, Khalistan Commando Force (Panjwar) and Khalistan Liberation Force, yet when all leading lights of Sikh militancy were mysteriously all being eliminated Dr Sohan Singh conveniently avoided death by the police. Indeed, one could argue that he may have been very astute and avoided arrest, but when he was arrested he spent barely a few weeks in custody and was then released and never formally charged. Today Dr Sohan Singh can be seen openly walking the streets of Chandigarh, yet many militants who are still alive today are still persecuted and pursued by the police. One can draw one's own conclusions. The elections of 1991 were crucial to the downfall of the insurgency and Dr Sohan Singh had a direct hand in this.

In the 1991 elections, the Baba Manochahal group made the farsighted decision to support the Sikh Student Federation group and participate in the elections. But this decision was opposed by some militant groups. They did not understand the earlier Government strategy of cancelling the elections and decided to boycott the elections, which proved to be a suicidal decision.

The Indian Central Government ordered elections for Punjab on February 19, 1992. A group of Sikh fighters under the Panthic Committee headed by Dr. Sohan Singh ordered the Sikhs to boycott the elections. Baba Manochahal on the other hand wanted the Sikhs to take part in the elections and by electing Panthic Singhs, showing that the will of the people was for Khalistan. Once a Panthic government was formed in Punjab, it could pass a motion for independence and show that Khalistan was the will of the people. Even if such a government were dismissed by the Central Government, the will of the people would have been expressed as being in favour of independence.

Baba Manochahl's stand was criticized by many and Dr Sohan Singh called him an agent of the government. Manochahal replied, *"The time will come when the Panth will know who is a government agent and who is not. But that time is unfortunately not going to come any time soon."* But short sightedness resulted in a boycott of the Punjab elections by the majority of Sikhs. Manochahal lamented, ***"The election boycott is going to have a deadly effect on us. It's going to throw the Sikh Movement decades behind. Just watch, those people who today are considering it an honour to invite us to their houses are not even going to give us food when we ask them for it, nor open their doors when we knock. We're going to be slaughtered, the Akali leaders are going to be thrown in prison and the entire struggle will be setback decades. We're going to boycott the elections and then we're going to see the big pillars of our movement drop, one by one."*** Baba Jee's words were nothing less than a prophecy of the bleak future.

The Congress Party won the elections on a turnout of about 25% and Beant Singh was appointed the Chief Minister, it has to be noted that Sikhs make up approximately 60% of the Punjab population. After the Beant government came to power, the genocide which took place in the villages left international human rights organizations horrified, but these atrocities did not affect the militants' determination and faith, even in the slightest.

After the election, the new Chief Minister of Punjab, Beant and the Punjab Police Chief KPS Gill had a meeting. Beant made it clear that the insurgency should be finished at all costs. KPS Gill said he could do the job, but he would need complete control over the police with no interference from anyone. No one should object to anything he did, based on human rights abuses or anything else. He could do the job, but it would be a bloody mess. Beant agreed. And so began the beginning of the end.

The legal framework to persecute the Sikhs had already been set by controversial draconian laws,

"Under an amendment to the National Security Act, the police in Punjab were permitted to enter and search homes without a warrant, to arrest and detain suspects for up to six months without giving a reason, and to imprison persons without a trial for as long as two years." [65]

The Terrorists and Disruptive Activities (Prevention) Act, 1985 (TADA) provided that the Indian State, within a legal structure, shall counter political opposition by introducing special courts. These special courts, used to try all TADA cases, empowered the state to prevent any public presence at the hearings and proceed with a presumption of guilt against the accused. The identity of witnesses was kept secret from the accused. Under TADA, the burden of proof was shifted from the prosecution to the defence. Confessions, even those extracted through torture, were made admissible in courts. By the end of 1987, there were about 4028 people charged under TADA.

---

[65] p.132 **"Indira Gandhi in 1984, Confrontation, Assassination & Succession."** Robert L. Hardgrave, Jr. (Asian Survey, Vol.XXV, No.1, January 1985)

KPS Gill thus had the above draconian laws to justify his cause but he also had the go-ahead to order his police to kill with immunity, he proceeded by ordering the police to extra-judicially eliminate anyone who got in their way. The police would harass and torture one and all, to draw out information about the militants. Many supporters of the insurgency were thus compromised, as many had to make hard choices of letting their whole families be wiped out or choose to talk, as the police were ruling with an iron fist and were very gung ho. The police thus recruited many infiltrators in this manner and they also set up their own death squads which were called Black Cats who were in essence bounty hunters with government patronage and support. Some Black Cats also imitated Sikh militants by growing their hair and wearing Sikh attire, committing heinous acts of rape and murder of Sikhs and Hindus. This was done to tar the image of the militant outfits, as the Black Cats would say that they belong to 'x' militant group, to the people that they would persecute.

In this manner the militancy was bought to an end, but today many militants live on and there are sporadic attempts of assassinations against the enemies of the Sikhs. More recently there was the Burail Jail break that highlighted that militant groups can still make a strategic impact. The movement is now more a political one and most people who are still struggling for justice are doing so within the confines of the Indian constitution. The most worrying factor is that the underlying issues that led to militancy in Punjab have still not been addressed, which were primarily about the economy and Sikhs are still discriminated against as a minority in India.

The declining water levels are a serious challenge to the agricultural dependent Punjab. There is a real possibility of Punjab becoming a dessert area in the future. The water table in the state fell by 42cm per year between 1997 &

2001. PPS Gill in the Punjabi Tribune of the 5th October 2004 argued that,

"When Punjab cries foul over SYL canal, saying if it was executed at least 9 Lakh acres in the South-West districts will become a desert is not without reasoning...Those who now talk of the declining water table forget that this is a manmade problem and it's solution lies with the policy-makers."

As previously argued much of Punjab's river water is diverted away from Punjab and there is increasing pressure on the Punjab government to build the controversial Satluj Yumana Link (SYL) Canal, which will divert more water away from Punjab. Captain Amarinder Singh in his last reign as Chief Minister of Punjab diligently avoided the construction of the SYL canal but it is not clear how much longer Punjab can hold out, as pressure from other states is building for the construction of the canal to be re-instated. The construction of the SYL canal was fundamental to the rise of militancy and whenever construction began, the contractors were killed by militants or farmers.

The religious wounds of the movement will never heal until the Sikhs get Khalistan, one can argue that there was not true consensus when the declaration of Khalistan was made, but regardless of this, it has now been made and many Sikhs are determined that the struggle for a free Sikh nation continues until Khalistan is realised. The wounds of Operation Blue Star remain fresh for many and it is now openly accepted that it was a direct attack on the faith and nation of Sikhs, but the wounds do not heal as they have eternal marks as was found by Mark Tully in a recent interview:

Mark: *My guide is Kiranjot Kaur, a member of the committee that manages the Sikh temples.*

Kiran: *This is the place where a lot of dead bodies were piled up, and later the municipal corporation was called in to remove the dead bodies, but you can still see the bloodstains on the floor of the marble, and these very white marble has bloodstains as if fresh blood has just been spilt on them.*

Mark: *Have you tried to remove the stains from here?*

Kiran: *These marks do not go away. They are like this since the last 20 years....*

Mark: *It seems extraordinary to me, you know, standing here, seeing all the peace and harmony and indeed sanctity of this place, that it can once have been a bloody battlefield.*

Kiran: *It is very unfortunate, but that is what the Indian government turned this into.*

In its history of about 400 years this temple has been demolished about 4 times, because this is the place from where Sikhs draw their spiritual power. And the ruler, any ruler, who tries to subjugate the Sikhs, for them this is one place where they feel if something is done to this place maybe they can subjugate the Sikh psyche and crush their spirit.[66]

Today the Sikh psyche is under attack from a number of quarters, but three so called *'holy men'*, have come to prominence and direct conflict with Sikhs in Punjab. They are Ashutosh (commonly referred to as Noormehlia, as one of his Deras is in Noormehal), Bhaniara Vala & Gurmit Ram Rahim; these individuals and their supporters have burnt the Sikh Scriptures and have questionable characters. They seem like a new version of the Nirankaris of Gurbachan which led to the Bloody Vaisakhi of 1978. Gurmit Ram Rahim re-enacted the 1699 Vaisakhi Initiation Ceremony with a pink milkshake which he had in a cauldron and he dressed in identical attire to that of Guru Gobind Singh, whilst conducting this pseudo-ceremony. A photo of him doing this was splashed across all the Punjab dailies and havoc and chaos followed on the streets of Punjab. Three Sikhs have attained martyrdom in protests against Ram Rahim. In 2010 Darshan Singh Lohara was martyred when peacefully protesting against an Ashutosh procession, when indiscriminate fire was made on Sikhs gathered. Thus on religious terms the ignition to re-light the fire is present again.

Finally, I would like to say that any ruler or government, who has attacked the Golden Temple and the Sikhs, has been extinguished from the face of India. First came the

---

[66] **After Blue Star,** Mark Tully, Final Script Programme 1, BBC Radio, 2004

Hindu Hill Rajas and the Mughals; they sowed their end with the martyrdom of the Sahibzade and they were soon routed and the Sikhs set up their own state under the leadership of Maharajah Ranjit Singh. Next it was the turn of the British, they cunningly waited for the demise of Maharajah Ranjit Singh before attacking the Sikh Empire, and they ruled most of what is now known as India, Pakistan and Bangladesh for about 100 years. It has to be noted that it was the Sikhs who led the freedom struggle in terms of sacrifices made, to stop British Imperialism.

Now it is the turn of the current legislative government of India - they have destructively attacked the Sikhs both as a faith and nation. The Sikhs will not stop until they are free citizens. I acknowledge that the dawn of Khalistan or Sikhs being treated as equal citizens seems a horizon very far away, but one only has to study Sikh history to see that struggles start and die down, but in the end the Sikhs are always victorious in their aims and they have never failed. The Sikhs will succeed in getting the freedoms they set out to achieve and the blood of the martyrs will only grow and invigorate the eternal flower of Sikhi.

The battle-drum beats in the sky of the mind;
Aim is taken, and the wound is inflicted.
The spiritual warriors enter the field of battle;
Now is the time to fight!
He alone is known as a spiritual hero,
Who fights in defence of religion.
He may be cut apart, piece by piece,
But he never leaves the field of battle.
(Bhagat Kabir Jee, Ang 1105, SGGS)

Annex 1

Baba Thakhur Singh Jee (1915-2004)

The Sikh nation's respected religious personality, Baba
Thakhur Singh Jee was born in 1915, village Eechogill, Dist
Lahore (Pakistan) to the respected Baba Bahadur Singh and
Mata Prem Kaur Jee.

Both his parents were Amritdharee, who recited many
prayers daily and had unshakeable faith in the Guru. After the
partition they came to India, where in village Sadaruala, near
Makhu, Dist Ferozepur, they started to live. From birth Baba Jee
was forever meditating, merciful, peaceful hearted, imbued with
spiritual energy and had unshakeable faith in the Guru. From a
young age He would not waste his time playing or talking.
When a little older, He started helping his mother and father in
running the household, whilst conducting his chores he would
forever attune his concentration to the one intoxicating Naam
Simran.

From childhood, Baba Jee used to share his earnings, food
and belongings with others as he saw Gods light in all and
always inspired others to become engrossed in Seva and Simran.
Baba Jee's mind forever longed to be in the presence and Seva
of a true Gursikh/Brahmgiani. They learnt through others that
Brahmgiani Sant Gurbachan Singh Jee Khalsa along with his
Jatha were doing Sikhi Parchar- who are respected as great
intellectuals and who have much blessings of Satguru Sri Guru
Gobind Singh Jee. Baba Jee left home and went to Bhindra in
Dist Moga where Khalsa Jee resided, whilst there Baba Jee took
Amrit from Panj Pyare. Khalsa Jee recognised Baba Jee's
spiritual state and thus put him in charge of Langar, this Seva
was performed with much love and commitment, after 2½ years
of Seva, Khalsa Jee accepted Baba Jee into the Jatha and taught
him the knowledge of God. Until Khalsa Jee went to Sachkand,

ANNEX 1

Baba Jee did Seva of Garveye (close associate) for 22 years, Khalsa Jee being happy with this Seva blessed Baba Jee with many gifts. They blessed him with a great spiritual state and said, *"A time will come, when you will perform the greatest Seva of all."*

After Khalsa Jee went to Sachkand, Baba Jee carried on his Seva of Langer of the Sangat/congregation with Sant Giani Kartar Singh Jee Khalsa and forever remained imbued in Naam Simran. Sant Giani Kartar Singh Jee had much respect for Baba Jee & would discuss decisions to be made, with Baba Jee. This time was a critical period for Sikhs as there were many efforts being made to silence the Sikh community, as a political and faith group. Sant Kartar Singh Jee Khalsa held 37 major processions which woke the sleeping Sikh masses to their identity. The government were trying to silence Sant Kartar Singh Jee Khalsa and were making plans to arrest him, Sant Jee said the following in response to this, *"If the government arrest me, then after me Baba Thakhur Singh Jee will be responsible for Damdami Taksal. They can give the Seva of leadership to whom they please."*

After Sant Kartar Singh Jee Khalsa Bhindra Vale ascended to Sachkand (left their mortal body), Baba Jee appointed Sant Giani Jarnail Singh Jee Khalsa the leader of Damdami Taksal, Sant Jee would always heed Baba Jee's advice.

In July 1982 Sant Jarnail Singh Jee Khalsa began the Dharam Yudh Morcha to free the Sikhs from oppression of the government and made Amritsar their permanent residence, and Baba Jee was given the Seva to look after Gurdwara Gurdarshan Parkash Mehta (the headquarters of Damdami Taksal). In June 1984 the government attacked Sri Harmander Sahib and Sri Akaal Takhat Sahib, martyring countless Singhs and Singhnia. After the attack Sant Jee went underground, in the absence of Sant Jee the leadership of Damdami Taksal Seva was taken up

2

ANNEX 1

by Baba Jee in accordance with Sant Jee's wishes, there are recordings of Sant Jarnail Singh in which he states that should he go missing the leadership of Damdami Taksal is in the hands of Baba Jee. Baba Jee led the Damdami Taksal from June 1984 to December 2004, during testing times and was an inspiration throughout this period.

He fought cases for arrested Singhs and assisted those still in jail, in whatever manner possible, Shaheed's families have been provided for and are still being supported. The children of Bhai Beant Singh (assassin of Indira Gandhi) made a press statement in 1999 stating that it was only Damdami Taksal who had supported them financially and emotionally throughout their childhood in the absence of their father and mother (who later died mysteriously). He restarted the great tradition of Sarbat Khalsa in 1986 and led the reconstruction of Sri Akaal Takhat Sahib with much physical fervour. Baba Jee will be remembered in history as the person who led the reconstruction of the Sri Akaal Takhat Sahib which reinvested pride and honour of the Sikh community that was damaged by the Indian Government when they reduced the Sri Akaal Takhat Sahib to ruins.

Gurdwara Shaheed Ganj B-block was built in Sri Amritsar in memory of the Shaheeds of the encounter with Nakali Nirankaris of 1978. At Sri Anandpur Sahib on Kiratpur Sahib Road a Gurdwara was built to benefit visiting sangats.

In terms of Baba Jee's spiritual prowess and daily living, Baba Jee never separated himself from the recitation of Gurbani. The recitation of Gurbani was kept continuous in the presence of Baba Jee and they used to talk with others very little, Sevadars used to recite Gurbani all day and night in accordance to Baba Jee's wishes. Even at night when Baba Jee used to sleep, which was never more than a couple of hours, the recitation of Gurbani

3

continued. Anyone who visited or met Baba Jee would bear witness to this.

In terms of Baba Jee's contribution to the freedom struggle not much has come into print or discussion and the reason for this is not due to Baba Jee's lack of involvement but to the contrary it is due to the highly skilled nature in which Baba Jee conducted himself and co-ordinated the activities of leading figures of the freedom struggle. Many Sikh Freedom Fighting outfits were seen to be aligned with Damdami Taksal most notably these were the AISSF, Khalistan Commando Force and Khalistan Bhindranvale Tiger Force. The leaders of these organisations sought the guidance and advice of Baba Jee.

In accordance with Baba Jee's influence and role, when Rajiv Gandhi came into power he wanted to try and diffuse the situation with the Sikhs and he sent a delegation to Baba Jee, to discuss bringing an end to the insurgency. Bhai Mokham Singh was well aware of the leading advisors coming to meet Baba Jee and he was quite concerned with the situation, he feared Baba Jee may just ignore the advisors and not even entertain dialogue with them. The meeting was arranged to take place at Mehta, Baba Jee was in Amritsar and thus he had to travel to get back to Mehta (about a 30 minute drive). When the advisors came they said that the government wants to discuss ending the Sikh insurgency, Baba Jee simply asked them:

Where have you come from?

Advisors: *We have come from Delhi*

Baba Jee: *Did you get stopped on your way from Delhi to Mehta?*

Advisors: *No*

ANNEX 1

Baba Jee: *Well I have just come from Amritsar and my car was stopped and searched 7 times, you want peace with us, stop this discrimination and then we will consider dialogue.*

Baba Jee did not entertain them with anymore conversation and they want back to Rajiv Gandhi with their tales between their legs.

Leading martyrs such as Bhai Harjinder Singh Jinda and Bhai Sukhdev Singh Sukha were very close to Baba Jee. The clothes they wore when they hanged were gifted to them from Baba Jee and they felt honoured to be wearing clothes gifted from Baba Jee for their hanging. Clothes from both of the families of the Singhs were placed upon them when they were subsequently cremated.

Gurdwara Gurdarshan Parkash, Mehta (headquarters of Damdami Taksal) was a hotbed of activity during the 80's and 90's and even recently Singhs involved in the insurgency have frequented the Gurdwara. During the 80's one could visit the Gurdwara and would see Singhs armed and ready for battle, this all occurred under the leadership of Baba Jee. In the year 2000 a Sikh wanted for militant activities was traced to be present at Gurdwara Gurdarshan Parkash and the police surrounded the Gurdwara. Baba Jee was furious and he came out shouting at the police, *"You think you can find something incriminating here, look where you want! Singh's open all the rooms so they can search"* Baba Jee was well aware of the presence of the Singh in the Gurdwara and he was discreetly taken to the back of the Gurdwara and he entered the village lanes and escaped unscathed.

Unfortunately many Singhs who could have narrated much more about Baba Jee's influence and role have been martyred or are choosing to remain quiet as people who are still alive may become incriminated. Baba Jee was a great soul and a shining example of a Khalsa. Those that question Baba Jee should try living one day like Baba Jee, i.e. they should try living one day in which they constantly meditate and then think of the high spirits one must be in, who did this on a daily basis. Photos of Baba Jee are on page 291.

Annex 2

Bibliography

1. Amar, Amardeep Singh, 2003, **Te Deeva Jaagdha Rahega,** Amritsar, Gurmat Pustak Bhandar

2. Amar, Amardeep Singh, 2004, **Keth Jo Mandeyo Soorma,** Amritsar, Gurmat Pustak Bhandar

3. Anurag Singh (Translated & Edited by), 1999, **Giani Kirpal Singh's Eye-Witness Account of Operation Blue Star,** Amritsar, B. Chattar Singh Jiwan Singh

4. Azad, Abul Kalam, 1988, **India Wins Freedom,** Delhi

5. Babbar, Gurcharan Singh, 1998, **Government Organised Carnage,** Delhi, Babbar Publications Pvt. Ltd

6. Baja, Maninder Singh, **Jujharoo Yode,** Amritsar, Gurmat Pustak Bhandar

7. Baja, Maninder Singh, 2005, **Pag Dee Laaj,** Amritsar, Gurmat Pustak Bhandar

8. Bal, S, 1990, **Politics of the Central Sikh League,** Delhi, Books N' Books

Annex 2

9. Chaddah, Mehar Singh, 1982, **Are Sikhs a Nation?,** Delhi Sikh Gurdwara Management Committee: Delhi

10. Chauhan, Ramesh K, 1995, **Punjab and the Nationality Question in India,** Deep and Deep Publications: New Delhi.

11. Cunningham, J.D., 1849, **History of the Sikhs,** Delhi: Low Price Publications (Reprint of 1996)

12. Devinderjit Singh, 1986, **Sikhs, Arms & Terrorism,** Cambridge: Cambridge University Sikh Society – Cambridge Research Papers on Sikhism.

13. Dhillon, G. S., 1992, **India Commits Suicide,** Chandigarh, Singh & Singh Publishers

14. Dhillon, G. S., 1996, **Truth about Punjab S.G.P.C. White Paper,** Amritsar, Shiromani Gurdwara Parbhandak Committee.

15. Effenberg, C. **The Political Status of The Sikhs During The Indian National Movement 1935 – 1947,** New Delhi, Archives Publishers Ltd.

16. Eliot, Charles, 1921, **Hinduism & Buddhism: An Historical Sketch,** London: Routledge & Kegan Paul, Vol.2

17. Gill, Pritam Singh, 1973, **Trinity of Sikhism,** New Academic Publishing Co. : Jullundhur.

18. Grewal, Manraj, 2004, **Dreams after Darkness,** New Delhi, Rupa & Co.

19. Grewal, J. S., 1996, **The Akalis a short History,** Chandigarh, Punjab Studies Publications.

20. Gulati, K. C., 1974, **The Akalis Past and Present,** New Delhi, Ashajanak Publications.

21. Gurharpal Singh & Ian Talbot (Ed.s), 1996, **Punjabi Identity – Continuity and Change,** Manohar: New Delhi

22. Gurmit Singh, 1989, **History of Sikh Struggles,** (4 Vol.s), Atlantic Publishers: New Delhi

23. Gurtej Singh, 1996, **Tandav of the Centaur,** Institute of Sikh Studies: Chandigarh

24. Harbans Singh, 1983, **The Heritage of the Sikhs,** New Delhi, Manohar.

25. Harbans Singh et al, 2002, **The Encyclopaedia of Sikhism,** Patiala, Punjab University.

26. Jaijee, Inderjit Singh, 1999, **Politics of Genocide 1984 – 1999**, Delhi, Ajanta Publications.

27. Jain, Sharda, 1995, **Politics of Terrorism in India – The Case of Punjab,** Deep and Deep Publications: New Delhi.

28. Kapur Singh, 1959, **Paraharprasna,** Jullundhur: Hind Publishers

29. Kapur, R.A. **Sikh Separatism: The Politics of Faith,** London, Allen and Unwin

30. Khalsa, Baljit Singh, 2002, **Hadi Handaya Ik Kooni Dahaka,** Amritsar, Gurmat Pustak Bhandar

31. Khalsa, Baljit Singh, 2005, **Punjab Dee Dharti Te Hindustani Atvaad,** Amritsar, Azaad Khalsa Parkashan

32. Kumar, Ram Narayan, 1997, **The Sikh Unrest and The Indian State,** Ajanta: New Delhi

33. Kushwant Singh et al, **The Punjab Story,** 1984, Rohli Books International, New Delhi

34. Kushwant Singh, 1953, **The Sikhs,** London: George Allen & Unwin

35. Lal, Shiv, 1994, **Dateline Punjab Lifeline Sikhs,** New Delhi, Election Archives

Annex 2

36. Macormack, P. M. (ed.), 1975, **Stories from Sikh History, Book VII,** New Delhi, Hemkunt Press

37. Mahmood, Cynthia, 2001, **A Sea of Orange,** USA, Xlibris Corporation

38. Mahmood, Cynthia, 1996, **Fighting for Faith & Nation,** Pennsylvania, University of Pennsylvania Press.

39. Mohinder Singh, 1988, **The Akali Struggle A Retrospect,** New Delhi, Atlantic Publishers

40. Narang, Gokul Chand, 1960, **Transformation of Sikhism,** 5th Ed., New Delhi: New Book Society of India

41. Nayar, Baldev Raj, 1966, **Minority Politics in The Punjab,** Princeton Press: Princeton.

42. Rai, S. M, 1984, **Legislative Politics and Freedom Struggle on the Panjab 1897 – 1947**

43. Rai, Satya M, 1986, **Punjab Since Partition,** Durga Publications: Delhi

44. Reddy et al, 1984, **Army action in Punjab, Prelude & Aftermath,** New Delhi: Samata Era Publication

45. Sandhu, Balbir Singh, **Kesri Kitab,** International Sikh Youth Federation (UK)

Annex 2

46. Sangat Singh, 1995, **The Sikhs in History,** New York.

47. Talbot, Ian, 1988, **Punjab and the Raj 1849-1947,** Delhi, Manohar Publications

48. Tatla, Darshan Singh, 1999, **The Sikh Diaspora The search for statehood,** London: UCL Press

49. Thursby, Gene, **Indo-British Review,** 15, 1, 1988, pp49-66

50. Tuteja, K. L., 1984, **Sikh Politics [1920-40],** Kurukshetra, Vishal Publications

51. Uday Singh (Professor), 1988, **Khalistan Dee Lehar Da Utra Te Chra,** 1988

52. Yagnik, I.K, 1943, **Gandhi, as I knew him,** Delhi

Printed in Great Britain
by Amazon